MW01032088

Integrating Faith
and Special Education

Integrating Faith
and Special Education

A Christian Faith Approach
to Special Education Practice

Edited by
BEN NWORIE

Dear Brother Chike,
May the grace of God abound for you.
And may He enlarge your territory more
and more. May His blessings overtake
you and your family, 1JN. Amen.
Ben Nworie 12/19/16.

WIPF & STOCK · Eugene, Oregon

INTEGRATING FAITH AND SPECIAL EDUCATION
A Christian Faith Approach to Special Education Practice

Wipf & Stock
An Imprint of Wipf and Stock Publishers
199 W. 8th Ave., Suite 3
Eugene, OR 97401

www.wipfandstock.com

PAPERBACK ISBN: 978-1-4982-3838-0
HARDCOVER ISBN: 978-1-4982-3840-3
EBOOK ISBN: 978-1-4982-3839-7

Manufactured in the U.S.A.   10/07/16

Contents

Acknowledgments

FIRST AND FOREMOST, I must acknowledge God, by whose grace and providence this work has become possible. Next, I must acknowledge all my students, my peers both past and present, as well as my teachers, all of whom have taught me a lot over the years.

I must also acknowledge my family, who because they very much believe in me and have high expectations of me, enable me to stay focused. Last and not the least, my thanks go to Dr. June Hetzel, dean of the Biola University School of Education for her support.

Preface

CHRISTIAN FAITH DOES NOT simply refer to spirituality, religion or faith in general. It is a specific faith that has a message (the gospel) and a mission (teaching and Christian action) and that centers on Jesus Christ and his love. There is an inherent connection between the Christian faith and special education. The great, critical issues of special education are issues that the Christian faith addresses, too. For example, both focus on the worth of the individual. Both also focus on fairness and on caring for or helping the weak. Similarly, both aim to "serve and edify others."[1] The ultimate aim of both is shalom as wholeness (not just peace). Shalom in this sense has strong relevance in both the Christian faith and special education.

The aim of this book is to help the reader perceive this integral relationship which exists between the Christian faith and the special education discipline. The aim of the book is also to utilize the chapters that stem from real-life professional experiences and scholarship of the contributors to model and encourage special education practice from a Christian faith perspective. It is our view that special education practiced from this faith perspective will transform what is currently accepted as best practice into a new system of special education experience that is wholesome, biblically based, and characteristic of shalom.

Special education best practice such as creating a positive and safe learning environment, understanding behavioral assessment and intervention, tracking each student's progress by monitoring successes and setbacks, mastering differentiated instruction, learning and teaching collaboratively, finding and utilizing students' strengths in creating best learning outcomes, all these and more, carried out from a Christian faith perspective of love,

---

1. D. S. Dockery, ed., *Faith and Learning: A Handbook for Christian Higher Education* (Nashville: B&H, 2012), 3.

caring, compassion, justice, equity and a sense of vocation, will morph into a new system of special education that will be evidenced by positive and measurable educational outcomes, less litigation, more thriving practitioners who teach not out of a sense of obligation, but out of a sense of calling to nurture flourishing students who experience love, justice, and shalom in fellowship (*koinonia*) with their teachers, peers and service providers. The book is, therefore, a proposal for a paradigm shift in the practice of special education that is christocentric and transformational.

Introduction

INTEGRATING FAITH AND SPECIAL education, specifically practicing special education from a Christian faith approach, is not a preoccupation of most Christian educators in the field of special education. This seeming apathy toward a faith-integrative disciplinary orientation exists for two main reasons. First, the postmodern, secular culture that dominates the educational landscape has a bent toward dichotomization of faith and reason. It is a scenario in which matters of faith are largely regarded as inferior and subordinate to matters of reason. Second, most people, including Christians who teach in the field of special education, seem to do it as a way of obtaining job employment, rather than as a vocation in the deeper sense of a life calling. Christians who opt to teach in the field of special education should see it as an opportunity to engage in critical and theological reflections on the discipline of special education, as an opportunity to engage in the serious questions of life, the important questions that usually transcend this life.

The chapters of this book contain information, materials and resources which by offering a new paradigm in the practice of special education encourage and help teachers, administrators and parents to reflect theologically on how the Christian faith informs and transforms special education. The chapters demonstrate the fact that teaching children with special needs from the Christian faith perspective ensures not only that the children are meaningfully informed, but that their transformation toward Christlikeness is enhanced. The contents of the book have been put together to illustrate how teaching from this purposive faith perspective makes meaningful difference and lasting contribution to the world of children with special needs.

In chapter 1, titled "What Is Special Education, and What Is Its Connection with Christian Theology," after giving a brief review of the development of the field of special education, and an in-depth definition of the discipline, the chapter undertakes an overview of special education by addressing various pertinent questions, such as: What differentiates special education from general or regular education? What is special education instruction? What is the goal of special education? What is special about special education? What advances have been made in the field of special education? What is the job of a special education teacher? What does the future of special education look like? And what is the connection between special education and Christian theology?

Chapter 2 focuses on the theology of special education by bringing attention to the intricate connection between special education and Christian theology as both of them deal with similar notions, concerns and assumptions. To register the importance of being guided by Christian theological perspectives in the practice of special education, the chapter finally focuses on the doctrine of God (especially creation and practical theology), Christology (especially regarding the person and work of Christ), and biblical anthropology (especially regarding the nature, worth and purpose of man) and shows the relevance and implications of these three aspects of Christian theology for special education.

Worldview plays a pivotal role in being an effective special educator. Chapter 3 demonstrates this by presenting an ethical view of love, worldviews, and special education practice from a Christian worldview perspective. The Christian world-view leads the faith-based special educator to develop an appropriate mission statement identified as a key to an effective, integrative special education practice.

Chapter 4 presents a Christian faith perspective on collaborative practices in special education. The chapter reports the analysis of a qualitative study of the practices and principles of thirty preservice special education teachers as they met state standards for collaborations in K–12 schools by utilizing good communication and servant leadership strategies to collaborate with general education teachers in schools, showing the positive impact of explicit faith connections.

Chapter 5 highlights the related factors that impede or promote the school outcomes of students with disabilities, especially those with emotional and behavioral disorders (EBD), and provides recommendations for looking at student outcomes from a biblical justice perspective as a way to accelerate and sustain positive educational outcomes. Chapter 5 and chapter 6 deal with the issues of equity and justice. Chapter 6, therefore, focuses on the status of the social, emotional, as well as educational experiences of diverse learners who are lesbian, gay, bisexual and transgendered (LGBT) and suggests ways of creating school success environments for them. Chapter 7 deals with the prevalent problems of depression and anxiety in the classroom for children with mild to moderate disabilities, and recommends practical strategies and ways for the school community and the family to help.

Chapter 8, titled "Three Models of Constructivist Learning Utilized by Jesus Christ," discusses constructivism as a learning theory that explains how learners construct knowledge and meaning from their experiences. The chapter highlights three known categories of constructivism: (1) inquiry-based learning (IBL); (2) discovery learning (DL); and (3) problem-solving learning (PSL) and discusses Jesus Christ's utilization of these three modes of constructivist learning in his teaching. Chapter 9 uses a personal story and reflective discourse to buttress the point that effective faith integration which goes beyond how we share our faith in our disciplines calls for a rigorous combination of competent professional practice that is infused with well-thought-out faith and grounded upon balanced, sound theological and doctrinal foundations. Through this chapter the writer clearly shows that faith integration is how we communicate the important topics, issues, and principles of our disciplines to our students using solid theological foundations through application of the Christian worldview and values. The writer provides reflection on how faith informs disciplinary practice as well as how practice informs faith.

Chapter 10, titled "Jesus, Justice, and Special Education Inclusion: A Case for the Shalom Model of Inclusion," is a theoretical discourse that proposes a justice-infused, biblically based special education inclusion model. The chapter discusses justice, inclusion, incarnationality, the Hebrew concept of *shalom*, and *agape* love, which form the foundational thinking for the proposed inclusive Shalom Model. The four domains of the Shalom Model of Inclusion discussed are: shared curriculum experience, shared strengths and needs, effective and differentiated pedagogy, as well as community and collaborative praxis. The concept that we are all created in the image of God (*imago Dei*) is at the center of the model and holds it together. The model is illustrated with the love, compassion and collaboration shared in the L'Arche communities where disabilities, instead of being viewed negatively as problems to be solved, are viewed as gifts, and opportunities to learn new ways to love, to be faithful, to live together in recognition of the naturalness and goodness of difference, as well as discover the importance of weakness and vulnerability. L'Arche is thus portrayed as a tangible demonstration of the practicality and effectiveness of shalom inclusion.

What Is Special Education, and What Is Its Connection with Christian Theology?

Ben Nworie, PhD, MDiv, LPC
Professor of Special Education
School of Education, Biola University

Abstract

THE CHAPTER AFTER GIVING a brief review of the development of the field of special education, and an in-depth definition of special education, undertakes an overview of the discipline by positing various pertinent questions such as: What differentiates special education from general or regular education? What is special education instruction? What is the goal of special education? What is special about special education? What is the goal of special education? What advances have been made in the field of special education? What is the job of a special education teacher? What does the future of special education look like? And what is the connection between special education and Christian theology?

Keywords: special education, definition, instruction, IDEA, disabilities

Introduction

As a result of people's diverse orientations, perceptions and experiences, special education means different things to different people. To some people special education is a place where students go or stay. This place sometimes has positive or negative associations. To some other people special education is associated with service or support as part of the educational system. Consequently, special education has been described, defined, and explained in a number of different ways.

The Development of the Field of Special Education

In the last half century, the field of special education has gone through rapid developments. In the process, it has seen a number of important changes.

Beginning of Special Education Discussions and Publications

The early part of the twentieth century marked the beginning of discussions and publications in favor of the education of individuals with disabilities. For example, this period witnessed the beginning of some special education publications such as the remarkable special education textbook *The Education of Handicapped Children* in 1924 by J. E. Wallace Waliin.[1] However, despite these remarkable achievements, over one million students with disabilities were denied a public education. Those in public schools were segregated from their peers without disabilities. The origin of legally mandated inclusive education can be traced back to the *Brown v. Board of Education of Topeka* Supreme Court decision in 1954.[2] Although the focus of the Brown case was on school desegregation and did not include students with disabilities, its impact greatly expanded and spilled over into special education. This landmark case clarified that "separate cannot be equal." Consequently, some professionals began questioning to what extent separate classes provided students with disabilities with what could be considered appropriate education.[3]

From the middle part of the twentieth century through the mid-1960s there were studies which assessed the efficacy of the traditional special

1. Wood, *Teaching Students in Inclusive Settings*.
2. Heward, *Exceptional Children*.
3. Friend, *Special Education*.

education by comparing the achievement and social adjustment of students with intellectual disabilities who were educated in special classes to that of their comparable peers who were educated in general education classes. The studies seemed to show that students with intellectual disabilities (called *mentally retarded students at that time*) who were in the general education setting achieved more academic gains than their peers in the special education setting.

As the civil rights movement intensified by the mid-1960s, some researchers, such as Lloyd Dunn[4] challenged educators to use research on helpful teaching methods and new technology to educate students with disabilities along with their peers.[5] Between the 1960s and the 1970s other professionals focused attention on not just academic instruction, but on the discriminating effect of some labels used in reference to the students with disabilities. It was apparent that special education went beyond being a means of assisting students with disabilities to becoming a means of discriminating against students who were seen as making the teacher's job more difficult.

Parent Advocacy and Litigation for Students Rights

At this same time that researchers were evaluating the quality and impact of special education on students, vocal parent advocacy groups supporting the rights of children with disabilities were emerging as a force to be reckoned with.[6] These parents wanted their sons and daughters to be educated in the public school system, not at home, in institutions, or private agencies.

Consequently, as a result of the combined effort of the professionals, the researchers, the parents and the advocacy groups in 1965 the Elementary and Secondary Education Act (ESEA) (PL 89–750) was enacted as the first federal legislation to address the education of students with disabilities.[7] ESEA provided funding to states to assist them in creating and improving programs and services for these students.[8]

4. Friend, *Special Education*.
5. Ibid.
6. Salend, *Creating Inclusive Classrooms*; Friend, *Special Education*.
7. Yell, *Law and Special Education*; Friend, *Special Education*.
8. Yell, *Law and Special Education*.

Re-Authorizations of the Law

Beginning with the Education of All Handicapped Children's Act of 1975 (PL 94–142), the federal legislation which guides special education practice was re-authorized in 1990 as the Individuals with Disabilities Education Act (IDEA). IDEA mandated access for all students to publicly funded, inclusive classrooms and the general education classroom. IDEA accords to all children with disabilities the right to a free, appropriate public education in the least restrictive environment. IDEA also grants all children with disabilities and their parents the right to due process under the law, which includes the rights to be notified of any decision affecting the child's educational placement, to have a hearing and present a defense, to see a written decision, and to appeal any decision. IDEA mandates schools to conduct *nondiscriminatory identification and evaluation* through the use of nonbiased, multifactorial methods of evaluation to determine whether a child has a disability and, if so, whether special education is needed.

IDEA has been reauthorized several times since 1975.[9] An important set of changes happened in 1986, with the expansion of special education then to include services to infants and young children. The 1990 reauthorization of IDEA clarified the need for transition supports as students move from high school to post school educational or vocational options.

The 1997 reauthorization of IDEA introduced several significant additions such as procedures for addressing discipline for students with disabilities, the expansion of parent participation and the clarification of the roles of general education teachers in educating students with disabilities. The 2004 reauthorization of IDEA was aimed at aligning it with other federal general education laws, especially No Child Left Behind (NCLB). Also additional strategies for dispute resolution with parents were specified.

On December 10, 2015, the US Congress reauthorized the Elementary and Secondary Education Act and the No Child Left Behind (ESEA/NCLB) by passing the Every Student Succeeds Act (ESSA) which makes new helpful provisions while eliminating some former provisions that were not considered particularly helpful. In general, the new law puts the states and local districts in charge of accountability, educator evaluations and school improvement instead of the federal government.[10]

---

9. Ibid.

10. Council for Exceptional Children, "CEC's Summary."

What Differentiates Special Education from General or Regular Education?

Special education is different from general or regular education. It is education specially planned and provided to children who have disabilities. Special education can, therefore, be described as the educational practice of specifically planning and providing for the individual differences and learning needs of students with disabilities. What differentiates special education from general education, therefore, is that special education is a specifically planned and individualized system of education. Special education enables students with special needs to meaningfully access the regular education curriculum. It enables the students with disabilities to successfully develop to their fullest potential by providing them free appropriate public education in the least restrictive environment, as provided by the legislation governing special education, the Individuals with Disabilities Education Act (IDEA) which was initially enacted in 1975 as PL 94–142.

Definition of Special Education

IDEA defines special education as: "Specially designed instruction, at no cost to the parents, to meet the unique needs of a child with a disability."[11] The specially designed instruction includes supports and services provided to students with an identified disability requiring an individually designed instructional program to meet their unique learning needs.[12]

The IDEA definition makes it clear that special education has two important component parts and priorities which distinguish special education from general education. These two important parts and critical components of special education which derive directly from the IDEA definition are *specially designed instruction* (*SDI*), and *instruction that addresses students' unique needs*.

Specially Designed Instruction (SDI)

SDI is tailored to meet the individual needs of students with disabilities. It is instruction that is significantly more intense and individualized than regular education. SDI is accompanied by closely and systematically

11. Loyd et al., *What Is Special Education?*
12. US Dept. of Defense, "Special Education."

monitoring of instruction and documentation of progress. It is not limited to students' academic skills. It may in addition address various other skills of students such as communication, behavior, social interaction, functional or vocational skills, as well as any other areas affected by the disability.[13] An example of teaching that can be easily described as special education in the SDI sense is specially designing the instruction of students who are visually impaired by providing them with large print reading materials, or braille. The work of Anne Sullivan teaching Hellen Keller[14] qualifies as a great example of special education as specially designed instruction. Another example of SDI is equipping students who have hearing impairments with hearing aids or providing their instruction in sign language. Other examples of SDI include: providing students who have physical disabilities with special equipment; providing the instruction of the students who have emotional, behavioral or intellectual disorders with smaller and more highly structured classes;[15] providing instruction and reinforcement schedules or activities that enable students with Autism improve communication skills, as well as skills for staying on task, etc.

SDI involves the modification of teaching methods and environments so that the maximum numbers of students are served in general education environments, are held accountable along with their regular education counterparts, with the goal of improving academic achievement for the maximum number of students, while reducing social stigmas for students with disabilities.[16] Though the delivery of SDI is primarily the responsibility of special education professionals, increasingly general education teachers share this responsibility with special education teachers as a result of collaborative and inclusive practices which are becoming more common. For the students who need special education, the best general education does not and cannot replace special needs education.[17]

Instruction That Addresses Students' Unique Needs

Special education is reserved for students who need it as a result of their unique needs arising from their disability. To meet such unique needs

13. Friend and Bursuck, *Including Students with Special Needs.*

14. Bateman et al., *What Is Special Education?*

15. Hallahan et al., *Exceptional Learners.*

16. Scruggs and Mastropieri, "What Makes Special Education Special?"

17. Hallahan et al., *Exceptional Learners.*

of students, it is often necessary to provide more than individualized instruction. A common way for educators and other professionals in special education to go beyond providing individualized academic instruction is by supplementing their instruction with *related services*. These are services necessary in enabling the students to benefit from special education.[18] Examples of related services are: adapted physical education, assistive technology devices and services (for restoring lost capacities or improving lost capacities), audiology (determining the range, nature and degree of hearing loss, and operating programs for treatment and prevention of hearing loss), counseling, occupational therapy (improving, developing or restoring functions impaired or lost through illness, injury or deprivation), physical therapy, school health services (provided by a school nurse or other qualified professional), as well as transportation to and from services and schools in a specialized vehicle or school bus.[19] A list of related services recognized by IDEA is given below.

Figure 1.1. Definitions of Related Services in IDEA

The related services apply to part B and students ages three through twenty-one unless we note that they belong to part C only and thus only to children ages birth through two.

- *Assistive technology and services*: acquiring and using devices and services to restore lost capacities or improve impaired capacities (part C, but also a "special consideration" for part B students' IEPs).

- *Audiology*: determining the range, nature, and degree of hearing loss and operating programs for treatment and prevention of hearing loss.

- *Counseling services*: counseling by social workers, psychologists, guidance counselors, or other qualified professionals.

- *Early identification*: identifying a disability as early as possible in a child's life.

- *Interpreting services*: various means for communicating with children who have hearing impairments or who are deaf-blind.

---

18. Turnbull et al., *Exceptional Lives*; Friend and Bursuck, *Including Students with Special Needs*.

19. Friend and Bursuck, *Including Students with Special Needs*.

- *Family training, counseling, and home visits*: assisting families to enhance their child's development (part C only).

- *Health services*: enabling a child to benefit from other early intervention services (part C only).

- *Medical services*: determining a child's medically related disability that results in the child's need for special education and related services.

- *Occupational therapy*: improving, developing, or restoring functions impaired or lost through illness, injury, or deprivation.

- *Orientation and mobility services*: assisting a visually impaired or blind student to get around within various environments.

- *Parent counseling and training*: providing parents with information about child development.

- *Physical therapy*: services by a physical therapist.

- *Psychological services*: administering and interpreting psychological and educational tests and other assessment procedures and managing a program of psychological services, including psychological counseling for children and parents.

- *Recreation and therapeutic recreation*: assessing leisure function, recreation programs in schools and community agencies, and leisure education.

- *Rehabilitative counseling services*: planning for career development, employment preparation, achieving independence, and integration in the workplace and community.

- *School health services*: attending to educationally related health needs through services provided by a school nurse or other qualified professional.

- *Service coordination services*: assistance and services by a service coordinator to a child and family (part C only).

- *Social work services in schools*: preparing a social or developmental history on a child, counseling groups and individuals, and mobilizing school and community resources.

- *Speech pathology and speech-language pathology*: diagnosing specific speech or language impairments and giving guidance regarding those impairments.

- *Transportation and related costs*: providing travel to and from services and schools, travel in and around school buildings, and specialized equipment (e.g., special or adapted buses, lifts, and ramps).

- *Vision services*: assessing vision in an infant/toddler (part C only).[20]

Another aspect of special education instruction that helps address students' unique needs is the inclusion of mandated Supplementary Aids and Services (SAS). These are various supports that enhance the participation of students with disabilities in general education, extracurricular activities, and other school settings. They ensure equal free access by all students to the educational curriculum.[21] Examples of SAS include: "preferential seating, access to computer technology, and instructional adjustments (e.g., more time to complete tests, simplified assignments, alternative but equivalent instructional materials)."[22]

To provide instruction that addresses students' unique needs, students with disabilities are allowed to receive accommodations and modifications as part of their instruction. Friend and Bursuck give the following helpful definition of accommodations and modifications.

> Accommodations are changes in *how* the student learns key curriculum. For example, a student may be learning the same math as classmates, but he may be assigned fewer math problems because he takes longer than other students to complete each one. Another student may respond to an essay question on a history test by writing bullet points instead of paragraphs, because it reduces the writing task and the goal is to determine what she has learned about history rather than to assess paragraph-writing ability. In each case, the curriculum has remained the same. Modifications refer to *what* the student learns and usually imply that some curriculum is removed. For example, a student with a significant intellectual disability may not learn all the vocabulary in a science unit, focusing instead on words that he is likely to encounter in day-to-day life. . . . Many students with disabilities need accommodations, but only those with significant intellectual disabilities usually require modifications.[23]

20. Turnbull et al., *Exceptional Lives*.
21. Friend and Bursuck, *Including Students with Special Needs*.
22. Ibid., 5.
23. Ibid.

The IDEA definition also highlights the specific objective of special education which is successful educational development of students, regardless of their disabilities or limitations. Special education should, therefore, be seen as a process of service rather than as a placement for a student. To understand what special education is, one must first realize how it came to be. In the last four centuries or more, the question of what to do with students who have special needs, or those who learn differently, has confounded parents, educators, administrators and politicians. A myriad of solutions, all varying in effectiveness, have been employed to support, and sometimes, segregate this special population.[24]

The first public use of the term special education appears to have occurred at a presentation by Alexander Graham Bell at a National Education Association meeting in 1884. However, the history of the field of special education, brought about by a mixture of philosophical, political, economic, legal, and sociocultural factors, and influenced by changing societal and philosophical beliefs about the extent to which individuals with disabilities should be feared, segregated, categorized, and educated, began long before the 1884 event.[25] It is especially illuminating for one to recognize that before IDEA was enacted, over 1 million students with disabilities were denied a public education. Those in public schools were segregated from their peers without disabilities. Those placed within special education were subjected to awful stereotypes, struggles, and stigmas. Similarly, those who served this population of students faced tremendous heartaches, and experienced only occasional triumphs. IDEA mandated access to inclusive classrooms and the general education program which is publicly funded. This becomes increasingly difficult when the list of those who qualify for special education continues to grow and differentiated instruction is increasingly more on-demand from parents and politicians for *every* child, not just those possessing what have been classified as "special needs."

IDEA 2004 has specified the following thirteen categories under which special education services are provided: specific learning disabilities, autism, emotional and behavioral disturbance, other health impairments, orthopedic impairments, speech or language impairments, mental retardation, traumatic brain injury, deaf/blindness, multiple disabilities, visual impairments, developmental delays, hearing impairments.

24. Salend and Duhaney, "Historical and Philosophical Changes."
25. Ibid.

Nearly seven million children, youth and young adults with disabilities in our public schools receive special education and related services under these categories as part of their publicly funded education.[26]

What Is Special about Special Education?

Special education is special because of the provision of additional services, additional supports, additional programs, specialized placements or environments to ensure that the educational needs of the students with special needs are provided for. The provision of those individually planned and systematically monitored teaching procedures, adapted equipment and materials, and other interventions and related services that help to make special education special, help learners with special needs achieve a greater level of success in school and community than would be possible if the student were only given access to the general education setting without those accompanying services and supports. The collaborative efforts of parents, various service professionals, and especially special education Teachers are behind what is special about special education!

What Advances Have Been Made in the Field of Special Education?

Great advances have been made in special education over the last seventy years. Some examples of the advances are: the great strides that have been made in early childhood education, early reading and math instruction, positive behavior supports, curriculum based measurement, transition, and the multitiered systems of support in general education which includes special education students. New special education teachers need to be aware of their role in this multitiered system of support (which is primarily part of the general education domain) and the relationship of the response to intervention (RTI) model to the full inclusion effort.

What Is Special Education Instruction?

The individualization of the education and services that students with disabilities need in order to succeed despite their academic, social, or physical challenges is the sine qua non of special education instruction.

26. Turnbull et al., *Exceptional Lives.*

The critical components of special education instruction that differentiate it from regular education include: Explicit and systematic instruction, intensive instruction (referring to pacing, group size as well as duration and frequency). Corrective feedback and reinforcement are also components of special education instruction.[27]

As correctly outlined by Scruggs and Mastropieri, the essential components of special instruction include:

> important knowledge areas (knowledge of laws, regulations, and issues; knowledge of the characteristics of exceptionality); and effective specialized teaching skills (task analysis; evaluation and assessment; explicit instruction; use of classroom peers; addressing significant psycho-educational challenges, such as attention, memory, organizational skills, motivation, and affect; and managing social behavior). In addition, special education teachers employ specialized adaptations and learning strategies specific to all areas of academic functioning, such as literacy, mathematics, science, and social studies.[28]

What Is the Goal of Special Education?

The focus of IDEA is to provide specialized instruction, services and supports which help children with disabilities to benefit from their education. IDEA 2004 shows that part of the main purpose of special education is to prepare children with disabilities for further education, employment and independent living.[29] See figure 1.2 below for the full list of the purpose of IDEA 2004. On the other hand, the focus of the No Child Left Behind (NCLB) law of 2001 was to seek the improvement of the education of all children, especially children from low-income families. The 2004 reauthorization of IDEA was more closely aligned with NCLB in an effort to set higher academic standards for all learners and improve educational outcomes. However, the effect of this close alignment of IDEA and NCLB is that the focus of special education seems to have been integrated more with the general education curriculum standards. Clearly special education is increasingly being pushed more in the direction of general education. The observation of Bateman, Lloyd, Tankersley and Brown about this is very

27. Pullen and Hallahan, *What Is Special Education Instruction?*
28. Scruggs and Mastropieri, "What Makes Special Education Special?," 33.
29. LD Online, "IDEA."

pertinent. "Today's emphasis on standards-based IEPs and formal academic assessment of all students' performance on state standards is resulting in increased efforts to teach the general education curriculum to more and more special education students."[30]

IDEA encourages inclusion of special education students in general education, though inclusion is not mandated in the law. Schools should definitely encourage the active participation of those students who appear to be able to meet the general education academic expectations. For one thing, including students with disabilities who through the utilization of specialized instructional techniques, supports and devices can be a part of, and benefit from the general educational classrooms should be encouraged because such efforts can sometimes help to narrow the achievement gap between general and special education students. However, schools should not give up on, or minimize the needs of, the many other students who are not likely able to meet such general education academic expectations. It is certainly appropriate to set high standards for all learners, yet success in the general education curriculum is not the only goal of special education. As Scruggs and Mastropieri very correctly pointed out, a more important and realistic goal of special education instruction for many students is

> learning to read and appreciate basic text independently (or recognize emergency words); exhibit appropriate interpersonal skills; make purchases, maintain bank accounts, and budget money; learn marketable career or technical skills; and participate in our democracy. Such goals and skills may in many cases easily be as significant and important as, for example, mastering a foreign language or learning trigonometry, and especially so when these latter goals are unlikely to be attained.[31]

Despite the great, ongoing advances that are being made in special education, especially through improved teacher preparation, professional development, instructional techniques and technological advances such as iPads, computer applications and various assistive technology devices and services which may in the future lessen the need for some special education services, yet special education is still very important for millions of children who have unique educational needs which cannot be met by general education. As Bateman, Lloyd, Tankersley and Brown, have rightly cautioned, "People who advocate the merger of general and special education or the

30. Bateman et al., "What Is Special Education?," 15.

31. Scruggs and Mastropieri, "What Makes Special Education Special?," 32.

dissolution of special education may prevail in the short term, but unless all children can be made substantially more like each other than they are now, special education will most likely survive or be reborn, perhaps with a different name."[32]

The specific objective of special education is successful educational development of students, regardless of their disabilities or limitations.[33] The goal of special education is not to morph into, or be subsumed by, general education. The single, most important goal of special education is discovering and building on the abilities of exceptional students through the careful establishment, and effective implementation of a student's Individualized Education Plan (IEP) objectives.[34]

Figure 1.2. The Purpose of IDEA 2004

- (1A) to ensure that all children with disabilities have available to them a free appropriate public education that emphasizes special education and related services designed to meet their unique needs and prepare them for further education, employment and independent living;

- (1B) to ensure that the rights of children with disabilities and parents of such children are protected;

- (1C) to assist states, localities, educational service agencies, and federal agencies to provide for the education of all children with disabilities;

- (2) to assist states in the implementation of a statewide, comprehensive, coordinated, multidisciplinary, interagency system of early intervention services for infants and toddlers with disabilities and their families;

- (3) to ensure that educators and parents have the necessary tools to improve educational results for children with disabilities by supporting system improvement activities; coordinated research and personnel preparation; coordinated technical assistance, dissemination, and support; and technology development and media services; and

---

32. Bateman et al., "What Is Special Education?," 13.

33. Scruggs and Mastropieri, "What Makes Special Education Special?"

34. Ibid.

- (4) to assess and ensure the effectiveness of efforts to educate children with disabilities.[35]

What Is the Job of a Special Education Teacher?

The job of a special education teacher is multifaceted.[36] The special education teacher serves as case manager who is charged with coordinating the different aspects and components of the services and needs of a student with special education identification for maximum effective outcomes. Additionally, the job of a special educator involves counseling, mentoring, surrogate parenting, advocacy, etc. The special education teachers also engage in individually planned, monitored, specialized, intensive, goal-directed instruction to ensure that all educational needs of the students with special needs are provided for.

Special education teachers present purposeful intervention efforts at three levels: preventive, remedial, and compensatory. Learning to carry out these various functions of the special education teacher with dedication, diligence and thoroughness is the key to a successful career as a special education teacher.

What Does the Future of Special Education Look Like?

The emergence of new vistas in technology and the explosion of technological information will continue to impact special education.[37] Diversity issues such as overrepresentation, LGBT, etc., will likely persist into the future. There will be probable dilution of special education in the future which will be accounted for by issues of funding, methods of accountability, methods of identification for services, instructional arrangements involving special education teachers in differential roles in the classroom, such as co-teaching contexts.[38]

35. LD Online, "IDEA."
36. Mamlin, *Preparing Effective Special Education Teachers.*
37. Dell et al., *Assistive Technology in the Classroom.*
38. Lloyd et al., "Whither Special Education?"

Conclusion: What Is the Connection between Special Education and Christian Theology?

Our conclusion will consist of a reflection on the connection between special education and Christian theology which hopefully provides a perspective on how best to view and practice special education. In their well-written article on faith integration in education, Lawrence, Burton, and Nwosu pointed out the long-standing connection between education and the Christian religion.

> Christianity did not create the combination of religion and education. As long as people of the world have passed on their culture from generation to generation, they have, in fact, been using some form of education to maintain, promote, and prolong their cultures, which almost always include some type of religion.[39]

Special education (just like education in general, and like disability studies) is intricately connected with Christian theology.[40] Indeed, there is something inherently Christian about special education as Anderson correctly affirms. Special education builds on certain assumptions and notions such as the assumption that the quest for knowledge and truth is possible, the notion of orderliness, fairness, justice, restoration, etc. all of which have basically theological underpinnings and dimensions. Yet the practice of special education has gone on for many years in a manner and environment that was considered "neutral." However, in reality there is no such thing as a neutral education. There is a worldview or worldviews governing every educational system and every educational curriculum. Every worldview has its belief system about God; either that he exists or that he does not. A neutral education stems from a worldview that sees God as either irrelevant or nonexistent. Either way the clear message of such a worldview is that there is no God since an irrelevant God is the same as no God at all.

In this case, the worldview of our "neutral" special educational system has predominantly been that of secular humanism which denies or minimizes the existence of God, exalts man as the architect of his own destiny, and affirms Darwinian evolutionism. In the world view of humanism, the natural world is the only one we can know; the here-and-now is all there is. In the humanistic worldview, mankind is the only source of truth, morals

---

39. Lawrence et al., "Refocusing on the Learning."

40. Anderson, *Toward a Theology of Special Education*; Yong, *Bible, Disability, and the Church*.

and values. The highest human achievement is to improve the human condition. The future will be better if people proceed ethically and rationally. The truth is that the utopia which humanism anticipates and promises has not materialized, and does not seem to be forthcoming.

The crucial point is that understanding and practicing special education from a biblical worldview perspective has the potential to lift the field and its practice to profound heights, and to unlock the huge prospect which the discipline has to ignite so much more dynamic and multi-dimensional accomplishments and benefits both for the students with disabilities, and those who care about their wellbeing. Thus, the special educator who practices special education from a Christian biblical worldview perspective sees their role not just as a profession, but as a call to service, as a choice to love and pursue justice (Micah 6:8), as a total life response to God.[41] With such a mindset, the special educator is best equipped to avoid the burnout that plagues the field, as well as to help the special needs students grow academically and in their discovery and development of their God-given aptitudes and abilities.

Bibliography

Anderson, D. W. *Toward a Theology of Special Education: Integrating Faith and Practice.* Bloomington, IN: WestBow, 2012.

Armstrong, T. *Neurodiversity in the Classroom: Strength-Based Strategies to Help Students with Special Needs Succeed in School and Life.* Alexandria, VA: ASCD, 2012.

Bateman, L., et al. "What Is Special Education?" In *Enduring Issues in Special Education: Personal Perspectives,* edited by B. Bateman et al., 11–20. New York: Routledge, 2015.

Council for Exceptional Children. "CEC's Summary of Selected Provisions in Every Student Succeeds Act (ESSA)." http://cecblog.typepad.com/files/cecs-summary-of-selected-issues-in-every-student-succeeds-act-essa-1 pdf.

Dell, A. G., et al. *Assistive Technology in the Classroom: Enhancing the School Experiences of Students with Disabilities.* Upper Saddle River, NJ: Pearson / Merrill-Prentice Hall, 2008.

Esqueda, O. J. "Biblical Worldview: The Christian Higher Education Foundation for Learning." *Christian Higher Education* 13 (2014) 91–100.

Fowler, J. W. "Practical Theology and Theological Education: Some Models and Questions." *Theology Today* 42 (1985) 43–58.

Friend, M. *Special Education: Contemporary Perspectives for Schools and Professionals.* 4th ed. Boston: Pearson, 2014.

Friend, M., and W. Bursuck. *Including Students with Special Needs: A Practical Guide for Classroom Teachers.* Boston: Pearson, 2015.

41. Anderson, *Toward a Theology of Special Education.*

Hallahan D. P., et al. *Exceptional Learners: An Introduction to Special Education.* Boston: Pearson, 2015.

Hasker, W. "Faith-Learning Integration: An Overview." *Christian Scholar's Review* 11 (1992) 234–48.

Heward, William L. *Exceptional Children: An Introduction to Special Education.* 10th ed. Upper Saddle River, NJ: Pearson, 2013.

Kang, S. S. "'Your Kingdom Come': Practical Theology as Living Out Three Great Pillars of Christianity." *Christian Education Journal* 8 (2011) 114–29.

Lawrence, T. A., et al. "Refocusing on the Learning in 'Integration of Faith and Learning.'" *Journal of Research on Christian Education* 14 (2005) 17–50.

LD Online. "IDEA." http://www.ldonline.org/features/idea2004.

Lloyd, J. W., et al. "Whither Special Education?" In *Enduring Issues in Special Education: Personal Perspectives*, edited by B. Bateman et al., 444–64. New York: Routledge, 2015.

Mamlin, N. *Preparing Effective Special Education Teachers.* New York: Guilford, 2012.

Pullen, P. C., and D. P. Hallahan. "What Is Special Education Instruction?" In *Enduring Issues in Special Education: Personal Perspectives*, edited by B. Bateman et al., 37–50. New York: Routledge, 2015.

Salend, S. J. *Creating Inclusive Classrooms: Effective and Reflective Practices.* 8th ed. Boston: Pearson, 2016.

Salend, S. J., and L. M. G. Duhaney. "Historical and Philosophical Changes in the Education of Students with Exceptionalities." Chapter 1 of *History of Special Education*, edited by A. F. Rotatori et al. Bingley, UK: Emerald, 2011.

Scruggs, T. E., and M. Mastropieri. "What Makes Special Education Special?" In *Enduring Issues in Special Education: Personal Perspectives*, edited by Bateman et al., 22–35. New York: Routledge, 2015.

Smith, D. J. "The Historical Context of Special Education: Framing Our Understanding of Contemporary Issues." In *Critical Issues in Special Education*, edited by Sorrells et al., 1–15. Boston: Pearson, 2004.

Turnbull, A., et al. *Exceptional Lives: Special Education in Today's Schools.* Boston: Pearson, 2016.

US Department of Defense Education Activity. "Special Education." http://www.dodea.edu/curriculum/specialeduc/index.cfm.

US Department of Education. "Building the Legacy: IDEA 2004." http://idea.ed.gov/explore/home.

Yell, M. L. *The Law and Special Education.* 4th ed. Upper Saddle River, NJ: Pearson, 2016.

Yong, A. *The Bible, Disability, and the Church: A New Vision of the People of God.* Grand Rapids: Eerdmans, 2011.

Wehmeyer, M. L. "Defining Mental Retardation and Ensuring Access to the General Curriculum." *Education and Training in Mental Retardation and Developmental Disabilities* 38 (2003) 271–82.

Wood, J. W. *Teaching Students in Inclusive Settings: Adapting and Accommodating Instruction.* 5th ed. Upper Saddle River, NJ: Merrill / Prentice Hall, 2006.

2

What Is the Theology of Special Education?

Ben C. Nworie, PhD, MDiv, LPC
Professor of Special Education
School of Education, Biola University

Abstract

TO ANSWER THE QUESTION "What is the theology of special education?"
this chapter calls attention to the intricate connection between special education and Christian theology as both of them deal with similar notions,
concerns and assumptions, such as the quest for knowledge and truth, the
notion of growth, compassion, orderliness, fairness, equity, and justice. A
brief historical overview of the tangled roots of education and religion
shows that the two have been closely connected from the earliest times to
fairly recent times when the establishment of most institutions of higher
education in the United States was based on Christian principles. To register the importance of being guided by Christian theological perspectives
in the practice of special education, the chapter finally focuses on theology
proper or the doctrine of God (especially creation and practical theology),
Christology (especially regarding the person and work of Christ), and biblical anthropology (especially regarding the creation, nature, worth and

purpose of man) and shows the relevance and implications of these three aspects of Christian theology for special education.

Keywords: theology, special education, Christology, anthropology, miracles

Introduction

Special education at its core is intricately connected with Christian theology. Special education builds on certain notions and assumptions, such as the quest for knowledge and truth, the notion of growth, compassion, orderliness, fairness, equity, justice, etc. all of which have basically Christian theological dimensions and implications. For example, in Christian theology, all knowledge stems from the omniscient God described in the Bible as a God of knowledge who no one can teach knowledge, but who knows the secrets of the heart (1 Sam 2:3; Job 21:22; Ps 44:21). Similarly, in Christianity, all truth emanates from God. The Bible indicates that God's word is truth (Ps 119:160; John 17:17), it also indicates that Jesus is the truth (John 14:6), and that the holy spirit of God is the spirit of truth (John 16:13). Indeed all truth is God's truth. God epitomizes perfection an aspect of which we aspire to through best practices in special education. God is also the epitome of justice, truth and uprightness or fairness (Deut 32:4; Mal 2:6). This connection between Christianity and special education is not a new or superficial phenomenon. The intricate connection between them is as old and deep rooted as the connection between education and religion.

The Intertwined Roots of Education and Religion

From the earliest times, humans have used education in some form or another to maintain, promote, prolong, transmit and disseminate their culture;[1] and religion is an integral part of human culture.[2] Beginning with the history of ancient Israel, we notice that for the Jews, both in the Old and New Testaments, education and religion were intricately interwoven. The Scriptures are resplendent with instances of God's people being taught God's word and God's law in the tabernacle, at home, in the temple, and in the synagogue. Instances also abound in which God's word is upheld

1. Lawrence et al., "Refocusing on the Learning."
2. Ilogu, *Christianity and Igbo Culture.*

as the vehicle for inculcating wholesome learning, wisdom and true knowledge (Deut 6:4; Ps 19:7–14; Amos 5:24; Matt 28:19–20; Col 3:16; Jas 1:22; 2 Tim 2:15; 1 Tim 5:17).

This trend of religion and education coexisting persisted for many years and eventually resulted in the emergence of a hybrid of theology and philosophy which for several centuries was recognized as the traditional approach to education. With the emergence of the Renaissance, and the rise in the level of authority ascribed to human thought; reason began to replace dogma. Belief in God and the Bible was demoted as the sole source and authority for education. Consequently, a trend ensured in which theology lost its position as the primal voice for faith and learning. This new trend continued, leading to Christian thought exercising limited influence in academic circles.[3] The weakening of Christian thought and influence in academic circles persisted through the period of the establishment of colleges and universities in the American colonies as religious institutions.

Historically, the establishment of most institutions of higher education in the United States was based on Christian principles. Many of them were established primarily for the propagation of the gospel or as training grounds for missionaries, clergy and other church workers.[4] As carefully detailed in the seminal book *The Dying of the Light*, by Burtchaell, over time, however, due to the influence of rationalism and non-biblical worldviews such as naturalism and post modernism, most of these institutions that were started by Christian denominations for the purpose of spreading the light of the Christian gospel have gradually abandoned their Christian identity. Others have relegated their Christian objectives to religious departments and seminaries.[5]

The Theology of Special Education

As a Christian educator how does the content of my faith intersect with the content of my discipline, and how does that fit into or affect what I do as a special education practitioner?

For a number of reasons, this is not a question that many Christian educators in the field of special education think seriously about daily, discuss or ask frequently. This question involves thinking theologically about

3. Lawrence et al., "Refocusing on the Learning."

4. Burtchaell, *Dying of the Light*; Esqueda, "Biblical Worldview."

5. Esqueda, "Biblical Worldview."

the discipline of special education. It involves thinking reflectively about the relationship of the Christian faith to the academic specialty of special education. The question involves what Hasker very correctly describes as reflecting deeply and clearly on the "integral relationship" which inherently exists between the Christian faith and the discipline. This question, therefore, involves thinking Christianly about special education as a discipline.

Thinking Christianly is an expression that has been well utilized in the literature on Christian faith integration, or faith and learning integration.[6] The idea of "thinking Christianly" is derived from the Apostle Paul's instruction in Philippians 2:5, to "let this mind be in you, which was also in Christ Jesus." It also relates to the Apostle Paul's teaching in Romans 12:2 to "be transformed by the renewing of your mind, that you may prove what is that good, and acceptable, and perfect will of God."

Thinking Christianly implies thinking biblically and viewing life from a Christian perspective. It implies an understanding of God as Creator and Redeemer. It also implies critically seeking after truth, and desiring to see how truths intersect. Dockery adds the following to the idea of Christian thinking: seeking "answers through curious exploration and serious wrestling with the fundamental questions of human existence."[7] Part of the aim of this book, therefore, is to create awareness of, and register the importance of, being guided by Christian theological perspectives in the practice of special education. Engaging in this important adventure of approaching the practice of special education through Christian theological perspectives is a serious endeavor that, as Hasker very correctly points out, is "a specifically scholarly task."[8]

The philosophical orientation guiding the way special education has been carried out from its inception is divergent from the time-tested and deeply rooted intricate connection between education and religion which was pointed out above. It is also divergent from the biblically guided viewpoint being advocated here. The practice of special education has gone on for many years in a manner and environment that was considered "neutral." For example, the Supreme Court moved from not allowing prayer in schools in 1962, to banning the Ten Commandments from being displayed on the walls in public school in the 1980 *Stone v. Graham* case.[9]

6. Lawrence et al., "Refocusing on the Learning."
7. Dockery, "Shaping a Christian Worldview," 13.
8. Hasker, "Faith-Learning Integration," 235.
9. Rosebrough, "Christian Worldview and Teaching."

This symbolic removal of the very basis for common law and morality in the public schools became the glaring evidence and verdict of neutrality in the American educational system. Consequently, special education has been rendered with a basically secular ethos and praxis where religious faith was not a factor. However, there is something inherently Christian about special education. The Christian theological perspectives relevant to special education are evident in *theology* proper or the doctrine of God (especially creation and practical theology), in *Christology* (especially regarding the person and work of Christ), and *biblical anthropology* (especially regarding the creation, nature, worth and purpose of man). There are also several biblical concepts and principles that are relevant to the essence and practice of special education. Some of them include the concepts of biblical worldview, biblical love, and compassion, as well as the principle of service or ministry (Greek, *diakonia*). However, in this chapter, we will concentrate on theology (especially creation and practical theology), Christology, and anthropology as they integrate with special education.

Theology (or the Doctrine of God)

Theology or the doctrine of God is broad. The aspects of theology most pertinent to our current discussion are creation and practical theology as they relate to special education. Erickson in his classical work on *Christian Theology* says it very well when he defines Christian theology as the study or science of God, which includes God's works, his relationship to them, which also seeks to "understand God's creation, particularly man and his condition, and God's redemptive working in relation to mankind."[10] The doctrine of God in relation to special education is best crystalized through focusing on practical theology, and through a look at the work of God in creation.

Practical Theology

The focus of practical theology is on everyday implications of Christian theological beliefs. The interest of practical theology is on useful application of the study of theology.[11] Theology in the form of practical theology

10. Erickson, *Word Became Flesh*, 21.

11. Fowler, "Practical Theology"; Kang, "Your Kingdom Come."

is something all Christians must do.[12] Consequently, as Kang very correctly articulated, "the question is *not whether* it is done or not, but *how well* it is done."[13]

Theology in special education should not be conceived in terms of the systematized study of the doctrine of God, focusing simply on academic reflections on Scripture. Theology in special education is more appropriately seen in terms of the discovery of, and reflection on, the characteristics and practical realities of God's involvement and superintendence in daily life. It is more of a reflection on what it means to be truly human, as well as an inquiry into the fullness of the truth of God. Theology in special education in this practical sense focuses on the implications of how faith guides understanding and actions in daily circumstances and in matters of practice within the field. Anderson summarizes the idea well when he says:

> Practical theology does not just ask "what is going on?" in a situation but, drawing on biblical revelation, goes on to ask "what should be going on?" "How are we to live?" "How should I respond to what is happening?" "Where is God in this experience or situation?" . . . In simple terms, practical theology is expressed in faith-based action flowing from the questions "What would God have me do?" and "What would God have me learn?" in any particular instance.[14]

Practical theology fits best into, and is best practiced in the context of a biblical worldview. Since creation is the beginning and central point of the biblical worldview, apart from creation then, no aspect of Christian thought has any validity.[15] Creation is, therefore, the valid central point of our discussion of theology in relation to the theology of special education.

Creation

One cannot agree more with the assertion of Claerbaut about creation, especially in contrast to evolution. He very correctly asserts that creation is "the central context in which all Christian thinking is placed. . . . Evolution is about the development of something already in existence, not the

---

12. Ibid.

13. Ibid., 117.

14. Anderson, *Toward a Theology of Special Education*, 50.

15. Claerbaut, *Faith and Learning on the Edge*.

beginning of that existence itself."[16] The biblical creation story answers the toughest questions of life that evolution does not, and cannot answer. The biblical creation account traces all reality to one ultimate reality, thus negating the artificial compartmentalization of reality in the various fields of knowledge.

In special education, just as in schools in general, as well as in the overall American society, there has been compartmentalization between the sacred faith and social life of individuals; a dichotomy between faith and reason. This lack of integrity between the life of the mind and the life of the spirit has a detrimental effect on the Christian faith and Christian higher education. It poses a hindrance to the ability to perceive the integrated nature and wholeness of God's truth.

There has been a search, especially in Christian higher education for a firm basis for properly fusing faith and learning together. The biblical narrative which begins with creation, presents the answer to this dilemma of an avenue for solid integration between the Christian faith and various academic disciplines, including special education. The creation narrative is the key to the wholesome integration (*shalom*) of faith and learning. Esqueda, spells it out well in this way:

> The Bible tells of the triune God who personally relates to his creation and serves as the unifying factor for everything that exists. God is the creator and sustainer of the world. . . .
>
> Because everything that exists came from God, there is really no distinction between sacred and secular: everything is sacred. Life was not compartmentalized, but had the creator God as the foundation for its complete unity (Is. 45:18). Therefore, what some have viewed as a dichotomy between sacred and secular has no place in a coherent philosophy of education.[17]

The biblical creation narrative is not only the basis of human unity and dignity, it provides a basis for the validation of our knowledge and our thinking. For Christians in general and Christians in the academy in particular, creation is the beginning of knowledge. For example, Claerbaut contends that "In the beginning God . . ." (Gen 1:1) is not just doctrine; but that "it is an epistemological statement."[18] He maintains that

16. Ibid., 147.
17. Esqueda, "Biblical Worldview," 93.
18. Claerbaut, *Faith and Learning on the Edge*, 154.

right there is the beginning point for humanity to learn all that needs to be learned. It is also the end of knowledge. . . . Everything we can learn now—whether it is of geological layering of ages past or of the latest economic models—is merely a derivative of the eternal Creator. "For in him we live and move and have our being" (Acts 17:28). The various forms of revelation become understandable to humankind, given the creation of the human brain with its ability to understand and communicate using symbols. It is through that complex brain that we alone among all living organisms can receive and decode the various forms of revelation. . . . Again, by Christian logic, it is not "I think, therefore I am," but rather, "I am (in the image of God), therefore I think." That "I am (in the image of God)" is the epistemological starting point of true knowledge.[19]

Creation defines who we are, why we exist, and how people should treat one another. Creation is a clear indication that there was meaning and purpose associated with the making of all things by God. As Claerbaut correctly asserts,

In the Genesis account, creation occurs in phases grounded in design and purpose. . . . Every aspect of the universe—from the placement of the stars to the balance of nature, from the rotation of the earth to the food chain, affirms the notions of order, objectivity, meaning, and purpose. Foundational to the notion of a designer is a purpose for what he designed. . . . The passage in Romans (8:28) stating that all things work in concert for good in the lives of those who love God reinforces human value. A sense of security is derived from the Christian notion that things do not happen by accident. There is a reason behind events, a reason that coheres with the will of God.[20]

The doctrine of creation clearly suggests that everything made by God was purposeful, and that nothing made by God is intrinsically valueless or worthless. Everything that God has made is good. Erickson is, therefore, accurate in his assertion that "there was nothing evil within God's original creation."[21] Some of the implications then of God's creation, as Erickson correctly points out, are that

19. Ibid.
20. Ibid., 155.
21. Erickson, *Christian Theology*, 375.

> Christians should be at the very forefront of the concern for the preservation and welfare of the creation, for it is not merely something that is there; it is what God has made. Everything within creation has its function; that of man is to care for the rest of God's world. . . . We must not despise any part of God's creation. As different as some creatures may be from us, they have integrity as part of God's plan.[22]

The truth expressed here by Erickson is at the core of the theology of special education. That is, the core impetus of special education is genuine concern for the educational preservation and welfare of the special needs students because they are God's creation, and "we must not despise any part of God's creation". All students, including those with disabilities, have integrity since they are included in God's creative plan. The consistent efforts of special education to seek ways and means to level the playing field for the children with disabilities should be seen as part of this divine plan.

Another implication of the doctrine of creation for our discipline is that God can, and does continue his creative activity through us. Thus our scholarly products and creative teaching strategies aimed at helping our students learn, should be seen as continuations of the creative acts of God. Erickson clearly agrees when he says:

> Creation does not preclude development within the world; it includes it. Thus God's plan involves and utilizes the best of human skill and knowledge in the genetic refinement of the creation. Such endeavors are our partnership with God in the ongoing work of creation.[23]

Christology (the Person and Work of Christ)

A brief examination of some of Jesus' healing miracles which were an integral part of his effective teaching ministry provides clues about the person and work of Christ. These healing miracles yield several constructive christological themes that are relevant to effective inclusive special education. The miracle healings inform us about Jesus' Christology of disability because these healing miracles of Jesus show him as (among other things)

22. Ibid., 385.
23. Ibid., 385–86.

loving, caring, compassionate, and inclusive of all types of people, including people who were disabled, and therefore, were marginalized.

Historically, people with disabilities have been marginalized.[24] As White very aptly pointed out, "During His time on earth, Jesus walked alongside all types of people, showing no partiality in His ministry. He saw *all* people as bearers of the image of God and desired to share His Kingdom with everyone, especially those whom society deemed unworthy."[25] The healing miracles of Jesus reveal that he truly loved and valued people above cultural norms. To engage in this short examination of the healing miracles of Jesus, I will randomly use three approaches: a disability-informed Christology approach, a disability hermeneutic approach, and a socio-rhetorical interpretive approach.

A disability-informed Christology adopts the view of a life-affirming God who "calls us to justice and peace of all and to all." It is a perspective of disability that helps us to see a "hidden" dimension of God. This Christology perspective views disabilities not as a problem to be solved, but rather as particular ways of being human that need to be understood, valued, and supported. It is a view that welcomes persons with disability and accepts them "as people with gifts who have divine dignity, meaning, and purpose."[26]

A disability hermeneutic approach which is fairly similar to the Christology of disability method is "an approach to the Bible that is informed by the experiences of disability."[27] Instead of leaving the presuppositions of non-disabled people unquestioned, this approach tries, rereads and retrieves the biblical traditions from the perspective of people with disabilities.[28]

A third approach, the socio-rhetorical interpretive method, has also been slightly employed.[29] The socio-rhetorical approach "brings together historical, sociological and literary methods of interpretation to provide a detailed exegesis of biblical texts. It weaves together strands from each of these approaches to provide a textured reading of scripture that attempts to give equal emphasis to the literary and historical perspectives."[30]

24. Clapton and Fitzgerald, "History of Disability."
25. White, "People with Disabilities in Christian Community," 11.
26. George, *God of Life, Justice, and Peace,* 545, 46–462.
27. Yong, *Bible, Disability, and the Church,* 13.
28. Ibid.
29. McColl and Ascough, "Jesus and People with Disabilities."
30. Ibid., 2.

At least one of these three approaches will be utilized in the analysis of each of the four healing stories to be examined. From these three perspectives, the paper will look at four of Jesus' miracle healings in the gospels to see what themes emerge from them. Effort will then be made to reconcile the themes that emerge from these gospel healing stories with concepts such as inclusion, love and compassion which are essential for an inclusive experience for students with disabilities in the special education context.

We begin in John, the fourth gospel, with the healing of the man born blind. The story found in John 9:1–41 was chosen because it represents one of the clearest and longest narratives in the four gospels involving Jesus healing a person with a disability. According to this healing story in John 9, Jesus, on a Sabbath day, heals a man who had been blind from birth. The man's parents confirm the healing (vv. 1–12) which ignites the fury of the Pharisees who engage the man in a drawn-out cross-examination. The bulk of the chapter focuses on this interchange (vv. 13–34). In the ending part of the story, Jesus meets up with the man after he has been excommunicated from the synagogue. In this concluding scenario (vv. 35–41), the man ultimately acknowledges and worships Jesus, while the Pharisees are reprimanded by Jesus as remaining in spiritual blindness, consequently being guilty of sin by virtue of their rejection of Jesus and his ministry.

This healing story when viewed from a disability hermeneutic perspective brings some interesting awareness to the front. First, contrary to how this man may be perceived from the perspective of the non-disabled, the blind man was not in a completely dismal or dependent condition since he was apparently able to find his way around fairly well, without the help of other people. For instance, when Jesus instructed him to "go, wash in the pool of Siloam," the man, according to John "went and washed" (v. 7). There was no indication from the text that someone else aided the man or that he groped his way about to the pool where he washed.

Second, the man clearly understood that his identity was not defined by his sight or lack of sight. Indeed, people's disabilities should not define them. While acknowledging that he was blind, and now seeing (v. 25), the now sighted man in response to the argument among his neighbors and the local people regarding whether or not he was the same as the blind beggar, by keeping on saying: "I am he" (v. 9) insisted that he was the same person. The man who was born blind was certain that neither blindness nor sightedness altered his personal identity.

Third, it is important from a theology of disability perspective to point out that Jesus rejected the assumption by his disciples that this man's congenital blindness resulted from ancestral sin. Jesus affirmed that "neither this man nor his parents sinned" (v. 3). Though certain parts of the Old Testament indicated that the sins of parents would be visited upon generations of their descendants (Exod 20:5; cf. Num 14:18), there are also indications, especially through the post-exilic prophets that God would no longer punish children as a result of their parents' sins (e.g., Ezek 18:2–4; Jer 31:29–30). Many first-century Jews strongly believed (John 9:2, 34), that sin was the root cause of disabilities. Similarly, as the history of special education and disability studies reveal, till very recently people in the United States (and elsewhere) commonly believed that people with disabilities were morally deficient or were suffering as a consequence of sin and were therefore discriminated against.[31] The response of Jesus, does not, however, nullify the consequences to sin. For example, as Yong correctly remarks:

> The intemperate uses of alcohol or illegal drugs have disabling implications not only for those who abuse such substances (think of the many fatal or tragic car accidents caused by intoxicated drivers) but also for their children (particularly if women persist in such activities while pregnant). Think also about sexual promiscuity and the disabling diseases that are contracted, or about the disabilities related to the wars that human beings fight. In a real sense there are ontological connections between sinful behaviors in a fallen world and the disabilities that sometimes result.[32]

Jesus found it necessary to clarify the disconnection between sin and congenital disability in the case of the man born blind, but does not altogether blur the connection between sin and disability. It is important to point out that in the healing story of a man crippled for thirty-eight years who was by the pool at Bethesda (John 5:1–18), Jesus' final caution to this lame man at the pool of Bethesda was, "See, you have been made well! Do not sin any more, so that nothing worse happens to you" (5:14). In this warning Jesus shows the connection between sin and really bad outcomes which may not necessarily manifest in the form of physical disability. Could Jesus in that final admonition to that man to desist from sinning any more not be referring to serious spiritual consequences associated with sin?

31. Smith, "Historical Context of Special Education"; Heward, *Exceptional Children*; Friend, *Special Education*; Smith and Tyler, *Introduction to Special Education*.

32. Yong, *Bible, Disability, and the Church*, 52.

The Synoptic Gospels (Mark, Matthew, and Luke) who also report Jesus miracle healings attribute to him a total of twenty-nine miracles. Three, of these healing miracles were also selected for this chapter. The first of the triple-tradition synoptic healing stories considered in this chapter is the story of the cleansing of the man with leprosy, found in Matthew 8:1–4, Mark 1:40–45 and Luke 5:12–16. In this story, Jesus, surrounded by a crowd, is approached by a man with leprosy, who kneels before Jesus and inquires whether Jesus was willing to heal him. Jesus heals the man with a touch, and then sends him to the temple so that the healing may be verified.

In New Testament times, leprosy (represented in the Bible by the Greek word *lepra*) was a serious disability which isolated the sufferers from all important societal nexus with their families, their communities and their religious practices. This fact of the social implications of the disease makes this healing story particularly significant from a Christology of disability perspective. Mark's story portrays Jesus as healing the leper out of compassion. Jesus here models the importance of compassion which has a huge place in schools. It is not an overstatement that "schools with compassionate leaders increase their students' potential for academic success. Compassionate learning environments, for example, lower a student's cortisol levels (decreasing stress levels), which increases his or her ability to learn."[33] Matthew's account of the healing of the leper is set in front of a crowd who act as witnesses, and the healing provides a remarkable demonstration of faith which was properly rewarded when Jesus recognized the faith of the man with leprosy and healed him. Luke's account of the story describing the man as "full of leprosy" indicates that he probably has an advanced stage of the disease, thereby amplifying the uniqueness of Jesus action of coming into physical contact with the leper. Luke's account also throws some light on possibly why the man would fall on his face, beseeching Jesus for his healing. The story ends with a detail included by Mark and Luke which Matthew omits, indicating that despite the charge to keep the healing silent, the story of the healing of the leper spreads widely, pulling great crowds to Jesus.

The second of the synoptic healing stories considered in this chapter is the story of the healing of a man with paralysis (Matt 9:1–8; Mark 2:1–12; Luke 5:17–26). All the Synoptic Gospels again record the healing. According to the healing story, four men are prevented from carrying their friend with a disability in through the crowd, and so they climb up to the roof and lower him down in front of Jesus. Jesus is impressed by the faith shown by

33. Berkowicz and Myers, "Leadership, Learning, and Compassion."

the four friends, he grants the forgiveness of sin to the man who was paralyzed, and asks him to take up his bed and go home. The healing happens as the man immediately rises and walks away and the crowd expresses their awe and amazement, and glorified God. It is important from a disability hermeneutic perspective to observe that in this miracle it was not Jesus or the man who needed healing that took the initiative. It was the friends of the man who was paralyzed that took the initiative for healing on behalf of their friend. In special education, as well as in disability studies, support and collaboration are huge and critical components.

The third Synoptic healing story (also the fourth and last healing miracle of Jesus) for this chapter is the healing of the woman bent over for eighteen years. This is one of four healing miracles recorded only by Luke. It bears similarities with other stories that are unique to Luke, such as the story of the woman who hemorrhaged for twelve years (Luke 8:43–48), and the story of the man with dropsy (Luke 14:1–6) which is the fourth and final healing episode in Luke in which controversy over Sabbath laws emerges.[34] This narrative represents not only Jesus' final healing event in Luke, it is also his last teaching experience in any synagogue.

Visiting rabbis were frequently asked to give the sermon or homily for the synagogue service (Luke 4:16–24).[35] In Luke's account, while Jesus was teaching in one of the synagogues on the Sabbath, he spotted a woman who had suffered for eighteen years from a condition that probably resulted from a fusion of the bones in her back (Luke 13:11).[36] This condition which caused the woman to be bent over has been identified by many commentators as *spondylitis ankylopietica*.[37] It is not necessary to assume that the woman may have been demon possessed because Luke does not indicate that a demon spoke or that Jesus cast out any demon.[38] The Greek literally says that the woman was "having a spirit of weakness."[39]

The woman's presence in the synagogue should not be a surprise when it is realized that though women were excluded from much of Israel's religious life, including access to the inner temple court (mainly to prevent possible ceremonial uncleanness or defilement) women were allowed to

---

34. McColl and Ascough, "Jesus and People with Disabilities"; Evans, *Luke*.

35. Garland, *Mark*.

36. See Evans, *Luke*.

37. Ibid.

38. Evans, *Luke*; Barton et al., *Luke*.

39. Garland, *Mark*.

participate in synagogue worship.[40] Jesus took the initiative in the healing of this woman, just as he had done in the story in John 9. This initiative taken by Jesus in the healing is significant from a Christology of disability perspective. Jesus is aware of and involved in the existential experiences of people with disabilities. He wants them not excluded, but included, and participating in the daily life experiences of their people.

He wants their needs addressed, not ignored or minimized as was exemplified by the synagogue ruler who did not want the woman to be healed on the Sabbath. After Jesus put his hands on the woman, she was immediately healed. Right away "she straightened up and praised God" (13: 13). Through this healing miracle and the spontaneous response of praise to God by the woman Jesus makes vivid the picture of the sense of joy and gratitude to God which people with disabilities experience when they feel included, cared about, genuinely or therapeutically touched, or reached out to in schools or in the community. From a socio-rhetorical interpretive perspective, the bent-over posture of the woman (13:11) has some symbolic significance. First, it portrays the posture of extreme subjugation, low standing and social tension. Second, it is suggestive of a posture which many animals assume, which may point to the relevance of the livestock analogy used by Jesus in the story.[41]

Emerging Themes and Perspectives

In general, the stories depict a lack of detail about the individuals with the disabilities. Typically we know their gender, and sometimes their age may be inferred. What seems to identify them mainly is their disability. This seems to mirror what obtains in contemporary discourse about disability where the tendency is to describe people in terms of their disability, not in terms of their "personhood"; in terms of their deficits, rather than in terms of their abilities.[42] In the school system, this tendency results in depersonalization and medicalization of students with disabilities or students who are different. It also results in the overrepresentation of the diverse students and students with exceptionalities in special education.[43]

40. Ibid.

41. McColl and Ascough, "Jesus and People with Disabilities."

42. Ibid.

43. Hallahan et al., *Exceptional Learners*; Coutinho and Oswald, "Disproportionate Representation in Special Education"; Blanchett et al., "Urban School Failure"; Sullivan,

Several themes and perspectives emerge from these four stories about Jesus' healing miracles concerning individuals with disabilities. In each of the healing stories, Jesus brings the people with disabilities who he cures away from the margins, and into the center, both physically and spiritually. In other words, Jesus does not only take away their infirmities or disabilities. He makes them well spiritually first by forgiving their sin, by commending their faith, and also by healing them physically, thus placing priority on the spiritual core or the image of God (*imago Dei*) in the individual, thereby restoring them to full health and overall well-being which connotes the meaning of the Hebrew word *shalom*.[44] The healing miracles of Jesus consistently evoke themes of inclusiveness, peace, love and harmony. Jesus treats the people with disabilities as whole persons; just as he would have treated other non-disabled people. In each of the four gospel healing accounts analyzed, by healing the person with the disability, Jesus restores the individual not only to health void of the former disability, but to full humanity, full standing in the religious and socio-cultural community.[45]

From the perspective of inclusion in the school setting, the healing miracles in the gospels repeatedly conjure themes of inclusiveness, advocacy and courage.[46] People with disabilities have historically been marginalized. As Clapton and Fitzgerald correctly observed, "People with disability are marginalized even by those who are themselves marginalized."[47] In the story of the man with paralysis lowered through the roof by his friends, Jesus' prompt and eloquent endorsement of the faith of the friends, offers a vivid perspective on inclusion, suggesting the high importance of the message of inclusion in comparison to the message of physical wholeness. This story further reminds us of the value, in special education, of collaboration, team work, provision of related services, care-giving and support to people with disabilities. These are essential components which are vital in the implementation of effective inclusive special education practice.

The efforts that the friends of the man with paralysis made to go through the roof is suggestive of the barriers that people with disabilities and their families, and /or care providers often have to overcome in order

Disproportionality in Special Education.

44. Fowler and Pacino, *Faith Integration and Schools of Education*; McColl and Ascough, "Jesus and People with Disabilities."

45. McColl and Ascough, "Jesus and People with Disabilities."

46. Ibid.

47. Clapton and Fitzgerald, "History of Disability," 1.

to access the services and amenities that other people enjoy. Before the enactment of the federal legislation, the Americans with Disabilities Act (ADA) in 1990, people with disabilities in the United States faced all kinds of barriers.[48] Similarly, before 1975 children with disabilities faced various insurmountable barriers to their learning.[49]

Another important reminder from this story of the man with paralysis is that no one needs to be abandoned or "left behind" on account of their disability as called for in another federal legislation, "No Child Left Behind," which was signed by President Bush in 2001. This law was designed to equip all students to be proficient in English and math, and all teachers to be highly qualified in order to provide effective, measurable learning outcomes to all students.[50]

An additional important correlate from the miracle healing stories of Jesus to the practice of inclusive special education is that it may be necessary, in some dire circumstances, to resist and/or disturb the status quo for the greater good of the student with a disability or exceptionality. Institutions will do well to closely examine the dynamics of their relationship with people with disabilities, and to adjust whatever structure (legal, political and economic) they have in place which may potentially constrain and impede the full participation of people with disabilities.

The three Sabbath healings provide very obvious examples. These stories suggest that for full inclusion to obtain in schools, parents, service providers and practitioners may occasionally act in unorthodox ways to seize opportunities which may present themselves from time to time, even when they are not in conformity with conventional practice or regulations adopted—in order to bring about enhanced well-being (*shalom*) of the person with disability. For example, sometimes in school or institutional settings, teachers, care givers or service providers may operate under some rules and guidelines provided by their governing agencies or bodies which may diminish the personhood, limit the freedom or stifle the creativity of an individual with disability. In working with people with disabilities, schools should be wary of insisting on maintaining the status quo instead of seeking to create and nurture environments that have room for flexibility aimed at bringing about the maximum benefits for the intellectual growth, and overall development of the individual child with disability, knowing

48. Yell, *Law and Special Education.*

49. Ibid.; Nworie, *Central Issues in Special Education.*

50. Nworie, *Central Issues in Special Education.*

that these children are also part of the determiners of the future of our society. As Willard and Black, wisely stated, "What our children learn or do not learn today is the primary determiner of the future of our society."[51]

In the Sabbath healing narratives, Jesus' healing was motivated by the compassion and sense of kinship he felt toward the people he healed. Jesus compassion and genuine love contrasts sharply with the lack of concern demonstrated by the Pharisees for the welfare of the people Jesus healed. Compassion is a key component of effective special education practice.

In another healing miracle not discussed in this chapter, the story of the man by the pool of Bethesda mentioned briefly above (John 5: 1–18), Jesus first inquires if the man wishes to be healed which suggests that Jesus deliberately wished to honor the man's autonomy and his will.[52] Just as God does not violate our freewill, Jesus' miracles were never forced on people. In special education it is best practice to, as much as possible, involve students in the formulation of their own individualized education plan. In that way the choice and autonomy of the student is respected. In asking this question, Jesus deflates the assumption that a full and satisfying life with a disability is not possible. With advances in modern science and technology today, it is very possible to live a full and satisfying life with a disability.

Concluding Thoughts on Jesus' Healing Miracles

Several implications from Jesus' healing miracles, integral to his ministry, were utilized to provide clues about Jesus' Christology of disability. For example, in the miracle of the healing of the man with paralysis, Jesus models the importance of compassion which has a significant implication for special education. The implication of Jesus' compassion which motivated his healings, is highlighted when it is recalled that, as pointed out in the chapter, compassion is indispensable for lowering student stress, and improving school success outcomes. Furthermore, it was demonstrated that a number of themes and perspectives emerging from the healing miracles of Jesus provide clues about Jesus' theology, which is compatible with inclusive special education practices. The following themes and perspectives emerged:

---

51. Willard and Black, *Divine Conspiracy Continued*, 131.

52. McColl and Ascough, "Jesus and People with Disabilities."

- Disability versus personhood. Jesus' loving attitude of recognizing the personhood of individuals with disabilities highlights the importance of the *imago Dei*.

- Inclusion versus marginalization. Jesus' evident habit of inclusion versus marginalization similarly reinforces two other vital components of Jesus' Christology which is Inclusive, namely the importance of community, and the importance of recognizing the value and worth of each individual.

- Social collaboration versus isolationism. The story of the four friends of the man with paralysis further reminds us of the value of collaboration, team work, provision of related services, and care-giving as well as support to people with disabilities in the inclusive practice of special education, certainly reinforcing.

- Barriers versus bridges. Another important reminder from the story of the man with paralysis is that no one should be abandoned, left out, or "left behind" on account of their disability.

- Status quo versus flexible methodology. Sometimes in school or institutional settings, teachers, care givers or service providers may operate under some rules and guidelines provided by their governing agencies or bodies which may diminish the personhood, limit the freedom, or stifle the creativity of an individual with disability. Such a situation might be an occasion to consider wisely challenging the status quo in the service of the individual with disability, and as an advocate for such an individual.

The miracles of Jesus are not only an illustration of Jesus' Christology of disability, they are his illustration of the main tenets of the Christian faith, such as love, compassion, collaboration, unity, service, etc. which are the practical out workings of the Christian gospel. This gospel, as Poe quite correctly points out, is the content of the Christian faith which is faith in Jesus Christ.[53] A close look at Jesus shows how his life and ministry portrayed the gospel in ways that were incisive, meaningful, practical, and helpful both spiritually and socially. As the British journalist Philip Yancey, who describes Jesus as the sinless friend of sinners, rightly observed, the Christ of the gospel commended a contrite tax collector over an arrogant, religious Pharisee. Yancey continues his thoughtful remarks by adding that "the first person to

53. Poe, *Christianity in the Academy.*

37

whom [Jesus] openly revealed himself as Messiah was a Samaritan woman who has a history of five failed marriages and was currently living with yet another man." He concludes by observing that with his dying breath Jesus "pardoned a thief who would have zero opportunity for spiritual growth"[54]

Jesus's miracles and ministry, his show of love and compassion, his genuine interest in, and life-changing interactions with various special needs people, as well as people considered sinners or outsiders by the contemporary Jewish religious leaders, shows Jesus' actions as both theologically and pedagogically significant. They show Jesus as an ideal role model for the special education practitioner. They challenge us to carefully reflect on our own practice models and motives. Following Jesus' ministry model, our own "ministry" with students with disabilities should be meaningful and significant both spiritually (theologically) and educationally.

This idea of special education practitioners following Jesus' ministry model calls for a determination to emulate Jesus as the master teacher, not only by submitting to a personal, redeeming relationship with Jesus, but also by having a practical and transforming relationship with the world as Jesus did. Just as Jesus came to save and to serve, as illustrated by his teaching in Nazareth where he openly proclaimed that he came to declare good news to the poor, liberty to the captives and recovering of sight to the blind, and to set at liberty those who are oppressed (Luke 4:18–19).

In the same way, special educators who adhere to the Christian faith are saved to serve. They should see themselves from an incarnational point of view. That is, as the extensions of Christ. This is a way for the special education practitioner to live out the purpose of God in their discipline. Erickson captures this idea when he boldly asserts that anyone who wholeheartedly believes in Jesus as the Son of God is thereby committed to a proper view of God, to a proper view of man, to a proper view of sin, to a proper view of redemption, to a proper view of the purpose of God in creation and history, to a proper view of human destiny.[55]

54. Yancy, *Jesus I Never Knew*, 258–59.
55. Erickson, *Word Became Flesh*.

Biblical Anthropology

Anthropology

After a brief introductory remark about anthropology in general, the discussion will focus on the creation, nature, worth and purpose of man from a biblical anthropological point of view. The compound word "anthropology" comes from two Greek words, *anthropos* (man) and *logos* (word, matter or thing). Anthropology, thus, refers to the study of man; it deals primarily with the comparative study of the physical and cultural characteristics of humanity across times and places.

Anthropology began in the mid-nineteenth century as a speculative study on the origin of human beings.[56] Early anthropology, as accurately pointed out by Whiteman, "was driven by an evolutionary paradigm conjecturing that human societies and cultures evolved from homogeneous to heterogeneous, from simple to complex."[57] One of the early anthropologists, James G. Frazer, proposed an evolutionary anthropological progression of human beings from belief in magic, to belief in religion, and eventually to science.[58]

Biblical anthropology, on the other hand, refers to the study of man and society as understood primarily within a biblical framework. It usually covers discussion of the creation of man, especially the creation of man in the image of God or imago Dei, the constitutional nature of man, the dignity of man, as well as the sexuality, freedom and depravity of man. Our discussion of biblical anthropology will focus especially on the creation, nature, worth and purpose of man.

The Creation, Nature, Worth and Purpose of Man

The creation narrative provides a vivid, summary commentary on the nature, worth and purpose of man. Man, though created from the dust of the earth, was made in the image of God. Consequently, as a bearer of that divine image, man is accorded intrinsic worth. Furthermore, being created by a purposeful God, there is attendant purpose and meaning in man's life (Gen 1:26–28). As made clear by Isaiah, the Old Testament prophet (Isa

---

56. Whiteman, "Anthropology and Mission."

57. Ibid., 398.

58. Ibid.

43:7), and as buttressed by J. I. Packer in *Knowing God*, which has become a classic of the Christian faith, God created man for the purpose of glorifying him, the Creator. One clear way of fulfilling that purpose of glorifying God is by living our lives in relationship and faithful service to God (Ps 100:2; John 17:4). It is clearly indicated in the Bible that God created us "for a life of good deeds, which he has already prepared for us to do" (Eph 2:10).

It seems obvious then that in the grand scheme of things, human life lived outside of this purposive plan by God of relationship and faithful service to him, quickly ends without much enduring import or substance. Given the brevity of human life on earth, that such a life will ultimately signify nothing is masterfully illustrated by William Shakespeare in this famous quotation in Macbeth:

> Out, out, brief candle! Life's but a walking shadow, a poor player that struts and frets his hour upon the stage and is heard no more. It is a tale told by an idiot, full of sound and fury, signifying nothing. (*Macbeth*, act 5, scene 5, 19–28)

This thought about the meaninglessness of human life lived outside God's purposive plan for man to relate with and faithfully serve God is also illustrated by King Solomon, who tried living for his own pleasure, yet at the end of his life he concluded that all was nothingness (or vanity) and that the only worthwhile life is one of honor and obedience to God (Eccl 12:8, 13–14). The implication of Solomon's conclusion is that there will be a final assessment by God of what people do on earth based on God's plan and purpose for man to honor God and give him faithful service, even by faithfully servicing others. The assertion by Rosebrough speaks clearly to this.

Rosebrough asserts that how people view themselves, including their view of the purpose of their existence, makes a difference in the classroom. For example, teachers who, though in a flawed world, see themselves as created by God for the purpose of serving God through serving other people, will honor their maker by faithfully serving their students, thereby furthering shalom (wholeness and justice) in their classrooms.[59] Perhaps by Jesus willingly choosing to become a humble servant of others God modelled what he expects of humans, including special education teachers (Matt 20: 28; Phil 2:6–8; cf. Isa 42:19; 53:5–6). It is within the repertoire of man to be of service to others and to be good to others.

---

59. Rosebrough, "Christian Worldview and Teaching."

There is inherent goodness associated with humanity. The creation account repeats five times that God saw that what he had made was good (Gen 1:10,12,18, 21, 25). Then at the conclusion, with the creation of man, God's verdict was that the entire creation was very good (Gen 1:31). The history of special education, however, reveals that the field was born out of an environment and mindset that predominantly saw those who require special education as not good, as a burden on our economic system, social services, health and educational systems or a challenge to conquer. This ideology is not only ostracizing to those students classified by the "special needs" title, it also conveys an understanding about students that is fundamentally discriminatory, unjust, and especially unbiblical. The Bible makes it clear that the fact that some people (such as people with disabilities) may look, learn, laugh or live differently, they are nevertheless fully human, and should not be treated as being somewhat less than others who seem "normal" or without disabilities. As Erickson very correctly contends, "The special status which God accorded to man by making him, in distinction from the animals, in God's own image, is extended to all members of the human race."[60] Jesus' theology of disability in the New Testament upholds this view that people with disabilities are not robbed of this imago Dei special status which God accorded to all humans. This affirmation that individuals with their disabilities are also God's image bearers is reflected particularly well in the account of Jesus' encounter with Zacchaeus. Jesus reaches out to Zacchaeus who was dwarfish in stature (Luke 19:3), and without healing Zacchaeus's physical "defectiveness" of shortness of stature, Jesus reaches out to Zacchaeus, includes him among the people of God just as he is, by extending salvation to him as a son of Abraham (Luke 19: 9–10). Similarly, in the story told by Jesus in Luke 16:19–26 of the rich man who lived in luxury daily but died and went to hades, and Lazarus, the poor beggar covered with sores who was carried by the angels to Abraham's side after he died, though Lazarus was not healed of his poverty and petrifying sores, he was still one of God's image bearers, and one of the people of God on Abraham's side.

It is helpful from a theology of disability perspective to look at the stories of Zacchaeus and Lazarus from the angle of the hermeneutics of physiognomy, which refers to the study of facial and other outer bodily characteristics, to discern inner temperamental and behavioral characteristics.[61]

---

60. Erickson, *Word Became Flesh*, 542.

61. *Merriam-Webster*, s.v. "physiognomy."

Among the Jews in the ancient world, just as among the ancient Greeks and Romans, it was commonly thought that people's outward physical features correlated anatomically with and represented their inward moral inclinations and physiognomies. Thus for the Romans, the epitome of normalcy was the body of the Roman male citizen. Among the Greeks physiognomic features such as facial frowns and furrowed brows symbolized inner emotions.[62] In the same way among the Jews, physical disabilities, deformities, skin diseases, etc., symbolized spiritual deformities and un-wholeness which disqualified such individuals from worshipping together with the rest of God's people (Lev 13; 21:18). However, in the stories of Zacchaeus and Lazarus, Jesus deviates from the common physiognomic perspective of his day.

In the case of Lazarus, seen from a physiognomic perspective, he would have been perceived as unclean, and valueless, but though he was not healed, his worth was not based on his poverty and advanced stage skin ulcers. In the same way, in Zacchaeus's case, as Yong very correctly points out, the physiognomic interpretation of his shortness of stature and the fact of him being a tax collector would have been to see him as "reflecting 'smallness in spirit,' small-mindedness, greediness, and other derogatory characteristics in the ancient world."[63] Jesus overlooked what others would have seen as flaws in Zacchaeus, thereby putting short Zacchaeus on equal footing with every other person.

It is important to stress, as we have just done, that this special status of being made in the image of God applies not only to people without disabilities, or to people who live in wealth. The status is accorded also to people with even the most severe forms of disabilities, as well as to people who live in poverty. Living with disabilities and living in poverty usually go very closely together. Hallahan, Kauffman, and Pullen put it this way: "Families particularly vulnerable to the stresses of raising a child with disabilities are those facing additional struggles arising from poverty or single-parent status. And both conditions are on the rise in the United States. . . . Unfortunately, a higher prevalence of disabilities exists in single-parent families and families in poverty.[64]

The Bible teaches a great deal about the poor. For example, the Bible declares that the poor will always be around (Deut 15: 11; Matt 26: 11;

62. Yong, *Bible, Disability, and the Church*.
63. Yong, *Bible, Disability, and the Church*, 67.
64. Hallahan et al., *Exceptional Learners*, 74.

Mark 14: 7). God specifically warns against mistreatment of the poor and oppressed (Deut 23:24–25; 24:6; Exod 22:25; Lev 25:39–40, 43). The Bible particularly stressed that great care was to be taken to ensure that justice was not denied to the poor (Exod 23:6; Amos 5:12). As Erickson rightly observed, Jesus chose to identify with the poor.[65] He came from a poor family (Lev 12:6–8; Luke 2:24) and he himself was one of the poor (Matt 8:20; Luke 9:58). James, the brother of Jesus, also gave some rather stern warnings against mistreating the poor within Christian circles (James 2:4–5). Special education practitioners should, therefore, heed the wise advice of Erickson which is to "adopt God's perspective on wealth and poverty and regard the rich and the poor alike."[66]

Conclusion

A theology of special education, just as would be the case for a theology of education,[67] has to inevitably rest upon a reflection on the nature of theology. It will involve the exploration of the theological implications of special education, as well as the implications for theology of the message and methods of special education. In an effort to elucidate the theological implications of special education, so as to practice special education from the Christian theological worldview lens, there must be both an inquiry into theology, as well as into special education. The endeavor to inquire into theology and special education is to see where and how they dovetail so as to generate maximum synergy. This endeavor seems to be best crystalized in applied or practical theology which focuses on everyday implications of Christian theological beliefs.[68] It is important to recognize that a nascent, relatively underdeveloped interdisciplinary field such as theology of special education is particularly susceptible to some loopholes that will be rectified with time.

The chapter started by calling attention to the close connection between special education and Christian theology. Both of them deal with similar notions, concerns and assumptions such as the quest for knowledge and truth, the notion of growth, compassion, orderliness, fairness, equity, and justice. The question of what is the theology of special education is not

65. Erickson, *Word Became Flesh*, 593.

66. Ibid., 551.

67. Hull, "What Is Theology of Education?"

68. Fowler, *Faith Integration and Schools of Education*; Kang, "Your Kingdom Come."

one that many Christian educators in the field of special education think seriously about daily or discuss frequently. The question involves thinking theologically, reflectively, deeply and clearly about the discipline of special education and its integral relationship to the Christian faith. The chapter, therefore, discussed thinking Christianly, since the question of what the theology of special education is also involves thinking Christianly about special education as a discipline.

A cursory look at the tangled roots of education and religion historically was undertaken to show that the two have been closely connected from the earliest times to fairly recent times, seen from the fact that the establishment of most institutions of higher education in the United States was based on the principles of Christian religion. Finally, the chapter gave some concentrated focus on theology (especially creation and practical theology), Christology (especially regarding the person and work of Christ), and biblical anthropology (especially regarding the creation, nature, worth and purpose of man) in an effort to show the intricate connection between Christian theology and special education which warrants the viewpoint that it is important for the practice of special education to be guided by Christian theological perspectives.

Bibliography

Anderson, D. W. *Toward a Theology of Special Education: Integrating Faith and Practice.* Bloomington, IN: WestBow, 2012.

Asiedu-Peprah, Martin. *Johannine Sabbath Conflicts as Juridical Controversy.* Tubingen: Mohr Siebeck, 2001.

Barton, B. B., et al. *Luke.* Life Application Bible Commentary. Carol Stream, IL: Tyndale, 1997.

Berkowicz, J., and A. Myers. "Leadership, Learning, and Compassion: The Indispensables of Education." *Education Week*, July 15, 2014. http://blogs.edweek.org/edweek/leadership_360/2014/07/leadership_learning_and_compassion_the_indispensables_of_education.html.

Blanchett, W. J., et al. "Urban School Failure and Disproportionality in a Post-Brown Era." *Remedial & Special Education* 26 (2005) 70–81.

Burtchael, J. T. *The Dying of the Light: The Disengagement of Colleges and Universities from Their Christian Churches.* Grand Rapids: Eerdmans, 1998.

Claerbaut, D. *Faith and Learning on the Edge: A Bold New Look at Religion in Higher Education.* Grand Rapids: Zondervan, 2004.

Clapton, J., and J. Fitzgerald. "The History of Disability: A History of 'Otherness'; How Disabled People Have Been Marginalized through the Ages and Their Present Struggle for Their Human Rights." *New Renaissance Magazine: Renaissance*

Universal. http://www.cds.hawaii.edu/sites/default/files/downloads/resources/diversity/TheHistoryofDisability.pdf.

Coutinho, M. J., and D. P. Oswald. "Disproportionate Representation in Special Education: A Synthesis and Recommendations." *Journal of Child & Family Studies* 9 (2000) 135–56.

Dockery, D. S. "Shaping a Christian Worldview." In *Shaping a Christian Worldview: The Foundation of Christian Higher Education,* edited by D. S. Dockery and G. A. Thornbury, 1–15. Nashville: Broadman & Holman, 2002.

Erickson, M. J. *Christian Theology.* Grand Rapids: Baker, 1985.

———. *The Word Became Flesh.* Grand Rapids: Baker, 1991.

Esqueda, O. J. "Biblical Worldview: The Christian Higher Education Foundation for Learning." *Christian Higher Education* 13 (2014) 91–100.

Evans, C. A. *Luke.* New International Biblical Commentary 3. Peabody: Hendrickson, 1990.

Fowler, J. W. "Practical Theology and Theological Education: Some Models and Questions." *Theology Today* 42 (1985) 43–58.

Fowler, M., and M. Pacino, eds. *Faith Integration and Schools of Education.* Indiana: Precedent, 2012.

Garland, D. *Mark.* Zondervan Illustrated Bible Background Commentary. Grand Rapids: Zondervan, 2002.

George, S. "God of Life, Justice and Peace: A Disability-Informed Reading of Christology." *Ecumenical Review* 64 (2012) 454–62.

Hallahan, D. P., et al. *Exceptional Learners: An Introduction to Special Education.* Boston: Pearson, 2015.

Hasker, W. "Faith-Learning Integration: An Overview." *Christian Scholar's Review* 11 (1992) 234–48.

Heward, William L. *Exceptional Children: An Introduction to Special Education.* 10th ed. Upper Saddle River, NJ: Pearson, 2013.

Hull, J. M. "What Is Theology of Education?" *Scottish Journal of Theology* 30 (1977) 3–29.

Ilogu, Edmund. *Christianity and Igbo Culture: A Study of the Interaction of Christianity and Igbo Culture.* New York: Nok, 1974.

Kang, S. S. "'Your Kingdom Come': Practical Theology as Living Out Three Great Pillars of Christianity." *Christian Education Journal* 8 (2011) 114–29.

Lawrence, T. A., et al. "Refocusing on the Learning in Integration of Faith and Learning." *Journal of Research on Christian Education* 14 (2005) 17–50.

McColl, M. A, and R. S. Ascough. "Jesus and People with Disabilities: Old Stories, New Approaches." *Journal of Pastoral Care and Counseling* 63 (2009) 3–4.

Nworie, B. C., ed. *Central Issues in Special Education: Engaging Current Trends and Critical Issues in Contemporary Practice.* New York: Pearson Custom, 2013.

Poe, H. L. *Christianity in the Academy.* Grand Rapids: Baker Academic, 2004.

Rosebrough, T. R. "Christian Worldview and Teaching." In *Shaping a Christian Worldview: The Foundation of Christian Higher Education,* edited by D. S. Dockery and G. A. Thornbury, 281–97. Nashville: Broadman & Holman, 2002.

Smith, D. J. "The Historical Context of Special Education: Framing Our Understanding of Contemporary Issues." In *Critical Issues in Special Education,* edited by A. M. Sorrells et al., 1–15. Boston: Pearson, 2004.

Smith, D. D., and N. C. Tyler. *Introduction to Special Education: Making a Difference.* Upper Saddle River, NJ: Merrill, 2010.

Sullivan, A. L. "Disproportionality in Special Education Identification and Placement of English Language Learners." *Council for Exceptional Children* 77 (2011) 317–34.

Vernon, G. M. *Sociology of Religion*. Columbus: McGraw-Hill, 1962.

White, G. F. "People with Disabilities in Christian Community." *Journal of the Christian Institute on Disability* 3 (2014) 11–35.

Whiteman, D. L. "Anthropology and Mission: The Incarnational Connection." *Missiology: An International Review* 31 (2003) 398–415.

Willard, D., and G. Black. *The Divine Conspiracy Continued: Fulfilling God's Kingdom on Earth*. New York: HarperCollins, 2014.

Yancey, P. *The Jesus I Never Knew*. Grand Rapids: Zondervan, 1995.

Yell, M. L. *The Law and Special Education*. 4th ed. Upper Saddle River, NJ: Pearson, 2016.

3

Being an Effective Special Educator from a Christian Worldview Perspective

An Ethical View of Love, Worldviews and Special Education Practice

Ben Nworie, PhD, MDiv, LPC
Professor of Special Education
School of Education, Biola University

Abstract

The teaching of special education from a Christian faith perspective has to be driven by a genuine love for God and others. To be effective, the special educator has to have some understanding of the meaning and demands of this love which is an integral part of the Christian worldview. For effectiveness the special educator also has to be knowledgeable about the current worldviews influencing education, as well as culture as a whole, and how these worldviews differ from the Christian worldview. This knowledge informs how a faith-based special educator should encounter the various worldviews that affect education and schools. This knowledge also leads the faith-based special educator to develop an appropriate mission statement which is a key to an effective, integrative special education practice.

Keywords: love, ethics, worldview, special education, mission statement

Love is at the heart of the Christian faith and practice. It was love that drew the plan of salvation, as clearly conveyed in the Bible, especially in the Gospels and the Epistles (John 3:16; John 15:13; Rom 5:8; Gal 2:20; Eph 5:2; 1 John 4:10–11) and as echoed in the old Gospel song:

> Oh, the love that drew salvation's plan!
> Oh, the grace that brought it down to man!
> Oh, the mighty gulf that God did span at Calvary![1]

In special education practice, especially the one operated from a Christian faith perspective, the special educator has to be driven by what the Bible describes as the first and greatest commandment which is to genuinely love God and others (Matt 22:37–40). Love is a commonly use word, but it has also been very commonly misunderstood. What love means to a lot of people is very different from what is being presented here.

For many people, love practically means, as Poe very well points out: a reciprocal agreement where you "rob my back and I rob yours." This common understanding of love goes sharply against what Christ taught as genuine love. As Poe very correctly stated, "Love is what you do in spite of what it costs you, not because of what it will gain for you.[2] This love that Christ taught and commands is an exceptional kind of love. It is agape, the God kind of love.

What Is Love?

Talking about this unique kind of love, Stowell very correctly identifies it as the love that is used of God for man. He says:

> It is a love that transcends emotion, feeling, and fact, yet at the same time, when practiced properly, creates an environment in which a depth of emotion and feeling can flow based on the fact of a solid, unwavering love commitment. . . . This *agape* love is the kind of love that chooses to understand the needs of another and

---

1. Newell, *At Calvary*.

2. Poe, *Christianity in the Academy*, 18.

then responds to those needs by expending available resources to meet those needs.[3]

The understanding and practice of this agape (love) makes it possible for the special educator operating from a Christian faith view point to effectively reach, teach and include all kinds of learners, including those that may be very different, such as students with severe autism, students with severe learning, physical and or emotional problems, students who are lesbian, gay, bisexual, and transgendered (LGBT) diverse learners and others.

The Teacher, Moral Ethics and the Command to Love

Deontological ethics is an approach to ethics that focuses on the rightness or wrongness of actions themselves. Deontological theories claim that certain actions like showing love and kindness; telling the truth; keeping promises; upholding one's teaching contract, are inherently right, without regard for the consequences. Deontologists believe that ethical rules obligate you to your duty. Deontological theorists maintain that rules (including the rule or command to love), rights, and principles are sacred and inviolable. The central thought of the moral philosophy of the German philosopher and deontologist Immanuel Kant, and of modern deontological ethics, is that a categorical imperative denotes an absolute, unconditional requirement that exerts its authority always (in all circumstances).

Kant's interpretations of the categorical imperative denied everything that is contrary to the command to love such as the right to steal, be lazy, lie or deceive for any reason, regardless of context or anticipated consequences. It is the consensus of deontologists that we have a responsibility to love. They see love as essential to ethical life.[4] Reilly, though operating primarily within a Buddhist context goes so far as to insist, in his brilliant work, that compassion or love of neighbor "is the basis of all moral value and, hence, of what it means to act justly or rightly."[5] Another aspect of acting justly or rightly which portrays love in action is the notion of rendering selfless service to others.

---

3. Stowell, *Shepherding the Church*, 182.

4. La Caze, "Love, That Indispensible Supplement"; Meyers, "Virtue of Cold-Heartedness"; Baron, "Love and Respect."

5. Reilly, "Compassion as Justice," 13.

A very critical question for every teacher, but especially the special education teacher who believes in the command to love, is: "What do I believe?" Everyone believes in something or someone. That is, we all have a philosophy of life or worldview, and what we believe colors how we conduct our lives, and it provides a distinct perspective that is perceptible to attentive students. Irrespective of the teacher's classroom setting, whether it is a private Christian college, a public high school, or a state university, the teacher's belief system or worldview, greatly matters. It makes a great difference in a student's life. Students look up to their teachers for more than academic instruction. Students being typically in their formative years and needing perspective, look up to their teachers to help them as they grapple with creating their own context of belief. The crucial point, as Rosebrough so poignantly pointed out, is that "this context of belief can be temporal or timeless, hopeless or hopeful, egocentric or transcendent, judgmental or redemptive."[6]

A teacher's worldview affects the way a student perceives and conceives of reality and human interactions. For example, teachers holding the Christian worldview who are honest will hold honest, direct communication with students which entails listening, talking, and acting in ways that communicate respect, caring, and confidence, both in themselves and in their students because students do test the teacher's honesty. Honesty is more than candor in expressing opinions and reporting facts accurately. Students want to know whether teachers are as good as their word.[7] Such teachers if they are also humble and compassionate may additionally model to their students a worldview of human beings that is humble, sensitive, caring and fair.

The worldview of a teacher affects students' sense of right and wrong. Since students look up to their adult teachers for perspective, a teacher's worldview can provide assurance to students that certain values are timeless, that morality has its bases on a transcendent standard and that their teacher who they consider a wiser role model has made a commitment to hold to that absolute standard.[8]

One of the challenges teachers face is to assess students with fairness, consistency and even with grace. Teachers, through their worldview, can more easily overcome this challenge; especially those who consistently hold

6. Rosebrough, "Christian Worldview and Teaching," 281.
7. Kauffman, *Characteristics of Emotional and Behavioral Disorders.*
8. Rosebrough, "Christian Worldview and Teaching."

a Christian worldview. Rosebrough rightly argues that though worldview and faith are not synonymous, to Christians worldview is meaningless without faith since faith inspires and glues the two together. Rosebrough suggests some ways to promote alternative teaching from a Christian worldview such as: "through a smile, a gesture of kindness, a simple presence in a room in a time of trouble, a humble act of servanthood, a word of encouragement, a show of sensitivity like knowing when to remain silent, a patient attitude in a time of stress."[9]

A teachers' worldview affects the way they teach. For example, from a constructivist worldview, the tendency of teachers is to do the work for students when the students should do the work themselves. It is perhaps pertinent here to point out that to the constructivist Swiss epistemologist Jean Piaget, learning is constructed by the learner. Rosebrough supporting this trend of thought says: "Recent neuroscience discoveries confirm that the human brain is a pattern-seeking device that craves variety, challenge, and structure. Let's teach less and allow our students to learn more."[10]

Worldview Definition

Our worldview is shaped by the totality of our experiences such as our education, the way we were nurtured, our culture, the literature we are exposed to, our media and movies consumptions, and more. It is the systematized way we knowingly or un-knowingly conceive reality. It has been correctly observed that the world is divided more by worldviews than by geographic boundaries.[11]

Some of the Secular Worldviews

The Christian educator has to be aware of the different worldview systems that influence education, particularly public education. He or she also has to be aware of the Christian worldview, and how it contrasts with the secular worldviews. Some of the many secular worldviews or systems of philosophy that currently impact public education are: naturalism, secularism, humanism, existentialism, new ageism, nihilism, postmodernism and

9. Ibid., 294–95.

10. Ibid., 295.

11. Colson and Pearcey, *How Now Shall We Live?*

pluralism. In general, these various non-Christian worldviews uphold the following viewpoints among others: (1) There is no God, there is no absolute truth; (2) There are many gods, and many truths; (3) Man is supreme in life, and is the center of the universe; (4) Man is worthless; he is the product of evolution and is struggling through the evolutionary process. Naturalism, humanism, and New Age-ism in some respects represent the rest.

Naturalism

Naturalism denies the existence of God. It believes that random chance and coincidence govern life rather than God's sovereign will and purposes.

In the naturalistic worldview, the universe explains everything about the whole of existence. Naturalism claims that this world is the only real world. In contrast to naturalism, the Christian worldview sees the transcendent God who precedes every existence and created everything as actively involved in this world. Naturalism has various forms such as moral relativism, multiculturalism, pragmatism, and utopianism.[12]

Secular Humanism

Humanism, a very broad world view which contains very many different elements, believes and upholds Darwinian evolutionism versus creationism. It underlies many theories like the death of God theology, the theory of a distant and uninvolved God.[13] The public school system has become the main vehicle for the propagation of humanistic philosophy.

The New Age Movement

In the New Age worldview, like the other secular worldviews, there is no belief in the existence of a transcendent God. The New Age movement is based on eastern beliefs and practices, especially the eastern belief that god is in all things (pantheism). Pantheism teaches that God and nature are identical. This worldview, therefore, pronounces the individual as divine; as someone who has god in him or her. As such, the New Age movement promises humanity the ability to create a new consciousness and a utopian

12. Ibid.

13. Sproul, *Lifeviews*.

society. The New Age practices currently permeate the elementary, secondary and college classrooms.[14]

How Should a Faith-Based Special Educator Encounter the Various Worldviews That Affect Education and Schools?

Vast numbers of people in schools today, especially in the Western world are influenced by these various worldviews. That is why the United States has been described as a post-Christian, secularized society. There is undoubtedly a cacophony of ideas in our culture. Sproul aptly describes the scenario in this way:

> The confusion of ideas and viewpoints became a national crisis when the Supreme Court ruled on the volatile issue of prayer in the public schools. The basic principle in view was that a religious view of life should not be imposed on the people by the state in a public schoolroom. . . . The solution to the crisis was formulated in the concept of a "neutral" education. . . . The only problem with the solution is that the ideal is impossible. There is no such thing as a neutral education. Every education, every curriculum has a viewpoint. That viewpoint either considers God in it or it does not. To teach children about life and the world in which they live without reference to God is to make a statement about God. It screams a statement. The message is either that there is no God or that God is irrelevant. Either way the message is the same there is no God. An irrelevant God is the same as no God at all.[15]

We certainly do not live in a homogenized culture in which the dominant influence is the Christian worldview. Most of the people that the special education practitioner comes in contact with are very likely to be individuals and groups that are influenced or impacted by the effects of the different secular belief systems mentioned. As the numbers of people imbibing these diverse philosophical and religious ideas have increased in the country, federal courts have reviewed several of the Christian practices that were formerly allowed in schools in cases that apply the First Amendment's Free Exercise and Establishment clauses to school situations. For example, practices like singing Christmas songs at school Christmas events, praying publicly at school graduations and varsity football games, and teaching the

14. Ibid.; Colson and Pearcey, *How Now Shall We Live?*
15. Sproul, *Lifeviews*, 23.

Genesis creation account have all been affected.[16] From a Christian world-view point, how should the special educator encounter these philosophical influences? First, be knowledgeable about the different worldview positions and their claims. Second, be tolerant so as to be able to function as an effective team player. And third, be wise by carefully deciding when to employ loving words and/or actions.

Christian Worldview

There are probably as many different shades of the Christian worldview as there are Christians. However, there are some basic elements which the majority of Christians affirm. Those fundamentals of the Christian faith make up the Christian worldview. They are: belief in God, the creator of heaven and earth; belief in Jesus Christ, his virgin birth, his crucifixion, death, burial, resurrection, ascension, and his second coming as judge of the living and the dead; as well as belief in the Holy Spirit, the universal church, the fellowship of saints, the forgiveness of sins, the resurrection of the body, and everlasting life in heaven or in hell. These affirmations make up what is called the Apostles' Creed. Some Christian denominations recite them regularly in church, others do not. Christians in general believe the foundational truths contained in that creed.

Integration of Faith and the Special Educator Practitioner

The faith integration journey should be part of an enjoyable lifelong learning process of connecting academic knowledge and skills with one's Christian faith experience as a Christian educator. The aim of this lifelong learning experience is discovering and applying the unity of God's truth. With this orientation in mind, the special education practitioner needs to adopt a mission statement that will steer the educator's practice based on his or her faith convictions, and job assignment.

Consequently, I guide my special education teacher candidates to learn how to construct helpful mission statements from a faith integration point of view. Below is a compilation of paraphrases of some personal mission statements from a few of my students:

16. Marshall, "Whose Religious Values?"

My personal mission statement as a special education teacher is to treat each child with a positive attitude and respect. I feel that no matter how the child functions I should remember that they are God's children and that they are created in his image. I feel it is my responsibility to give my students the tools so that they can succeed in life. I feel that God lead me to this work, so that I may help my students find hope, values, love and faith. I am determined to make a difference in my student's lives.

We, as special education teachers, need to be "highly qualified" to teach, and be accountable for teaching core academic subjects to special education students. One scripture I have found pertinent is Romans 15:1: *Now we that are strong ought to bear the infirmities of the weak, and not to please ourselves.* Another Scripture I found helpful is Romans 15:7: *Wherefore receive ye one another, even as Christ also received you, to the glory of God.* We represent Christ to our students and their families—it is an awesome responsibility!

I recommend this next statement as a model mission statement for a special educator:

I believe that every child is special and unique. My role as a teacher is to facilitate learning—to help each student discover his/her strengths, and to encourage them to discover a plan for their life. My students will know that I love them and care about them; a high trust level will be built between us.

I believe that, as a teacher, I am to serve my students. I will reach and teach each child in their own individual way, and in their own individual learning style.

I believe in providing structure, stability, and a positive learning environment for my students. I will have class rules and procedures that they can count on. I believe in the use of positive reinforcement to encourage and motivate.

I will be an advocate for my students, if necessary, to make sure they receive all the services they need to learn and grow. I will speak on their behalf when needed. I will never "give up" on a student—I will keep trying and trying until they learn! I will get to know my student's parents because we need to be a "team" working together and wanting the best for their child. I need to encourage the parents, too, because raising a "special needs" child is not always easy. I want them to know that I am on their side!

The type of attitude and love conveyed in this mission statement so clearly vocalizes what Anderson so aptly describes as "the point of intersection between faith and the discipline.[17] As Dockery very appropriately expressed, "Students and educators, who are committed to a faith and learning paradigm, seek knowledge in order to serve and edify others."[18] This attitude of loving, caring service aimed at both informing and transforming others serves as the core aim of Christian faith and learning in special education. As a bye product then, this attitude helps to shield the practitioner that engages in authentic integration from experiencing the burnout that is endemic in the field of special education practice.

The job of a special education practitioner is not easy. That is why there is a high burnout rate, high school migration rate, and high annual turnover rate in the field of special education.[19] Despite this trend, the work of the special educator could be enriching. Spiritual self care such as fellowship with other Christians is, therefore, very important so that the teacher can share his or her thoughts and beliefs, draw strength from others, as well as learn from others and their experiences. Consequently, membership in authentic Christian and professional support organization is highly encouraged. Here are a few suggestions or examples:

1. The National Association of Christians in Special Education (NACSPED): http://nacsped.com/home.htm.

   NACSPED provides support, encouragement and professional growth for all educators, particularly special educators and for families of students with disabilities. (This author was a former NACSPED national president.)

2. The International Christian Community for Teacher Education (ICCTE): http://iccte.org.

   The ICCTE promotes communication and encouragement among Christian teacher educators; it promotes research-based and theoretically informed conversation about a range of topics related to the preparation of educators; and it promotes broader awareness of the importance and value of Christian thought and practice in relation to the broad field of education. The ICCTE hosts a biennial conference, allowing for scholarly exchange, fellowship and networking opportunities for Christian teacher educators and for those who are in related fields.

---

17. Anderson, *Toward a Theology of Special Education*, xviii.

18. Dockery, *Faith and Learning*, 3.

19. Boe et al., "Teacher Turnover."

3. The Council for Exceptional Children (CEC): http://www.cec.sped. org/AM/Template.cfm?Section=About_CEC.

The CEC is the largest international professional organization for improving the educational success of individuals with disabilities and/ or gifts and talents. The CEC provides excellent resources for parents and special educators.

Bibliography

Anderson, D. *Toward a Theology of Special Education: Integrating Faith and Practice.* Bloomington, IN: WestBow, 2012.

Baron, M. W. "Love and Respect in the Doctrine of Virtue." In *Kant's Metaphysics of Morals: Interpretative Essays,* edited by Mark Timmons, 391–407. Oxford: Oxford University Press, 2012.

Boe, E. E., et al. "Teacher Turnover: Examining Exit Attrition, Teaching Area Transfer, and School Migration." *Exceptional Children* 75 (2008) 7–31.

Colson, C., and N. Pearcey. *How Now Shall We Live?* Wheaton, IL: Tyndale, 1999.

Dockery, D., ed. *Faith and Learning. A Handbook for Christian Higher Education.* Nashville: B&H, 2012.

Kauffman, J. M. *Characteristics of Emotional and Behavioral Disorders of Children and Youth.* 8th ed. Upper Saddle River, NJ: Merrill / Prentice Hall, 2006.

La Caze, Marguerite. "Love, That Indispensable Supplement: Irigaray and Kant on Love and Respect." *Hypatia: A Journal of Feminist Philosophy* 20 (2005) 92–114.

Marshall, J. M. "Whose Religious Values?" *School Administrator* 65 (2008) 28–29.

Meyers, C. D. "The Virtue of Cold-Heartedness." *Philosophical Studies* 138 (2008) 233–44.

Newell, W. *At Calvary.* 1895. Retrieved from http://library.timelesstruths.org/music/ At_Calvary.

Poe, H. L. *Christianity in the Academy.* Grand Rapids: Baker Academic, 2004.

Reilly, Richard. "Compassion as Justice." *Buddhist-Christian Studies* 26 (2006) 13–31.

Rosebrough, T. R. "Christian Worldview and Teaching." In *Shaping a Christian Worldview: The Foundation of Christian Higher Education,* edited by D. S. Dockery and G. A. Thornbury, 281–97. Nashville: Broadman & Holman, 2002.

Sproul, R.C. *Lifeviews.* Grand Rapids: Revell, 1986.

Stowell, J. M. *Shepherding the Church: Effective Spiritual Leadership in a Changing Culture.* Chicago: Moody, 1997.

4

Collaborative Practices in Special Education

A *Christian Perspective*

Dr. Yvette Latunde, EdD
Professor of Special Education
School of Education, Azusa Pacific University

Abstract

COLLABORATION IS A LEGAL mandate for special educators.[1] Special educators with a Christian worldview have both a legal and spiritual obligation to collaborate because working together is what Jesus would do. Preservice special educators at faith-based institutions know that collaboration is beneficial to students. They many not, however, be aware of the ethical and spiritual implications of collaboration.[2] This study utilized an observational method to analyze the practices and principles of thirty preservice special education teachers as they met state standards for collaborations in K–12 schools. Preservice teachers utilize good communication and servant leadership strategies to collaborate with general education teachers in schools.

1. Wrightslaw, *IDEA 2004*.
2. Chittister, *Wisdom Distilled from the Daily*; Keith, *Case for Servant Leadership*.

Teacher preparation programs at faith-based universities have opportunities to make faith connections explicit.

Immediately after his IEP meeting Sam's special education teacher, Mrs. Cormier, and his general education teacher, Ms. Goss, coordinate their schedules to co-plan his instruction and assessments. Because of Ms. Goss's expertise in math and Mrs. Cormier's expertise in teaching math to struggling learners, they have decided to co-teach during Sam's math period. Mrs. Cormier provides Ms. Goss with ideas for differentiating Sam's math lessons while Ms. Goss trains Mrs. Cormier on the scope and sequence of the general math curriculum. Both believe this is the right way to help Sam overcome challenges associated with dyscalculia and meet his individualized education program goals in the general classroom.

The purpose of the article is to help Christian educators develop a better understanding of the ethical and spiritual implications of collaboration as they work to serve students with disabilities in the general education setting. According to the National Center for Education Statistics, students with disabilities spend more than 80 percent of their day in inclusive classrooms.[3] The Individuals with Disabilities Education Act (IDEA), a federal law that protects students with disabilities, requires that the supports and services students with disabilities need to gain access to the general curriculum be provided in the least restrictive environment via an individualized education program (IEP). IDEA requires that those who provide support collaborate with an IEP team.[4] According to Johnson and Ridley, the ethical professional collaborates and works to create a respectful partnership aimed at meeting the needs of students.[5]

Throughout the Bible when people collaborated in doing God's will, God blessed them and their efforts. Collaboration improves the skills of both general and special educators.[6] Improvement in educators' skills results in improved student outcomes because a synergy is created during collaboration that produces results not possible when working in isolation.[7] Because special and general educators serve some of the same students and have their own pedagogical limitations, collaboration is critical not only

3. National Center for Education Statistics, *National Assessment of Educational Progress*.

4. *Building the Legacy*; Wrightslaw, *IDEA 2004*.

5. Johnson and Ridley, *Elements of Ethics for Professionals*.

6. Dettmer et al., *Collaboration, Consultation, and Teamwork*.

7. Ibid.

for the implementation of IDEA, but also for the teachers' spiritual development.[8] Since collaboration requires good listening, humility, ability to put others first, and the coming together of gifts, it is an exercise in faith.

Christ-centered collaboration hinges on humility and the ability to put others before one's self (Phil 2). Humility means critically analyzing one's self while empowering, inspiring, and allowing others to utilize their strengths and gifts; "those who lack [humility] are dogmatic and egotistical."[9] Humility marks a degree of moral maturity, and the absence of humility is a sign of an impoverished spirit. Spiritual impoverishment results in cold hearts and a mean spirit. Regular practice of spiritual disciplines produces humility.

Humility implies the valuing of diverse abilities and perspectives. God has gifted each person uniquely, and the perspectives and approaches of educators to teaching and learning are likely to vary widely, as they are influenced by schooling, gender, age, race, parenting, philosophy and faith affiliations. The many gifts of all teachers should be used to help spread hope, love, justice, and God's grace to students with disabilities.

Philippians 2:2 provides guidance for how Christian educators should collaborate. It reads, "Fulfill ye my joy that ye be likeminded having the same love, on one accord, of one mind." Preservice teachers should develop common goals and a plan for both the collaboration process and IEP implementation.[10] The Scriptures continues by saying, "Let nothing be done through strife but in humility consider others above yourself" (Phil 2:3). This requires preservice teachers to be responsive listeners, to respect others, value diverse perspectives, practice good communication, and seek opportunities to serve.[11]

However beneficial collaboration is, it is challenging. Some negative school cultures, individual personalities and spiritual malnourishment make collaboration between teachers difficult.[12] Absence of administrative support, lack of humility, lack of planning time, poor communication, gossip, slander, and territorialism are common barriers to collaboration (Prov

---

8. Austin, "Teachers' Beliefs about Co-teaching"; Covey, *8th Habit*.

9. Hooks and West, *Breaking Bread*, 50.

10. Friend and Cook, *Interactions*.

11. Chittister, *Wisdom Distilled from the Daily*.

12. Ibid.; Kardos, "New Teachers in New Jersey Schools."

18).[13] The dispositions necessary for collaboration do not come naturally; they must be developed.

In response to teacher accreditation and federal requirements, the teacher preparation program in this study emphasizes developing the teacher candidate's mind (building skills, defining program learning outcomes, and designing assessments). Because the program is faith-based it also addresses the development of the student's spirit. According to Stephen Covey, author of *The 7 Habits of Highly Effective People*, the spirit is one of the most important components of a person. The spirit gives meaning to teachers' work and guides what they do. faith-based: teacher education programs are uniquely able to develop the spiritual intelligence of teacher candidates by making the ethical and spiritual implications of collaboration more explicit.

Collaborative Theologies

Professionals working in Christian teacher education programs have a good reason for encouraging candidates to collaborate: if Jesus were teaching in a classroom setting, he would collaborate.[14] Both Trinitarian and relational theologies provide biblical perspectives on why and how Christians should collaborate with others. These theologies have implications for Christians working with both Christians and non-Christians.

The doctrine of the Trinity is fundamental to the Christian faith. In the Trinity can be seen the original collaborative ministry among God the Father, God the Son, and God the Holy Spirit.[15] The Bible says that each is a distinct being, yet the three are one (John 14:9–11). According to the Scriptures, each person of the Trinity has specific functions yet they work collaboratively. God the Father initiated the plan of salvation, and God the Son fulfilled the plan through the power of the Holy Spirit.

It is within the confines of a relationship with Christ that Christian preservice teachers can collaborate in ways that glorify God. Consider a relational theology, a movement in the evangelical Christian world that helps to frame the motivations that should move Christians toward

13. Dettmer et al., *Collaboration, Consultation, and Teamwork*; Friend and Cook, *Interactions*.

14. Chittister, *Wisdom Distilled from the Daily*; Johnson and Ridley, *Elements of Ethics for Professionals*.

15. Yong, "Relational Theology and the Holy Spirit."

collaboration.[16] Relational theology stresses the interconnections between God and humans. It is largely based on a spiritual bond between people because of their bond in Christ, in love.[17] Relational theology asserts that God's love extends beyond love *to* humans to include love *through* humans to other humans. Thus love without service is impossible. Throughout the Bible, God commands those who love him to act as he does, and Jesus' example shows that he serves others (Matt 20: 25–28; John 13:12–17).

Relational theology sees each person as made in the image of God (Genesis). Because all humans are made in the image of God each person is due the highest consideration.[18] Thus Christians are charged to speak to others with care, paying attention to their words and asking God for grace to know what to say and when. This consideration of others is fundamental to relational theology. People made in the image of God are not to speak evil of other people. Believers are commanded to be kind and to forgive others as Christ forgave them (Eph 4:32). Due to their interconnectedness, Christians are charged with using their skills, talents, and strengths to serve others in love (1 Pet 4:10).

Dr. Martin Luther King, Sojourner Truth, Muhammad Ali, Frederick Douglas and other great leaders/educators practiced a relational theology grounded in their faith. Many of their faith traditions were based in love, care, service, and respect for others. The philosopher and activist Cornel West wrote that Christian narratives and stories empowered him to do what seemed impossible. He observed, "We are human to the degree which we love, care, and serve."[19]

This article explores the integration of a Christian worldview in the practices of preservice special educators.

The study was guided by the following questions:

1. How do preservice special education teachers establish appropriate communication with general educators to establish continuity of services and remediation?

2. What principles do preservice teachers use to establish communication with general educators and nurture relationships?

---

16. Callen, "John Wesley and Relational Theology."

17. Chittister, *Wisdom Distilled from the Daily*; Oord, "Relational Love."

18. Powell, "Image of God."

19. Hooks and West, *Breaking Bread*, 51.

Methodology

In the qualitative study reported in this article, documents were collected that described the collaboration activities of preservice teachers as they established communication and nurtured collaborative relationships with general education teachers. This is the type of field research in which written materials are collected and organized and the results reported in writing.[20] Records documenting the activities of thirty preservice special education teacher candidates enrolled in clinical practice were gathered at the end of their three-unit field experience course. Data were collected from documents dated 2008–2012.

While enrolled in the course, candidates were given a syllabus that described the California Teaching Program Standards 4.1–4.5; these standards are related to communication and collaboration.[21] These standards were unchanged from 2008 through 2012. The syllabus instructed candidates to document the activities in which they engaged that met the specific standards. The syllabus did not specify the activities the student needed to do to meet the standard; it required only that they document what the activity was, the number of hours the teacher engaged in the activity, the location in which the activity occurred, and which standard corresponded with the activity. Students could document between ten and one hundred hours of activities for any specific state standard.

This study took place in a special education teacher program at a faith-based private university in California. The program offered a collaboration course as part of its preliminary credentialing preparation. The collaboration course covered various topics regarding teaching in K–12 school settings, including models, theories, theology, roles, communication, negotiation, team teaching skills, and ethics. This course utilized faith-based textbooks and activities. One of the required texts for the course was *Wisdom Distilled from the Daily: Living the Rule of St. Benedict Today.*[22] It speaks to the call from Christ to live in community, share gifts, and put others first and it discusses the importance of listening and cultivating humility. Another text used in the course, *The Elements of Ethics for Professionals*,[23] describes ethical practices such as collaboration, terminating services no longer needed,

20. Lofland, "Styles of Reporting Qualitative Field Research."
21. California Commission on Teacher Credentialing.
22. Chittister, *Wisdom Distilled from the Daily.*
23. Johnson and Ridley, *Elements of Ethics for Professionals.*

and benefice. Program designers considered it important that students and faculty examine information on collaboration and the teaching profession from a Christian worldview.

In addition to the collaboration course and other classes, the program required a three-semester-unit university-supervised clinical practice course. Standards for collaboration with general educators, other professionals, and families were embedded requirements. Program standard 4 was "communication and collaborative partnerships." Program standards 4.2 and 4.3 directly related to communication and collaboration between general and special educators as they serve children with disabilities. Standard 4.3 concerned the student's ability to nurture supportive relationships with general education teachers. This article describes findings regarding standards 4.2 and 4.3.

The study analyzed the self-reported clinical practice activities of thirty former special education teacher candidates. All thirty student teachers held bachelor's degrees and were enrolled in the special education teacher education program; 80 percent were pursuing a master's degree. The participants were of two types: some were interns—they had state-issued intern credentials and were acting as the teacher of record—and others were teaching under the supervision of a master teacher. The two types of students were responsible for the same coursework, syllabus, and state standards. All participants were in the last semester of their credential program and were assigned a university mentor who provided them with individualized support, including site visits to nearby urban schools. The mentors visited the students regularly and provided support that varied according to the needs of the students and the mentors' experience and background.

During clinical practice, the student teachers were asked to document activities over a period of eighteen weeks that specifically addressed establishing communication and nurturing relationships with general education teachers for the purpose of providing appropriate services to students with disabilities. Data were collected on the self-reported activities of the special education teacher candidates related to questions regarding collaborating with general education teachers. Document analysis is appropriate for answering the question of what principles and practices preservice teachers use when collaborating with general education teachers.[24] Documents are

---

24. Creswell, *Educational Research*.

easily accessible and low risk for the participant.[25] In order to answer the research questions, a close examination of completed assignments based on the standards was necessary. The documents examined are considered extant because they were produced in a natural setting and in alignment with the course standards and guidelines.

Preliminary research questions and related literature guided the analysis process. The data were coded and subcoded. Coding is used in research to "allocate passages to topics" and is the "hack work of the qualitative researcher, labeling text according to its subject."[26] The research was conducted according to the following guidelines:

1. Data were collected and analyzed at the same time.

2. Data were divided into categories and codes and subcodes were created for the categories.

3. Codes were constantly compared and categories were also constantly compared.

4. The researcher wrote field notes.

5. The researcher offered interpretations or explanations of actions based on literature and experience.

Both the unique and commonplace activities recorded on the documents were used to create themes for this study. Two major themes emerged from the analysis of the data: communication and servant leadership.

Results and Discussion

The results of this study support the literature on the practices preservice special education teachers use when collaborating with general educators in inclusive settings. This study expands on the literature related to the principles preservice teachers use when collaboration since little is known about this topic.[27] This information can be useful in other teacher education programs in which teacher educators are concerned about teacher motivations, dispositions, and collaboration skills. Preservice teachers unconsciously integrated their faith in practice. A Christian worldview of

25. Ibid.
26. Richards, *Handling Qualitative Data*, 8.
27. Dettmer et al., *Collaboration, Consultation, and Teamwork.*

collaboration encourages teachers to practice good communication, put others before themselves, and value diverse perspectives. In this study, teachers evidenced ongoing efforts to establish good communication and servant leadership.

Communication

The subject of inclusion evokes both positive and negative attitudes in teachers. Therefore it is important that educators keep the lines of communication among colleagues open to develop mutual understanding. The preservice special educators in the study spent a significant amount of their time communicating with general education teachers to develop common goals for including students with disabilities in the general classroom. The communication was both formal and informal. Of the preservice teachers, 51 percent utilized email and any available pocket of time to communicate with general education teachers about their students. They met after school, before school, on breaks, and in passing:

"Talked to English teacher during her prep time regarding writing age-appropriate goals for a senior student reading on a second-grade level" (participant #3, 2008).

"Every morning before serving any student our team would meet and discuss the day and if there were any special circumstances" (participant #2, 2010).

Servant leaders listen and respond to the needs of others.[28]

Study participants frequently used formal meetings for initiating or maintaining communication related to students. The types of meetings preservice teachers utilized most often to establish communication were faculty, staff, and grade-level meetings. Face-to-face interactions are the most effective way to communicate.[29] More than half (55 percent) of the communication between the preservice participants and general education teachers took place face to face. Meetings were generally focused on students' behavior or goals or the pedagogy involved in teaching them. Leo and Cowan found that it was uncommon for collaborating teachers to focus on instruction.[30] They state it is often the last dimension of collaboration to be developed. Proverbs 31:8–9 encourages preservice special

28. Keith, *Case for Servant Leadership*.

29. Dettmer et al., *Collaboration, Consultation, and Teamwork*.

30. Leo and Cowan, "Launching Professional Learning Communities."

educators to speak up for those students who cannot speak for themselves and to judge fairly. Dialogue around instruction, goals, and methods are necessary for collaborators to gain mutual understanding[31] and effectively implement the IEP.

Servant Leadership

"Servant leadership starts with the desire to serve."[32] Jesus came to serve, not to be served (Matt 20:28). Servant leaders have the heart to serve. They serve and lead simultaneously. Jesus was a good example of this. He healed, washed feet, taught, and led all at the same time. Servant leaders utilize diversity to reconcile opposites.[33] Jesus utilized disciples who represented a variety of backgrounds, experiences, and skills to complete some of his most important work. Christianity is not the only faith system to value servant leadership; serving while leading is extolled across many cultures and religions.[34]

Many general educators do not believe they have the proper training to serve some included students.[35] Preservice special educators have an ideal opportunity to change attitudes toward inclusion by demonstrating a heart of service and love, and Christian educators are encouraged by their faith tradition to extend care and respect.[36] The practices of the preservice special educators in the study demonstrated a desire to serve both students and fellow teachers. Of the participants, 72 percent mentioned engaging in some type of collaboration as a means of nurturing the relationship with the general education teacher to ensure services for children with disabilities. For example, one participant reported: "Spent time in the general education class discussing how we would instruct our autistic student to help

---

31. Bandura, *Social Foundations*; Dettmer et al., *Collaboration, Consultation, and Teamwork*.

32. Keith, *Case for Servant Leadership*, 5.

33. Trompenaars and Voerman, *Harnessing the Strengths of the World's Powerful Philosophy*.

34. Ibid.

35. Austin, "Teachers' Beliefs about Co-teaching"; Kardos, "New Teachers in New Jersey Schools."

36. Hooks and West, *Breaking Bread*.

him meet his goals" (participant #5, 2011). Keith noted that "throughout history the servant leader has emphasized serving those in greatest need."[37]

In the study, 23 percent of preservice special education teachers co-planned with general education teachers as a means to nurture their relationships and ensure delivery of remediation and services to students with disabilities: "Collaboration daily to ensure that our included students received appropriate instruction and that the teacher felt supported" (participant #7, 2011). Ten percent of the participants reported providing consultation to general education teachers to serve not only students, but also teachers who they believed needed support. One participant noted, "Went to observe and document behavior of a student in a regular class. We met after and I gave her ideas to improve the behavior" (participant #6, 2011). Preservice teachers evidenced humility and servant leadership when they utilized their gifts and strengths to support and develop others.[38]

More than 55 percent of the participants reported learning something new from the collaborating teacher. Austin found that when preservice special educators and general educators collaborate, the general education teachers gain accommodations skills and experience less anxiety.[39] On the other hand, preservices special educators learn more about curriculum and specific pedagogy from general education teachers. It was evident in the study that resources were shared in the process of collaboration: "I went to her class and she showed me how to use Touch Math and gave me resources too" (participant, #21, 2010). According to Keith, servant leadership is not about position, but influence. "Leadership requires love."[40]

Interestingly, participants did not report much regarding evaluation of the interactions, communication, or collaboration. Research suggests that evaluation is a key component of collaboration.[41] Jesus often checked in with the disciples to hear their perspectives. He asked, "Who do you say that I am?" because he wanted to ensure that they still believed in what he had called them to do.[42] "Servant leaders gather feedback in as many

---

37. Keith, *Case for Servant Leadership*, 3.

38. Eph 4:12; Keith, *Case for Servant Leadership*.

39. Austin, "Teachers' Beliefs about Co-teaching."

40. Keith, *Case for Servant Leadership*, 47.

41. Dettmer et al., *Collaboration, Consultation, and Teamwork*; Friend and Cook, *Interactions*.

42. Latunde, personal communication, May 2013.

ways as possible from their colleagues and those they serve."[43] They obtain feedback through informal conversations about how things are working or by scheduling regular times for evaluation. One explanation for the omission of evaluation in this study could be that preservice teachers did not see evaluation as an activity that was directly related to nurturing relationships or communication. If that is the case, university mentors can help preservice teachers see the importance of evaluation to collaboration through their guidance, consultation, and modeling.

Implications and Recommendations

Faith-based special education teacher preparation programs present optimal opportunities within their preservice induction programs to be explicit about the ethical and spiritual implications of collaboration. Preservice teachers at faith-based institutions are asked to demonstrate how they integrate their faith in their practice, but many integrate their faith unconsciously. To support teachers in articulating the connection between faith and teaching, clinical practice can be carefully linked to spiritual standards and learning outcomes. Faith-based institutions may consider adding spiritual or faith-based learning objectives to both the clinical practice experience and the course work to make the connections more explicit. Although preservice teachers in this study were not asked to complete specific faith-based activities regarding collaboration, it was evident that they were integrating a Christian worldview in practice. The researcher believes that the modeling from faculty and the inclusion of discussions of faith in the courses impacted teacher practices.

Christian teacher preparation programs may need to infuse more collaborative theological models into their coursework with special attention to the connections between learning outcomes, activities, and assessments.[44] It is important that teachers recognize that collaboration is not only a legal requirement, but a necessity for spiritual development.[45] When the conversation about the need for collaboration is limited to legislation, teachers may operate from a framework of fear rather than love. Shippen, Crites,

---

43. Keith, *Case for Servant Leadership*, 37.
44. Dettmer et al., *Collaboration, Consultation, and Teamwork*.
45. Johnson and Ridley, *Elements of Ethics for Professionals*.

Houchins, Ramsey and Simon found high levels of anxiety in teachers related to inclusion and collaboration that stemmed from fear of litigation.[46]

According to Covey, educators need to develop spiritual intelligence to be their best. The hope is that the spiritual intelligence of preservice special educators will contribute to changing negative school cultures. Collaboration helps to develop spiritual maturity by forcing teachers to navigate communication and collaboration with colleagues whose perspectives may differ from theirs. Servant leaders encourage and respect diversity.[47]

Although church and public schools must remain separate, there is no law that hinders teachers from applying their faith to their teaching practices. Faith can be integrated into the ways that communication happens, motivations for teaching, problem-solving processes, relationship building strategies, and acts of service. None of the participants in the study mentioned eating together, playing together, or meeting for coffee or tea as practices for nurturing relationships or initiating communication although these activities would foster both relationships and communication. Jesus often shared meals and traveled with his disciples and those whom he served. Playing together and sharing meals are great opportunities for teachers to build rapport needed for collaboration.

Evil communication corrupts good manners, so it is important that preservice teachers center communication around what is good. Teacher education programs at faith-based institutions can stress the need to avoid communication that involves gossip, slander, and lies (Prov 6 and 18). According to the scriptures, Satan is the father of lies and those who lie are helping him achieve his agenda (John 8:44). A Christian worldview challenges people to speak God's truth in love (Jas 4:11).

Establishing faith-based new teacher groups may be beneficial to preservice teachers. These groups can help new teachers learn to overcome communication or planning challenges and address other collaboration issues in ways that reflect a relational theology and servant leadership. According to Belmonte, teachers who rely on other teachers experience more longevity in the profession than teachers who do not.[48] New teacher groups have been effective in reducing the stress that is common to new teachers, increasing collaboration, and promoting problem solving.[49]

46. Shippen et al., *Preservice Teachers' Perceptions*.

47. Keith, *Case for Servant Leadership*.

48. Belmonte, *Teaching on Solid Ground*.

49. Durn, "No Teacher Left Behind."

Using theology and spiritual frameworks to motivate preservice teachers to collaborate may prove more effective than merely using the legal impetus. When encouragement of collaboration is limited to models, frameworks, and legal aspects teachers tend to operate from fear with a minimalistic approach: "What is the least that I need to do?" Helping preservice special educators to understand their sphere of moral, ethical, and spiritual influence may enable them to improve the culture of their schools and add meaning to their work.[50] Teachers who have developed their spiritual intelligence usually ask, "What can I do in this situation to improve it?" Since will is an important component in the implementation and effectiveness of collaboration, teachers who believe that there are spiritual implications to collaborating may be more likely to collaborate and may collaborate more effectively.[51]

Conclusion

The purpose of this chapter was to help Christian educators make important connections between their faith and teaching. Specifically this chapter examined the role of faith in the principles and practices used to collaborate while serving students with disabilities. Faith-based special education teacher preparation programs present optimal opportunities within their preservice induction programs to be explicit about the ethical and spiritual implications of collaboration. One of the underutilized areas for making these connections is clinical practice. While mentors can be a great source for helping to facilitate these connections, more explicit learning objectives, faith related activities may also be useful is solidifying these ideas. The use of theological frameworks as a means of understanding working with others, God's way, may also prove beneficial to pre-service teachers.

Bibliography

Austin, V. L. "Teachers' Beliefs about Co-teaching." *Remedial and Special Education* 22 (2001) 245–55.

Bandura, A. *Social Foundations of Thought and Action: A Social Cognitive Theory.* Englewood Cliffs, NJ: Prentice Hall, 1986.

50. Covey, *8th Habit.*

51. Chittister, *Wisdom Distilled from the Daily*; Johnson and Ridley, *Elements of Ethics for Professionals.*

Barkley, E. F., et al. *Collaborative Learning Techniques: A Handbook for College Faculty.* San Francisco: Jossey-Bass, 2005.

Belmonte, D. *Teaching on Solid Ground: Nuance, Challenge, and Technique for the Emerging Teacher.* Thousand Oaks, CA: Corwin, 2006.

Building the Legacy: IDEA 2004. Retrieved February 2, 2012, from http://idea.ed.gov.

California Commission on Teacher Credentialing. *Standards: Common and Program.* Retrieved from http://www.ctc.ca.gov/educator-prep/program-standards.html.

Callen, B. L. "John Wesley and Relational Theology." In *Relational Theology: A Contemporary Introduction,* edited by B. Montgomery et al., 7–10. Eugene, OR: Wipf & Stock, 2012.

Chittister, J. *Wisdom Distilled from the Daily: Living the Rule of St. Benedict Today.* San Francisco: HarperCollins, 1991.

Covey, S. *The 8th Habit: From Effectiveness to Greatness.* New York: Free Press, 2004.

Creswell, J. W. *Educational Research: Planning, Conducting, and Evaluating Quantitative and Qualitative Research.* 2nd ed. Upper Saddle River, NJ: Prentice Hall, 2004.

Dettmer, P., et al. *Collaboration, Consultation, and Teamwork for Students with Special Needs.* 7th ed. Upper Saddle River, NJ: Pearson, 2012.

Dettmer, P., et al. *Collaboration, Consultation, and Teamwork for Students with Special Needs.* 6th ed. Columbus: Pearson, 2009.

Durn, J. L. "No Teacher Left Behind: Effectiveness of New Teacher Groups to Facilitate Induction." Unpublished doctoral dissertation, Indiana University of Pennsylvania, 2010. Retrieved from http://dspace.iup.edu/bitstream/handle/2069/243/?sequence=1.

Friend, M., and L. Cook. *Interactions: Collaboration Skills for School Professionals.* Upper Saddle River, NJ: Prentice Hall, 2012.

Hooks, B., and C. West. *Breaking Bread: Insurgent Black Intellectual Life.* Cambridge, MA: South End, 1999.

Johnson, W. B., and C. R. Ridley. *The Elements of Ethics for Professionals.* New York: Palgrave Macmillan, 2008.

Kardos, S. M. "New Teachers in New Jersey Schools and the Professional Cultures They Experience: A Pilot Study." Unpublished special qualifying paper, Harvard University Graduate School of Education, 2001.

Keith, K. M. *The Case for Servant Leadership.* Westfield, IN: Greenleaf Center for Servant Leadership, 2008.

Leo, T., and D. Cowan. "Launching Professional Learning Communities: Beginning Actions." *Issues . . . About Change* 8 (2000).

Lofland, J. "Styles of Reporting Qualitative Field Research." *American Sociologist* 3 (1974) 101–11.

National Center for Education Statistics. *National Assessment of Educational Progress.* 2005. Retrieved from http://nces.ed.gov/nationsreportcard/mathematics/2005mathacctype.asp.

Oord, T. J. "Relational Love." In *Relational Theology: A Contemporary Introduction,* edited by B. Montgomery et al., 24–27. Eugene, OR: Wipf & Stock, 2012.

Powell, S. M. "The Image of God." In *Relational Theology: A Contemporary Introduction,* edited by B. Montgomery et al., 28–30. Eugene, OR: Wipf & Stock, 2012.

Richards, L. *Handling Qualitative Data: A Practical Guide.* Thousand Oaks, CA: Sage, 2005.

Shippen, M. E., et al. "Preserve Teachers' Perceptions of Including Students with Disabilities." *Teacher Education and Special Education* 28 (2005) 92–99.

Trompenaars, F., and E. Voerman. *Harnessing the Strengths of the World's Most Powerful Management Philosophy: Servant Leadership across Cultures.* San Francisco: McGraw Hill, 2010.

Wrightslaw. *IDEA 2004: IEP Teams Members and IEP Team Attendance.* Retrieved from http://www.wrightslaw.com/idea/art/iep.team.members.htm.

Yong, A. "Relational Theology and the Holy Spirit." In *Relational Theology: A Contemporary Introduction,* edited by B. Montgomery et al., 18–23. Eugene, OR: Wipf & Stock, 2012.

5

___

Outcomes for Students with Disabilities, Especially Those with Emotional and Behavioral Disorders

A Justice and Equity Perspective

Ben C. Nworie, PhD, MDiv, LPC
Professor of Special Education
School of Education, Biola University

Abstract

THIS CHAPTER HIGHLIGHTS THE related factors that contribute to the outcomes of students with disabilities, especially those with emotional and behavioral disorders (EBD). A brief analysis of the disproportionate representation of minorities in special education, especially African Americans in EBD, and its impact on their outcomes is presented from a justice and equity perspective. Recommendations for looking at student outcomes from a biblical justice perspective as a way to accelerate and sustain positive educational outcomes are discussed.

Keywords: outcomes, special education, disproportionality, justice, equity

Introduction

Poor school performance by students (especially students with disabilities) over a protracted period of time gave rise to the high stakes tests requirements. Part of the congressional findings in IDEA 1997, and IDEA 2004 was that low expectations adversely affected student outcomes.[1] Shortly after passage of the No Child Left Behind Act, a significant enough number of students in every disability category underperformed in reading and math to justify concern over their ability to perform high school work.[2] Research findings from the National Center on Educational Outcomes (NCEO) on the 2007–2008 school year indicate that the average scores of students with disabilities across over forty states were lower in reading and mathematics than general education students.[3] The prolonged low academic performance of students with and without disabilities led congress to mandate changes requiring strict accountability standards from all students, including students with disabilities.[4] Consequently, students with disabilities (SWDs) who were formerly excluded from measures of educational performance began to be explicitly acknowledged in federal and state accountability systems.

The 1997 amendments to the Individuals with Disabilities Education Act (IDEA) led the way in mandating that students with disabilities take part in state- and district-wide high stakes standardized tests (with appropriate accommodations or take part in alternate assessments), and that their participation and performance be reported along with their peers without disabilities.[5] The Elementary and Secondary Education Act (ESEA), which was reauthorized as the No Child Left Behind law (NCLB) of 2001 further reinforced this accountability requirement for SWDs. The NCLB established SWDs as a specific student subgroup for the purpose of helping to determine if and to what extent schools made adequate yearly progress (AYP). Additionally, the Individuals with Disabilities Education Act (IDEA) amendments of 2004 further reinforced this accountability

1. McLeskey et al., "Inclusion of Students with Learning Disabilities."

2. Blackorby et al., "Academic Performance"; Hettleman, *Road to Nowhere*.

3. Bremer, "Public Reporting."

4. Wrightslaw.

5. Salend, *Creating Inclusive Classrooms*; Katsiyannis et al., "High-Stakes Testing"; Darling-Hammond, "Race, Inequality and Educational Accountability"; Harr-Robins, "Inclusion of Students."

requirement for SWDs to take part in state- and district-wide high stakes standardized tests along with their peers without disabilities.

Impact of High-Stakes Tests on Special Education Outcomes

As pointed out above, a couple of concerns about the status of special education instruction gave impetus to the high stakes tests mandates. They are:

- the relatively poor academic outcomes for children with disabilities.[6]

- the lack of accountability mechanisms that focus on outcomes rather than processes.[7]

Certain accommodations are allowed by law for the children with disabilities who are being mandated to take these high stakes test. However, the accommodations are often insufficient to mitigate the limiting effects posed by the disabilities; and as Brinckerhoff and Banerjee have strongly argued, misconceptions about the accommodations review process employed by testing agencies add to the anxiety that many test takers feel around obtaining approval for high-stakes test accommodations. Most of the children in special education facing rising educational mandates and high-stakes testing are facing great challenges. These children experiencing handicapping conditions already face special challenges in mastering educational requirements. Many of these young people are minority youths attending schools with inadequate support and limited resources.[8]

The imposition of higher standards on these children places them at even greater risk of educational failure. This seems especially true for children with emotional and behavioral disorders (EBD) and those suffering from family abuse and neglect. These children usually populate the foster care and juvenile justice systems where educational programs typically provide only the bare minimum of instruction. The high level of resources and instruction that the new tests and mandates presume often does not exist

---

6. Salend, *Creating Inclusive Classrooms*; Johnson et al., "Cross-State Study"; Moody et al., "Reading Instruction"; Schulte et al., "Effective Special Education"; Harr-Robins, "Inclusion of Students with Disabilities."

7. Carnine and Granzin, "Setting Learning Expectations"; Johnson et al., "Cross-State Study"; McLaughlin and Warren, *Resource Implications of Inclusion*; Shinn, "Does Anyone Care."

8. Christenson et al., "Consequences of High-Stakes Assessment."

in many programs educating these children with special needs. Donlevy, agrees with this thought when he says:

> The current high-stakes environment is philosophically and morally inimical to the interests of children and cannot be sustained in its current form. It is a one-sided development governed by questionable assumptions and uninformed by the demands of practical experience. . . . High standards are desired by everyone. But the path to achieving them should not be littered with the dashed hopes of disappointed children unaware of the high stakes manipulations being orchestrated beyond their grasp.[9]

The overuse of standardized testing does not ensure that students are achieving higher standards of learning.[10] To the contrary, some test critics have argued that state tests often assess low levels of learning[11] and have led to "dumbing down" or "watering down" the curriculum so students can be more successful. African American children and youth who happen to be over-represented in the special education category of emotional disturbance undoubtedly face a double jeopardy. They are already exposed to differential instructional approaches characterized by low teacher expectations and myths about the needs of students from a non-dominant culture. These students also put up their own barriers to academic achievement by adopting racial identities or behavioral characteristics in opposition to school expectations and codes.[12] As a result, multiple barriers operate singly and in combination to undermine the academic achievement of these students with disabilities, especially those with EBD.

The impact of high-stakes testing on students with disabilities has been viewed from different angles. While significant positive outcomes have been recorded (as we will point out later), some negative outcomes have also been documented. To begin with, there are strong views that NCLB has produced meager gains in achievement, and that students with disabilities made greater progress before the NCLB mandate. For example, it has been documented that

> despite enormous pressure to raise reading and math test scores, the rate of progress on the National Assessment of Educational

9. Donlevy, "Dilemma of High-Stakes Testing," 336.

10. Darling-Hammond, "Race, Inequality and Education Accountability."

11. Hilliard, "Excellence in Education."

12. Fordham and Ogbu, "Black Students' School Success"; McKenna, "Disproportionate Representation of African Americans."

Progress (NAEP) at grades 4 and 8 was generally faster in the decade before NCLB took effect than under this law. . . . Increased testing coupled with punitive sanctions caused a wide range of damage. The harm includes narrowed curriculum, teaching to the test, pushing out low-scoring children, and cheating.[13]

The argument is that for the students with disabilities, the high-stakes tests have resulted in damage to both educational quality and equity. Tanis, a special education teacher and a mother of two children on the autism spectrum, claims that these tests actually prevent many students with disabilities from receiving the individualized education that meets their needs.[14]

The impact of high-stakes testing on students with disabilities is sometimes not clear-cut. The California High School Exit Examination (CAHSEE) which in 2005 was already being described as an accountability fad that was rapidly moving across the nation[15] presents a somewhat good illustration of the point that the impact of high-stakes testing on students with disabilities sometimes seems ambiguous.

For example, according to data released by the state of California the passing rate for 2008's graduating class of the California High School Exit Examination (CAHSEE) was 90.2 percent. The CAHSEE was created in 1999 and first implemented as a graduation requirement for the graduating class of 2006. CAHSEE is a standards-based test which is used to test students' mastery of key skills in English language arts and mathematics before graduating from high school. The 90.2 percent figure of 2008 shows a decrease from the previous year's 94 percent.[16] This is said to be the lowest rate of passage since three years before when the test became mandatory to earn a diploma. According to the state officials the estimated passage rate dipped because for the first time special education students were required to take the exam to receive diplomas, and their test results were included in the Academic Performance Index (API) score. The API score performance is important to schools because it is a principal factor in determining the accountability rating assigned to each school by the state of California. Nearly half of the students in the different special education categories such as learning disabilities, speech or language impairments, other health impair-

13. Ravitch and Chubb, "Future of No Child Left Behind."
14. Tanis, "Pushing Back against High Stakes."
15. Brinckerhoff and Banerjee, "Misconceptions Regarding Accommodations."
16. Slater, "Schools of Chief Jack O'Connell."

ments, mental retardation (intellectual disability), emotional disturbance, autism and multiple disabilities were unsuccessful in passing the exam.

Among special education students, however, 53.8 percent passed the exam, which is an increase from the 49.6 percent who passed the previous year. At the same time the May 2008 figures indicated that the class of 2008 without the special education students, showed a small increase to 93.6 percent in those who passed.[17] More recent reports from the California Department of Education (CDE) have shown continued improvements in the performance on the CAHSEE. However, the same CDE reports on CAHSEE show that performance has remained consistently low for students with disabilities.[18]

Other research findings also show a pattern of significant outcome discrepancies between students with disabilities and their non-disabled peers. For example, a research report by Bremer, Albus, and Thurlow indicates that in reading, special education students experienced a gap in scores on regular assessments that progressively widened, in comparison with their regular education counterparts, as they moved through school, rising as high as 38.9 percent in high school reading. A fairly similar trend was observed in Mathematics where middle school students with disabilities performed with a 36.8 percent score gap in comparison to the regular education students.[19] Students with disabilities in the Baltimore city public school system in 2003–2004 showed equally low proficiency scores compared to their regular education peers. The gaps of 35 percentage points in reading and 29 percentage points in mathematics in Baltimore are somewhat typical of the national trend.[20]

Factors That Contribute to Poor Outcomes

What factors contribute to the consistent pattern of poor outcomes in schools for young people with EBD and other disabilities? Are these poor outcomes inevitable, or are there aspects of their school programs or support services that could help students with disabilities have relatively more positive experiences? Both research and practice experience point to several factors that seem to be responsible.

17. Mehta, "Fewer California Students"; Nworie, "High-Stakes Testing."
18. http://www.cde.ca.gov/ta/tg/hs/documents/cahsee14evalrpt.pdf.
19. Bremer et al., "Public Reporting of 2007–2008."
20. Hettleman, *Road to Nowhere.*

Poor Attendance (Especially in Lower Grades)

One of the many reasons for poor learning outcomes among students with disabilities is lack of consistent school attendance, especially in the lower grades. This poor attendance usually caused by health concerns and secondary logistical obstacles for families such as transportation difficulties, child care issues, and the issue of half-day preschool schedules has been identified as one of the reasons for poor learning outcomes, especially for students with EBD and other disabilities. A 2014 study in Chicago shows that preschool students who come in with low levels of prior skills (such as those with disabilities) who miss a significant number of preschool days end the year with poor learning outcomes, both during preschool and in second grade.[21] For example, students who miss the majority of their preschool days at age four, score lower on math and letter recognition at the end of the school year. Conversely preschool students (such as those with disabilities) with low incoming skills who maintain regular attendance do show significant academic gains. Overall students who miss school for many years between preschool and second grade usually need intervention to read at grade level by third grade. By the end of second grade students who are chronically absent between preschool and second grade have significantly lower learning outcomes than their counterparts who are not chronically absent in preschool. Consequently, second-graders who yearly have persistently missed school beginning from preschool, by third grade do most likely need intensive reading intervention in order to be reading at grade level.[22]

Similarly, consistent school attendance in grades 8 and 9 are significantly associated with positive outcomes such as graduating on time. For example, a recent study in Oregon on early warning signs of students who may drop out or fail to graduate from high school on time indicates that grade 8 attendance rates below 80 percent, (and grade 8 grade point average (GPA) of less than 2.0), as well as grade 9 attendance rates below 80 percent, (and grade 9 GPA of less than 2.0) are valuable early warning signals about both students who did not graduate on time, as well as students who dropped out of high school.[23]

21. Ehrlich et al., "Preschool Attendance in Chicago."
22. Ibid.
23. Burke, "Early Identification of High School Graduation Outcomes."

Other issues and factors that contribute to poor special education outcomes include: *challenging behaviors, teacher quality, teacher attitude and expectation, bias in the rating or reporting of achievement outcomes of students with disabilities, overrepresentation,* and *poor students' attitudes.*

Challenging Behaviors

Students with challenging behaviors and negative attitudes are typically at risk for decreased academic success.[24] Besides, students' characteristics have been found to be several times more powerful than school characteristics in limiting or enhancing academic success, such as reading achievement.[25] Poor student engagement in academic responding significantly contributes toward poor outcomes such as obvious gaps in academic achievement.[26]

Teacher Quality

There is research evidence that poor student outcomes can sometimes be attributed to lack of teacher effectiveness.[27] Though about 90 percent of special education teachers for preschool and school-age students with disabilities are considered highly qualified, yet in the past several years, half of district special education administrators have reportedly experienced difficulty regularly in finding qualified applicants for special education positions.[28] Specifically, Robinson found that as the number of students with disabilities per highly qualified teacher increased, student reading achievement decreased. There are reports of instances where teachers were exposing students with significant cognitive disabilities to academic content, such as physics and algebra that were well beyond the academic repertoire and scope of competence of such students. Lack of understanding from teachers on how to properly adapt content to enhance student achievement has negative impact on student outcomes.[29]

24. Johns, *15 Positive Behavior Strategies.*

25. Singh, "Longitudinal Study."

26. Greenwood, "How Should Learning Environments Be Structured."

27. Robinson, "Highly Qualified Teacher Status"; Kahn and Lewis, "Survey on Teaching Science."

28. Bradley et al., "IDEA National Assessment Implementation Study."

29. Karvonen et al., "Academic Curriculum for Students"; Kahn and Lewis, "Survey

Teacher Attitude and Expectation

Research confirms that teacher attitudes and expectations do affect teacher practice and student achievement.[30] Consequently, negative teacher attitude and expectation do result in poor student outcomes.[31] If a teacher develops attitudes and expectations based on a student's characteristics, documented past behavior, and observations, then the teacher's interactions with the student can be affected by these attitudes and expectations. Depending on the self-image, and self-efficacy of the student, the student's behaviors can confirm these teacher attitudes and expectations, allowing the teacher to maintain the expectation and attitude that has been formed. This can in turn lead to a self-fulfilling prophecy kind of situation. "Self-fulfilling prophecy" is used to describe expectancy effects where as a result of a false evaluation of a situation or person, a new behavior makes the originally false perception come true.[32]

Teacher attitude and expectation affect student achievement as a result of the Pygmalion effect which is a phenomenon by which expectation is often communicated through unintended, nonverbal behavior which can have significant impact on the individual to whom the expectation is unintentionally communicated. As accurately reported by Klehm, studies of the Pygmalion effect in the classroom have shown that students in the classes where teachers expected more intellectual growth showed a significantly greater improvement in test scores, higher scores on classroom performance and achievement tests, and receiving of more praise and less criticism than the students in the class where the teacher had no such high expectation of the students. Klehm points attention to other findings which suggest that teachers may have negative attitudes that they may not be aware of, even when those attitudes are affecting the achievement of students with dyslexia.

A national online survey of 1,088 K–12 science teachers by Kahn and Lewis found that attitudinal barriers inhibit the success of students with disabilities. Hornstra, Denessen, Bakker, Van den Bergh and Voeten,[33] examined the attitudes of thirty regular education teachers toward dyslexia

---

on Teaching Science."

30. Klehm, "Effects of Teacher Beliefs."
31. Kahn and Lewis, "Survey on Teaching Science."
32. Klehm, "Effects of Teacher Beliefs."
33. Hornstra et al., "Teacher Attitudes toward Dyslexia."

and found that the effects of the teacher attitudes and expectations have direct implications for the academic achievement of students with dyslexia in comparison to students without learning disabilities.

Bias in the Rating or Reporting of Achievement Outcomes of Students with Disabilities

Teachers who usually play an important role in rating students' work sometimes exhibit bias in the rating or reporting of achievement outcomes of students with disabilities. In a study by Mastergeorge and Martinez in which trained teachers rated student performance in language arts and mathematics in third, fifth, and ninth grades, the findings showed greater inconsistency when rating papers from students with disabilities. The findings of the study suggest that individual teachers may show some bias when scoring students with disabilities.[34]

A teacher's decision to refer a student for special education was one of the highest predictors of learning disabilities (LD) placement. Over-identification was one of the reasons for increases in the incidence of LD. This happened partly because due to bias there were many "false-positive" LD cases where students who actually did not have LD were labeled with an LD.[35] The newer IDEA mandated LD identification and placement criteria were put in place to, among other things, curb such bias driven over-identification of students as LD.[36]

A recent study that used a statewide longitudinal sample to examine mathematics achievement gaps and growth in students with and without disabilities, found that regardless of which of the various identification criteria was used, the students with disabilities subgroup showed lower average achievement and slower growth than students without disabilities. The results thus suggested the possibility of the presence of bias in the present way of identifying the students with disabilities subgroup in reporting achievement outcomes.[37]

---

34. Mastergeorge and Martinez, "Rating Performance Assessments."
35. Goodman and Webb, "Reading Disability Referrals."
36. Turnbull et al., *Exceptional Lives.*
37. Schulte and Stevens, "Once, Sometimes, or Always."

Overrepresentation

Overrepresentation refers to the disproportionate representation of cultur-ally diverse students in special education programs.[38] The over represen-tation of minority children in special education and the quality of their educational experience have been regarded as among the most significant issues faced by the US public school system in the past forty years.[39] The disproportionate number of minority students in special education pro-grams affects the outcomes of these minority students in special education.[40] Blanchett, Mumford, and Beachum, in their discussion of this endemic system of disproportional minorities' representation in special education, have correctly observed that "ultimately, the system generates a group of students who underachieve, drop out, and become marginally employed or moderately successful."[41]

Poor Students' Attitudes

The school outcomes of students with disabilities are also affected by stu-dents' attitudes. While positive attitudes tend to enhance positive school outcomes, negative attitudes seem to equally result in poor students' out-comes. For example, a study by Decker, Dona, and Christenson showed a close association between improved student attitudes (as measured by in-creased student-teacher relationship quality) and increased positive social, behavioral, engagement and academic outcomes for students.

Factors That Contribute to Improved Outcomes

Despite the ambiguities and the challenges associated with the require-ments of the accountability standards on the special needs students, the imposition of the higher standards required by the laws are helping many students with disabilities to achieve positive outcomes at levels not previ-ously thought possible.[42]

Examples of the improved outcomes include:

38. Artiles and Trent, "Representation of Culturally/Linguistically Diverse Students."
39. Hallahan et al., *Exceptional Learners.*
40. McKenna, "Disproportionate Representation of African Americans."
41. Blanchett et al., "Urban School Failure."
42. Smith and Tyler, *Introduction to Comtemporary Special Education.*

- The school dropout rate of students with disabilities is fewer as it has shown a decrease of 21 percentage points within a ten-year period.

- Students with disabilities show a 43 percent increase in graduation rate as an increased number of students with disabilities graduate with a regular diploma since 1996.

- The number of students with disabilities attending postsecondary education has increased from 15 percent in 1987 to 40 percent in 2005.

- Post high school employment outcomes have increased as more students with disabilities than ever before hold jobs.

What factors contribute toward making these positive outcomes possible for students with disabilities, especially those with EBD? A number of factors have combined to bring about such improvements in the lives of special needs students who learn differently and who need a specialized education. Those factors include: *early intervention, effective inclusion,* and *effective instructional practices.*

Early Intervention

Early intervening by providing to students additional learning supports as soon as needs are recognized prevents the "wait to fail" approach to providing special education supports to students. This proactive, early intervention, approach prevents early learning difficulties and behavior problems from becoming disabilities later, and helps to ensure desired students' schooling outcomes. For example, there is research evidence that providing all students with two years of schooling in prekindergarten (ages 3–5), adds significant beneficial impacts on children's later life outcomes.[43]

Early intervention in the field of special education often refers to educational intervention services provided for very young children who are two years and under. Early childhood special education which the federal government has very vigorously pursued since the first reauthorization of IDEA in 1990 includes the provision of educational and related services to preschoolers who are between three to five years of age. The broad concept of early intervention encompasses the provision of a wide variety of therapies, health, social and educational care, and family supports designed to help prevent or minimize the incidence of eventual developmental,

43. Greenwood, "How Should Learning Environments Be Structured."

educational or social problems, particularly for children believed to be at risk for such problems.[44]

Early Intervention and Students At Risk for EBD

The consensus of special education research literature shows that special education students, especially those at risk for emotional and behavioral disorders such as anger, aggression, and conduct disorders are at a greater risk for poorer secondary school outcomes than other youths with disabilities as a whole. EBD students are at greater risk than youths in the general population.[45] One clear implication of this research information for special education is that early identification and early intervention should be considered essential for improved student outcomes, and should be vigorously pursued.[46]

A recent research report showed that reading and behavior problems are risk factors for each other. This research found that children with reading problems in first grade were significantly more likely to display poor task engagement, poor self-control, externalizing behavior problems, and internalizing behavior problems in third grade. The research also found that children displaying poor task engagement in first grade were more likely to experience reading problems in third grade. Such research findings lead to the obvious conclusion that the most effective types of interventions, especially for at risk kids, are not only those that target problems with academic tasks and task-focused behaviors simultaneously, but those that begin as early as possible.[47]

Kauffman put it very correctly when he said that "a persistent and self-defeating response of educators and parents is to let emotional or behavioral problems fester until they become disorders of serious if not dangerous proportions."[48] As Ysseldyke, Algozzine, and Thurlow rightly pointed out, the two fundamental assumptions underlying early intervention for young children (both with and without disabilities) are developmental plasticity and cost effectiveness. Developmental plasticity is the notion that the

44. Heward, *Exceptional Children*.

45. Heward, *Exceptional Children*; Kauffman, "Characteristics of Emotional and Behavioral Disorders"; Ysseldyke et al., *Critical Issues in Special Education*.

46. Nworie, "Early Intervention."

47. Morgan et al., "Are Reading and Behavior Problems."

48. Kauffman, "Characteristics of Emotional and Behavioral Disorders."

brain grows, that intelligence results from an active interaction between the individual and his external environment. It is also the conception that the developmental progress of a child can be positively changed, and that behavior is changeable. The idea of cost effectiveness lines up with the adage "the sooner, the better." It lines up even better with the wise saying "a stitch in time saves nine."[49] The new constituencies for early special education intervention include drug- and alcohol-exposed infants, low-birth-weight survivors, as well as AIDS babies, among others. The research literature suggests that the eventual costs of dealing with and servicing these children would be considerable.[50]

Effective Inclusion

One of the many benefits to effectively including special education students in the general education population is that expectations usually rise, leading to children with disabilities achieving more.[51] With the focus of the general education classroom on the general curriculum, inclusion in the general education setting seems to provide more encouragement toward skill development in the general curriculum.[52] Another benefit of inclusion is that effective inclusive programs tend to yield increased accomplishment of IEP objectives often evidenced by increased student outcomes.[53] For example, in a comparative study by Tremblay of two instructional models (co-teaching inclusion and solo-taught special education) for students with learning disabilities (LD) with regard to their effect on academic achievement and class attendance, significant differences were observed in the effects on student outcomes in reading/writing and on attendance, as the inclusion model was shown to be globally more effective compared with the special education setting.[54]

The fact that special education students who are placed in mixed-ability groups tend to have fewer discipline issues, and tend to participate more in class activities means that more of the teachers' time can be spent in direct instruction to students rather than managing behavior or engaging

49. Nworie, "Early Intervention."

50. Ysseldyke et al., *Critical Issues in Special Education.*

51. Salend, *Creating Inclusive Classrooms.*

52. Huefner, "Placements for Special Education Students."

53. Salend, *Creating Inclusive Classrooms.*

54. Tremblay, *Comparative Outcomes of Two Instructional Models.*

in discipline issues.[55] In addition, as student's transition time is curtailed in the inclusive classroom, instruction time is better utilized as the student stays in one classroom for services.[56]

Effective Instructional Practices

Multiple Tiers of Support

As useful as early intervention is, it leads to even better student outcomes when the school is structured to provide Multiple Tiers of Support (MTS). MTS is a way of differentiating the instruction of individual learners not making adequate progress in the general education curriculum or providing progressive levels of intervention as a way to accelerate the progress of such learners who need to make expected progress.[57] A good example of MTS is the Response to Intervention (RtI) process. The RtI is a means to improve educational outcomes and decision-making by supporting instruction in general classroom with scientifically proven high quality intervention and monitoring individual student outcome.

Clear Learner Goals and Expectations

Other effective instructional practices for increasing outcomes include making learner goals and expectations clear at the school and district levels by

> specifying objectively what the learner needs to know and do in alignment with appropriate standards, providing instruction focused on these skills that is explicit, providing multiple opportunities to respond using a mix of teacher- and peer-led lesson formats and materials that keep things interesting, differentiating instruction based on learners' response to instruction, and arranging useful consequences for correct responding and appropriate classroom conduct.[58]

---

55. Ibid.
56. Nworie, "Early Intervention."
57. Spencer et al., "Tier 2 Language Intervention."
58. Greenwood, "How Should Learning Environments Be Structured."

Self-Determination

Since the 1990s, there have been research findings suggesting a direct relationship between student self-determination and school-based outcomes, such as academic skills, access to the general education curriculum, as well as student involvement in transition planning.[59] Recent research evidence indicates that exposure to self-determination interventions in secondary school may lead to more stability in student outcomes over time.[60]

Justice, Equity, and Improved Special Education Outcomes

All the factors considered above help to bring about improved special education Outcomes. Additionally, the factors discussed above lead to higher expectations, result in more positive attitudes about what these individuals can accomplish, reduce or eliminate barriers, and foster innovative and effective instructional practices that facilitate students' classroom performance.[61] The value of justice works in combination with these factors not only to help many students with disabilities achieve positive outcomes, but justice (especially biblical justice) can act as catalyst to accelerate and guarantee improved outcomes for students with disabilities.

Justice Defined

What is justice? There seems to be some confusion among people today about the real meaning of justice because the term seems to mean different things to different people. For example, currently some people commit violent crimes against children, women and innocent citizens in the name of "peace and justice." One wonders if the confusion about justice might have anything to do with the fact that there is no article in the latest *Encyclopedia Britannica* under the heading "justice." Justice is often defined in the dictionary as fairness in protection of rights and punishment of wrongs. It is commonly thought of as a principle or means by which people are treated fairly. As a noun, it is the quality of being fair and reasonable.[62]

---

59. Shogren et al., "Relationships between Self-Determination and Post School Outcomes."

60. Ibid.

61. Smith and Tyler, *Introduction to Contemporary Special Education*.

62. *Oxford Dictionary*, s.v. "justice."

The Need for Justice in the School System

Usually students bring with them to school a variety of concerns and challenges which they are confronted with in their homes and in their neighborhoods. Educators are expected to exhibit fairness and justice in the way they serve these students and their families, including the handling of the various attending apprehensions and challenges. Besides, as the student demographics are rapidly growing and changing, so are the diverse needs of students growing and changing while resources are becoming increasingly limited. Minority students (which usually includes special needs students) make up about 40 percent of the total school enrollment.[63] As Warren and Pacino correctly observed, "The high school students and parents of students at all levels openly share with educators the challenges of discrimination and even disease that they face as gay, lesbian, bisexual, or transgendered individuals; more children with special needs are integrated into the regular education classroom, often with limited support; and *traditional* family structures in which students live with both biological parents throughout their schooling are not necessarily the norm."[64] The growing issue of bullying, the need for some educators to review their personal beliefs, prejudices and practices, add to the mounting need for Justice in the school system.

Social Justice

There are various types and systems of justice (such as legal and ethical). However, social justice and biblical justice are more applicable to education. Brackette, Rezaei, and Kuyinu point out that "social justice involves the belief in equity and fairness, and is concerned with the treatment of disenfranchised individuals and groups of people in society who do not possess equal societal power." They add that "working with social justice involves a continuum of activities, including advocacy, raising awareness, and engaging in practices to impact legislative action."[65] There are social justice implications of the IDEA law governing special education practice, based on this understanding of justice as "fairness." However, the idea of justice in special education should not be limited to the IDEA requirement

63. Warren and Pacino, "Faith Integration."

64. Ibid., 91.

65. Brackette et al., "Engaging in Social Justice Practices."

of educating students with disabilities in the least restrictive environment by effectively including the students with special needs in the general education curriculum.[66] Justice calls for going beyond obeying the letters of the law to recognizing and following through with the spirit of the law. Justice in special education which is a precursor for quality special education outcomes, therefore, needs to include a biblical, more sustainable dimension of justice for a just and equitable education system.

Biblical Justice

Though IDEA lays emphasis on the "rights" of students with disability, human rights derive not from legal mandates, but from the love of God for human beings.[67] Thus, while social justice and biblical justice are both applicable to education, biblical justice is more closely applicable to special education. Keller correctly points out that according to the Bible what it means to do justice includes the following: care for the vulnerable, reflection of the character of God, right relationships, and generosity.

Biblical justice is founded on the character and nature of God. Just as God's justice is not about what is fair, but about what is right, biblical justice goes beyond simply granting other people their rights to vigorously seeking to establish the rights of others. Biblical justice helps educators to create and operate on a positive environment, which in turn helps students to flourish and perform at their optimal level. Anderson captures this idea well when he says: "biblical justice will help educators recognize that each student should receive what he or she needs, giving due consideration to each one's strengths and weaknesses, while avoiding negativity that results from focusing attention only on limitations or differences."[68] When students flourish and perform at their optimal level, in a barrier free environment, that is shalom.

The biblical concept of shalom connotes completeness or true flourishing which can most certainly be realized in the context where justice obtains in the biblical sense. A biblical justice educational setting creates a barrier free environment for all students by challenging practices and ideologies that militate against leveling the playing field in order to promote positive outcomes for students with disabilities.

66. Ferguson et al., "Family Portraits."

67. Anderson, *Toward a Theology of Special Education*.

68. Ibid., 203.

The discussion of these essential components of biblical justice will follow a brief analysis, from a justice perspective, of the disproportionate representation of minorities, especially African Americans in EBD, in special education and its impact on their outcomes.

Disproportionality and Special Education Outcomes

What Is Disproportionality in Special Education?

Disproportionality in special education being one of oldest issues in the field has been defined and described in various ways,[69] but simply put, disproportionality or overrepresentation in special education happens when the percentage of an ethnic group in a disability category exceeds that group's percentage of the overall population.[70] This is the case regarding African American students, who are disproportionately represented in the emotional and behavioral disorder (EBD) disability category, in the specific learning disabilities, as well as in the intellectual disability (ID) categories.[71] While African Americans account for over 17 percent of public school students, 27.3 percent receive educational services under the EBD category. 44.2 percent are served under the specific learning disability category, and 13.6 percent are served under the intellectual disability category.[72]

Causes of Disproportionality in Special Education

Just as there are various possible contributors to the disproportionate representation of minorities in special education, there are equally many possible causes of the disproportionate representation of African Americans in EBD. The overrepresentation of many African American students in the EBD disability category is an indication that possibly many of these students may have been misidentified or mislabeled.[73]

According to Piechura-Couture, Heins, and Tichenor, the main reason for placing students into special education is through behavioral issues

69. Reid, "Disproportionality in Special Education."

70. McKenna, "Disproportionate Representation of African Americans."

71. Ibid.; Turnbull et al., *Exceptional Lives.*

72. McKenna, "Disproportionate Representation of African Americans"; Reid, "Disproportionality in Special Education."

73. McKenna, "Disproportionate Representation of African Americans."

and slow academic achievement. Misinterpreted behavior of students from different cultures increases the amount of referrals to special education.[74] For example, sometimes, teachers place their judgments on the actions of African American students for being disruptive when they talk out of turn.

Among the other numerous possible contributors to the disproportionate representation of African Americans in EBD identified by researchers, some of them include: problems associated with the definition of EBD, issues of wrong placement decisions, such as those not based on a merging of evidence collected from multiple sources over time, educator perceptions, such as when the predominantly white, middle-class, female teacher population perceives the behavioral differences of minority students as unsolved behavior problems and developmental skill deficits, this can create a disconnect in appropriate expectations and lead to referrals to special education. Other contributors to disproportionality are: socioeconomic factors such as poverty which by affecting nutrition and health may also pose risks for learning disabilities, failure to use evidence-based practices, such as the use of inappropriate instructional methods, and school demographic factors.[75]

Impact of Disproportionality on Outcomes

The objective of special education services is to improve student outcomes by helping students perform at their highest possible level. However, placing the students in these more restrictive educational environments (such as EBD, LD, and ID) usually results in poor outcomes as a result of the provision of inadequate learning opportunities.[76] The fact that African American students who receive services as individuals with EBD experience various negative educational and life outcomes has been well documented. For example, 50 percent of the African American students served under the EBD category do not earn a diploma before dropping out of school. Of these 73 percent are arrested within three to five years.[77]

74. Irvine, "Complex Relationships."

75. McKenna, "Disproportionate Representation of African Americans."

76. Ibid.

77. Ibid.

Equity, Disproportionality and Special Education Outcomes

Educational equity is one of the main ideals that educators try to promote in the field of special education. Educational equity refers to all students being given equal opportunities and outcomes for success.[78] Public education under IDEA promises all students equal access to high-quality learning opportunities. Consequently, educational equity is one of the main ideals that educators try to promote in the field of special education. To accomplish this objective of educational equity, as well as increase educational effectiveness and produce positive outcomes for all learners (regardless of race, ethnicity, or disability status), collective and coherent action is required. Education stakeholders need to identify equity concerns, such as the disproportionate representation of minorities in special education programs, and prioritize ways to intentionally and intelligently address criteria for developing improved equity and quality in special education which in turn will increase positive learner outcomes.[79]

In the past, equity and quality seemed to have conflicting goals. Many advocates, professionals and other stakeholders calling for increases in quality seemed not to be concerned with equity. Similarly those calling for increased equity appeared not to be very concerned with improved quality. The following criteria for developing a robust special education process in which equity and excellence coexist should be encouraged: (1) universal access, such as the use of Universal Design for Learning (UDL), and the utilization of appropriate bilingual resources for testing and instruction; (2) individualization, especially in the effective use of the IEP process; (3) generic problem-solving, including the use of the Collaborative Problem Solving intervention framework for solving difficult problems and developing deficient skills;[80] (4) family and/or community partnerships, especially as making families aware of parental rights can significantly help their children in the education process; and (5) best practices, such as the use of Multiple Tiers of Support (MTS) for instruction.

---

78. De Valenzuela et al., "Examining Educational Equity."

79. Education Northwest; Irvine, "Complex Relationships"; Smith and Tyler, *Introduction to Contemporary Special Education.*

80. McKenna, "Disproportionate Representation of African Americans."

Recommendations for Looking at Student Outcomes from a Biblical Justice Perspective

As noted above, teachers' attitudes and biases can negatively affect students' outcomes. Serving students from a biblical justice perspective of not just fairness, but being right, and recognizing that the students derive their worth from God, enables educators to be willing to examine their own beliefs, biases, and practices to ensure that they are impacting the students in the most positive manner.

Also as noted earlier, educators have the power to influence students with their unintended messages that can affect the student's capabilities and potential. With time students come to believe in the hidden messages from their teachers and act on them.

Biblical justice requires that though they may be different, the various contributions, gifts and abilities of individual students be recognized, encouraged and celebrated. Biblical justice also encourages "greater emphasis on providing the instructional accommodations each person needs in order to learn and grow, rather than forcing students with a disability to be assimilated into the dominant classroom culture in a way that denies their individuality and their special needs."[81]

As Warren and Pacino, have so clearly and correctly recommended, "Educators must model the virtues of biblical justice, valuing and believing in the potential of all of God's children."[82] Warren and Pacino, also offer the following guidelines:

> Seeking justice within the education system includes striving to ensure the highest possible educational attainment for every learner. This is revealed at the classroom level with effective pedagogical practices. . . . High educational attainment for all learners requires a curriculum and strategies which help close the achievement gap.[83]

From a biblical justice perspective, the following elements which have been identified by researchers as factors that help struggling learners become successful will help to close the achievement gap and help students experience positive outcomes:[84]

81. Anderson, *Toward a Theology of Special Education*, 198.
82. Warren and Pacino, "Faith Integration," 100.
83. Ibid., 100–101.
84. Ibid., 101.

- Positive teacher attitudes and beliefs that nurture student motivation;

- Interpersonal relationships that draw on the social constructivist aspects of teaching;

- Social activist approaches to address racism, social injustices, conditions and opportunities to learn, and disparate expectations;

- Safe instructional environments which promote moral and spiritual development along with justice awareness;

- Creation of a cultural context for learning based on students' backgrounds; and

- Powerful, culturally responsive instruction and assessment.

Other pedagogical practices that align with biblical justice principles include: engaging learners in activities that facilitate and support student inquiry, meaning-making, proper student engagement,[85] and effective inclusive practices.[86] The caution by Anderson is helpful. He says:

> When not built upon principles of biblical justice, what is typically considered an inclusive classroom may instead promote a sense of isolation, distress or powerlessness (or at least distance, discomfort, and weakness) among students with disabilities, especially if those students are the recipient of "service" or "help" from others which, though well-meaning, emphasize the limitations caused by the disability.[87]

Additional pedagogical practices that align with biblical justice principles include: clarifying expectations, communicating clearly and honestly with students, working on effective classroom management, careful instructional planning, on-going assessment of student learning, and utilization of universal design for learning (UDL) for effective instruction of students who learn differently.

Clarifying Expectations

One way to clarify expectations is by teacher asking questions that elicit students clear understanding of teacher's expectations of them.

85. Greenwood, "How Should Learning Environments Be Structured."
86. Salend, *Creating Inclusive Classrooms*.
87. Anderson, *Toward a Theology of Special Education*, 200.

Communicating Clearly and Honestly with Students

Clear and honest Communication with students entails the teacher listening, talking, and acting in ways that convey respect, caring, and confidence, from the teacher to the students because students do test the teacher's honesty which is more than candor in expressing opinions and reporting facts accurately. Students want to know whether teachers are authentic.[88]

Working on Effective Classroom Management

Teachers who develop strong skills in creating safe, supportive classroom environments, especially by establishing the guidelines and boundaries in the classroom, are better able to positively influence students' motivation, behavior and academic achievement.[89]

Careful Instructional Planning

Careful instructional planning entails utilizing effective instructional strategies and best practices such as understanding behavioral assessment and intervention, finding and utilizing each student's strengths in creating an educational plan that works best for the student.

Ongoing Assessment of Student Learning

Curriculum based measurement is an effective tool for ongoing assessment of student learning. Tracking each student's learning progress by monitoring successes and setbacks, so as to quickly provide intervention plans for sustained success is an integral part of the tiered system of instruction and intervention used in general education, and extended to special education also.

88. Kauffman, *Characteristics of Emotional and Behavioral Disorders.*
89. Wong and Wong, *First Days of School.*

Utilization of Universal Design for Learning (UDL) for Effective Instruction of Students Who Learn Differently

UDL provides a way of designing instructional materials and activities so as to accommodate learner differences and ensure that diverse learners and students with disabilities can access the general education curriculum.[90]

There are some research proven conditions in schools which help reduce achievement gaps and which are in line with biblical justice principles.[91] They include: positive teacher beliefs, attitudes, and expectations; research based multi-tiered intervention systems; positive interpersonal relationships in an environment in which everyone does not necessarily receive equal treatment, but one in which everyone does receive what he or she needs; an environment where there is collaboration and mutual support that builds motivation, positive student identity and self-image.

The biblical justice principle of seeing each one as someone loved and endowed with worth by God is helpful in fostering a healthy learning environment where helpful learning strategies such as peer assistance can be profitably utilized. Anderson is very correct in shedding light on the fact that without biblical justice, "even the use of peer assistance can have the unwanted effect of accentuating the disability and creating a one-way relationship."[92]

In a biblical justice context, it is more likely that the overall moral, emotional, intellectual, spiritual and physical needs of the student will be cared for. The important example from Warren and Pacino is a timely reminder: "children who are hungry and fear walking to school because of gang violence do not come to school ready to learn because, . . . their physical and safety needs have not been met."[93] Anderson is in agreement that schools need to become "communities in which all students feel valued, safe, connected, and cared for."[94]

Rightly answering these searching questions from Warren and Pacino will make for a school climate and climate which has a biblical justice focus.

90. Turnbull et al., *Exceptional Lives*.

91. Smith et al., *Teaching Students with Special Needs*; Greenwood, "How Should Learning Environments Be Structured"; Warren and Pacino, "Faith Integration"; Salend, *Creating Inclusive Classrooms*; Anderson, *Toward a Theology of Special Education*.

92. Anderson, *Toward a Theology of Special Education*, 201.

93. Warren and Pacino, "Faith Integration," 103.

94. Anderson, *Toward a Theology of Special Education*, 201.

Do school employees spend time connecting with the community around the school? How are students' families treated by school staff, particularly those who may be different from those working at the school? Is the school climate welcoming for students and families? . . . Does the talk in the teachers' lounge reflect positive comments about students and their families, or is it centered on blaming children and parents for their inadequacies? Teachers who hear colleagues engage in conversations which demean children must have the courage to speak up against such injustices. What action is the school taking to ensure justice? Is this justice based on love, like God's love, for all children regardless of ethnicity, language, economic status, gender, sexual orientation, religion, or physical/mental condition?[95]

In an educational environment in which biblical justice prevails, the parents, as well as community agencies and organizations are invited and seen as partners with the school in building just and equitable schools. In such an educational environment students tend to feel surrounded with support, which enables them to put in their best efforts in their learning, and which in turn helps them to experience positive outcomes.

Questions for Discussion

1. Discuss the impact of high stakes tests on special education outcomes

2. What factors contribute to poor outcomes in schools for students with disabilities? Are these poor outcomes inevitable, or are there aspects of their school programs or support services that could help students with disabilities have relatively more positive experiences?

3. What factors contribute to positive outcomes for students with disabilities?

4. What is educational equity, and how should education professionals and other stakeholders address it so as to increase outcomes?

5. What is justice? In what ways can biblical justice help to improve special education outcomes?

---

95. Warren and Pacino, "Faith Integration," 103.

Bibliography

Anderson, D. W. *Toward a Theology of Special Education: Integrating Faith and Practice.* Bloomington, IN: WestBow, 2012.

Annamma, S. A. "Disabling Juvenile Justice: Engaging the Stories of Incarcerated Young Women of Color with Disabilities." *Remedial and Special Education* 35 (2014) 313–24.

Artiles, A. J., and S. C. Trent. "Representation of Culturally/Linguistically Diverse Students." In *Concise Encyclopedia of Special Education*, edited by C. R. Reynolds and E. Fletcher-Jantzen, 513–17. New York: Wiley, 2002.

Blackorby, J., et al. "The Academic Performance of Secondary School Students with Disabilities." 2003. http://www.nlts2.org/reports/2003_11/nlts2_report_2003_11_ch4.pdf.

Blanchett, W. J., et al. "Urban School Failure an Disproportionality in a Post-Brown Era." In *Remedial & Special Education* 26 (2005) 70–81.

Brackette, C. M., et al. "Engaging in Social Justice Practices: The Role of Christian Clinicians." *Journal of Psychology & Christianity* 34 (2015) 73–78.

Bradley, M., et al. IDEA National Assessment Implementation Study. Final Report. National Center for Education Evaluation and Regional Assistance, July 2011.

Bremer, C., et al. "Public Reporting of 2007–2008 Assessment Information on Students with Disabilities: Progress on the Gap Front." Technical Report 57. National Center on Educational Outcomes, University of Minnesota, 2011.

Brinckerhoff, L. C., and M. Banerjee. "Misconceptions regarding Accommodations on High-Stakes Tests: Recommendations for Preparing Disability Documentation for Test Takers with Learning Disabilities." *Learning Disabilities Research & Practice* 22 (2007) 246–55.

Burke, A. "Early Identification of High School Graduation Outcomes in Oregon Leadership Network Schools." National Center for Education Evaluation and Regional Assistance. April 2015. http://ies.ed.gov/ncee/edlabs/regions/northwest/pdf/REL_2015079.pdf.

Carnine, D., and A. Granzin. "Setting Learning Expectations for Students with Disabilities." *School Psychology Review* 30 (2001) 466–72.

Christenson, S. L., et al. "Consequences of High-Stakes Assessment for Students With and Without Disabilities." *Educational Policy* 21 (2007) 662–90.

Connor, D. J. "Who 'Owns' Dis/ability? The Cultural Work of Critical Special Educators as Insider-Outsiders." *Theory and Research in Social Education* 41 (2013) 494–513.

Darling-Hammond, L. "Race, Inequality and Educational Accountability: The Irony of 'No Child Left Behind.'" *Race, Ethnicity & Education* 10 (2007) 245–60.

De Valenzuela, J. S., et al. "Examining Educational Equity: Revisiting the Disproportionate Representation of Minority Students in Special Education." In *Exceptional Children* 72 (2006) 425–41.

Decker, D. M., et al. "Behaviorally At-Risk African American Students: The Importance of Student-Teacher Relationships for Student Outcomes." *Journal of School Psychology* 45 (2007) 83–109.

Donlevy, J. "The Dilemma of High-Stakes Testing: What Is School For?" *International Journal of Instructional Media* 27 (2000) 331–37.

Education Northwest. "Equity Priorities in the Northwest and Pacific: A Regional Dialogue." 2014. http://educationnorthwest.org/sites/default/files/resources/dec-2013-ednw-equity-convening-proceedings.pdf.

Ehrlich, S. B., et al. "Preschool Attendance in Chicago Public Schools: Relationships with Learning Outcomes and Reasons for Absences." University of Chicago Consortium on Chicago School Research, 2014. https://consortium.uchicago.edu/publications/preschool-attendance-chicago public-schools-relationships-learning-outcomes-and-reaso-0.

Ferguson, D. L., et al. "Family Portraits: Past and Present Representations of Parents in Special Education Text Books." *International Journal of Inclusive Education* 17 (2013) 1326–41.

Fletcher, T. V., and L. A. Navarrete. "Learning Disabilities or Difference: A Critical Look at Issues Associated with the Misidentification and Placement of Hispanic Students in Special Education Programs." *Rural Special Education Quarterly* 3 (2011) 30–38.

Fordham, S., and J. Ogbu. "Black Students' School Success: Coping with the Burden of 'Acting White.'" *Urban Review* 18 (1986) 176–206.

Goodman, G., and M. A. Webb. "Reading Disability Referrals: Teacher Bias and Other Factors That Impact Response to Intervention." *Learning Disabilities: A Contemporary Journal* 4 (2006) 59–70.

Greenwood, C. R. "How Should Learning Environments (Schools and Classrooms) Be Structured for Best Learning Outcomes?" In *Enduring Issues in Special Education: Personal Perspectives*, edited by B. Bateman et al., 303–21. New York: Routledge, 2015.

Hallahan, D. P., et al. *Exceptional learners: An Introduction to Special Education.* 13th ed. Upper Saddle River, NJ: Pearson, 2015.

Harr-Robins, J., et al. "The Inclusion of Students with Disabilities in School Accountability Systems: An Update." National Center for Education Evaluation and Regional Assistance, October 2013. https://ies.ed.gov/ncee/pubs/20134017/pdf/20134017.pdf.

Herbert, M. "Common Core's Implications for Special Ed Students." *District Administration* 47 (2011) 10.

Hettleman, K. K. *The Road to Nowhere: The Illusion and Broken Promises of Special Education Instruction in the Baltimore City Public Schools and Elsewhere.* Baltimore: Abell Foundation, 2004.

Heward, W. L. *Exceptional Children: An Introduction to Special Education.* 10th ed. Boston: Pearson, 2013.

Hilliard, A. "Excellence in Education versus High Stakes Standardized Testing." *Journal of Teacher Education* 51 (2000) 293–304.

Hornstra, Lisette, et al. "Teacher Attitudes toward Dyslexia: Effects on Teacher Expectations and the Academic Achievement of Students with Dyslexia." *Journal of Learning Disabilities* 43 (2010) 515–29.

Huefner, D. S. "Placements for Special Education Students: The Promise and the Peril." In *Enduring Issues in Special Education: Personal Perspectives*, edited by B. Bateman et al. 215–30. New York: Routledge, 2015.

Irvine, J. "Complex Relationships between Multicultural Education and Special Education: An African American Perspective." *Journal of Teacher Education* 63 (2012) 268–74.

Johns, B. H. *15 Positive Behavior Strategies to Increase Academic Success.* New Delhi: Sage, 2015.

Johnson, D. R., et al. "Cross-State Study of High-Stakes Testing Practices and Diploma Options." *Journal of Special Education Leadership* 20 (2007) 53–65.

Kahn, S., and A. Lewis. "Survey on Teaching Science to K–12 Students with Disabilities: Teacher Preparedness and Attitudes." *Journal of Science Teacher Education* 25 (2014) 885–910.

Katsiyannis, A., et al. "High-Stakes Testing and Students with Disabilities." *Journal of Disability Policy Studies* 18 (2007) 160–67.

Kauffman, J. M. "Characteristics of Emotional and Behavioral Disorders of Children and Youth." 8th ed. Upper Saddle River, NJ: Merrill/ Prentice Hall, 2006.

Karvonen, M., et al. "Academic Curriculum for Students with Significant Cognitive Disabilities: Special Education Teacher Perspectives a Decade after IDEA 1997." 2011. http://eric.ed.gov/?id=ED521407.

Keller, T. "Generous Justice: How God's Grace Makes Us Just." New York: Riverhead, 2010.

Klehm, M. "The Effects of Teacher Beliefs on Teaching Practices and Achievement of Students with Disabilities." *Teacher Education and Special Education* 37 (2014) 216–40.

Konrad, M., et al. "Setting Clear Learning Targets to Guide Instruction for All Students." *Intervention in School & Clinic* 50 (2014) 76–85.

Lloyd, J. W., et al. "Whither Special Education?" In *Enduring Issues in Special Education: Personal Perspectives*, edited by B. Bateman et al., 444–64. New York: Routledge, 2015.

Mastergeorge, A. M., and J. F. Martinez. "Rating Performance Assessments of Students with Disabilities: A Study of Reliability and Bias." *Journal of Psychoeducational Assessment* 28 (2010) 536–50.

McKenna, J. "The Disproportionate Representation of African Americans in Programs for Students with Emotional and Behavioral Disorders." *Preventing School Failure* 57 (2013) 206–11.

McLaughlin, M. J., and S. H. Warren. *Resource Implications of Inclusion: Impressions of Special Education Administrators at Selected Sites.* Palo Alto, CA: Center for Special Education Finance, 1994.

McLeskey, J., et al. "Inclusion of Students with Learning Disabilities: An Examination of Data from Reports to Congress." *Exceptional Children* 66 (1999) 55–66.

Mehta, Seema. "Fewer California Students Pass High School Exit Exam." *Los Angeles Times*, September 10, 2008. http://articles.latimes.com/2008/sep/10/local/me-exam10.

Mithaug, Dennis E. "Equity and Excellence in School-to-Work Transitions of Special Populations." *Centerfocus* 22 (1994) 1–5.

Moody, S. W., et al. "Reading Instruction in the Resource Room: Set Up for Failure." *Exceptional Children* 66 (2000) 305–16.

Moore, M. L. "The Effects of Increased Accountability Standards on Graduation Rates for Students with Disabilities." PhD dissertation, University of Southern Mississippi, 2012.

Morgan, P. L., et al. "Are Reading and Behavior Problems Risk Factors for Each Other?" *Journal of Learning Disabilities* 41 (2008) 417–36.

Nworie, B. C. "High Stakes Testing and Special Education Instruction." In *Central Issues in Special Education: Engaging Current Trends and Critical Issues in Contemporary Practice*, edited by B. Nworie, 91–94. Boston: Pearson Learning Solutions, 2013.

Nworie, B. C. "Early Intervention: Early Childhood Intervention and Students At Risk for Emotional and Behavioral Disorders." In *Central Issues in Special Education: Engaging Current Trends and Critical Issues in Contemporary Practice*, edited by B. Nworie, 113–14. Boston: Pearson, 2013.

———. "Inclusion and Collaboration Issues: An Overview." In *Central Issues in Special Education: Engaging Current Trends and Critical Issues in Contemporary Practice*, edited by B. Nworie, 213–16. Boston: Pearson, 2013.

Piechura-Couture, K., et al. "The Boy Factor: Can Single-Gender Classes Reduce the Over-Representation of Boys in Special Education?" *Journal of Instructional Psychology* 38 (2011) 255–63.

Ravitch, D., and J. Chubb. "The Future of No Child Left Behind: End It? Or Mend It?" *EducationNext*, summer 2009. http://educationnext.org/the-future-of-no-child-left-behind.

Reid, D. "Disproportionality in Special Education: A Persistent Reality for African American Students." *Justice, Spirituality & Education Journal* 3 (2015) 1–14.

Robinson, H. "Highly Qualified Teacher Status and the Reading Achievement of Students with Disabilities." *American Secondary Education* 39 (2011) 42–66.

Salend, S. J. *Creating Inclusive Classrooms: Effective and Reflective Practices*. 8th ed. Boston: Pearson, 2016.

Salend, S. J. "Determining Appropriate Testing Accommodations: Complying with NCLB and IDEA." *Teaching Exceptional Children* 40 (2008) 14–22.

Saunders, A. F., et al. *Teaching Exceptional Children* 45 (2013) 24–33.

Schulte, A. C., et al. "Effective Special Education: A United States Dilemma." *School Psychology Review* 27 (1998) 66–76.

Schulte, S., and J. I. Stevens. "Once, Sometimes, or Always in Special Education: Mathematics Growth and Achievement Gaps." *Exceptional Children* 81 (2015) 370–87.

Shogren, K. A., et al. "Relationships between Self-Determination and Post School Outcomes for Youth with Disabilities." *Journal of Special Education* 48 (2015) 256–67.

Shinn, M. R. "Does Anyone Care What Happens after the Refer-Test-Place Sequence: The Systematic Evaluation of Special Education Program Effectiveness?" *School Psychology Review* 15 (1986) 49–58.

Singh, M. "A Longitudinal Study of a State-Wide Reading Assessment: The Importance of Early Achievement and Socio-Demographic Factors." *Educational Research and Evaluation* 19 (2013) 4–18.

Slater, P. "Schools Chief Jack O'Connell Announces California High School Exit Exam Results for 2007–08." California Department of Education News Release, 2008. http://www.cde.ca.gov/nr/ne/yr08/ yr08rel117.asp.

Smith, D. D., and N. C. Tyler. *Introduction to Contemporary Special Education*. Boston: Pearson, 2014.

Smith, T. E. C., et al. *Teaching Students with Special Needs in Inclusive Settings*. 7th ed. Boston: Pearson, 2016.

Spencer, Trina D., et al. "Tier 2 Language Intervention for Diverse Preschoolers: An Early-Stage Randomized Control Group Study Following an Analysis of Response to Intervention." *American Journal of Speech-Language Pathology* 24 (2015) 619–36.

Tanis, B. "Pushing Back against High Stakes for Students with Disabilities." *American Educator* 38 (2015) 19–23.

Tremblay, P. "Comparative Outcomes of Two Instructional Models for Students with Learning Disabilities: Inclusion with Co-Teaching and Solo-Taught Special Education." *Journal of Research in Special Education Needs* 13 (2013) 251–58.

Turnbull, A., et al. *Exceptional Lives: Special Education in Today's Schools.* 8th ed. Boston: Pearson, 2016.

Uecker, R., et al. "Implementing the Common Core State Standards." *Knowledge Quest* 42 (2014) 48–51.

Wagner, M. M. "Outcomes for Youths with Serious Emotional Disturbance in Secondary School and Early Adulthood." *Future of Children* 5 (1995) 90–112.

Wakeman, S., et al. "Changing Instruction to Increase Achievement for Students with Moderate to Severe Intellectual Disabilities." *Teaching Exceptional Children* 46 (2013) 6–13.

Warren, S. R., and M. Pacino. "Faith Integration and the Educator's Resposibility to Equity and Justice." In *Faith Integration and Schools of Education*, edited by M. Fowler and M. Pacino, 90–109. Indiana: Precedent, 2012.

Wong, H. K., and R. T. Wong. *The First Days of School: How to Be an Effective Teacher.* Mountain View, CA: Wong, 2009.

Wrights Law. 2004. http://www.wrightslaw.com/idea/law/section1400.pdf.

Ysseldyke, James E., et al. *Critical Issues in Special Education.* 3rd ed. Boston: Houghton Mifflin, 2000.

6

Creating School Success Environments for Diverse Learners Who Are Lesbian, Gay, Bisexual and Transgendered

Ben C. Nworie, PhD, MDiv, LPC
Professor of Special Education
School of Education, Biola University

Abstract

THIS CHAPTER TAKES A look at the lesbian, gay, bisexual, and transgendered (LGBT) diverse group of learners and examines the status of their social, emotional, as well as educational experiences. The chapter explores perspectives on homosexuality from a Christian worldview point, and proposes a model for the creation of school success environments which promote positive school outcomes for LGBT students.

Keywords: LGBT, homosexuality, school success, outcomes

Introduction

The number of diverse learners in the United States today is significant. Discussion about diverse learners covers a wide spectrum of concerns. It covers issues of cultural, linguistic and geographic diversity. The discussion also covers issues of diversity based on ability/disability (or exceptionality), and on sexual orientation.

Who Are LGBT Diverse Learners?

The focus of this chapter is on students who are diverse primarily based on their classification as a sexual minority, as well as students who are diverse both as a sexual minority and as those with exceptionality or disability. According to the 2010 United States Census, diverse exceptional learners account for over 21 percent of the US population between fifteen and twenty-one years.[1] The number of students who are diverse based on their sexual orientation is growing. Students who are lesbian, gay, bisexual or transgendered (LGBT) make up more than 10 percent of a schools population.[2] While the estimate is that in schools there are currently between 10 to 20 percent of students who can be classified under the LGBT rubric, it is difficult to determine the exact number of these students who identify as LGBT learners. One of the reasons is because some of the students in this group go back and forth, not being quite decided yet where they belong, and another reason is because a good number of these students find it difficult to face the social stigma associated with revealing their sexual identity.[3] For the same reasons and more, it is difficult to quantify the number of youth with disabilities who also identify as LGBT students. It seems apparent, however, that there is a disparity between the percentage of LGBT learners in the regular population and those in the population of students with disabilities.[4]

Several reasons account for this disparity. For example, while some higher functioning students with disabilities, such as those served under the special education categories of emotional and behavioral disorders,

1. Kattari, "Idenitity and Sexual Communication"; Smith et al., *Teaching Students with Special.*
2. Friend, *Special Education*; Fisher et al., "Promoting School Success."
3. Ibid.
4. Morgan et al., "Creating Safe Environments for Students with Disabilities."

learning disabilities, or other health impairments who identify as LGBT may be reluctant, for privacy or confidentiality reasons, to self-disclose their disability status to researchers, other students with more severe disabilities, such as those with autism or intellectual disabilities, may not be afforded the opportunity to share their sexuality because issues of sexuality are often considered off the table for them based on the belief that they are asexual or would not be engaged in sexual relationships in the future.[5]

In either case, it does not make it easy to estimate the number of students with disabilities who may be identified as part of the LGBT population. Regardless of the difficulty of establishing numbers, it is reasonable for special education professionals to expect that there will be students with disabilities who may also come under the LGBT grouping. Such sensitivity can lead to the creation of classroom environments that are positive and supportive of the needs of all students.[6] Overall, it is estimated that LGBT students are likely to be in most middle schools, and in every classroom in every secondary school in the United States, even if they do not openly identify as LGBT.[7]

Status of the Social, Emotional, and Educational Experiences of LGBT Learners

Many LGBT learners are subjected to very high levels of stress and pain in their social, emotional, and educational experiences.[8] They face difficult times both at home and at school. These young people show their frustration through some extreme behaviors such as suicide or running away. It is estimated that in some places within the country the LGBT runaways may be up to 40 percent of the entire teen homeless population.[9]

There have been repeated reports of various forms of unfair treatment against LGBT students, as well as youth who are curious about their sexual identity.[10] Some examples of this unfair, discriminatory treatment include: verbal ridicule such as name calling (e.g., names such as "fag," "faggot," or "gay"), damage of their property, bias-related physical assaults, and alien-

5. Ibid.
6. Ibid.
7. Fisher et al., "Promoting School Success."
8. Biegel and Kuehl, "Safe at School."
9. Ibid.
10. Salend, *Creating Inclusive Classrooms.*

ation sometimes by friends and family.[11] These harsh treatments against the LGBT young learners are associated with significant adverse consequences in their experience. For example, it is estimated that as a result of their isolation and victimization, nearly 50 to 80 percent of LGBT youth have had suicidal thoughts while nearly 30 to 40 percent have had suicidal attempts.[12] Significantly higher incidents of depression, hopelessness, and suicidal inclinations are reported among LGBT youth than among their heterosexual peers. Also LGBT young people are more vulnerable to drug use and abuse, more vulnerable to forced or coerced teenage sexual encounter, and more likely than none LGBT teens to become victims of sexual assault or assault with a deadly weapon.[13] Furthermore, Wolff, Himes, Kwon, and Bollinger report that

> emerging epidemiological research suggests that LGB youth who live in geographic areas with higher densities of conservative religions are more likely to abuse alcohol and have more sexual partners than heterosexual youth, even when controlling for other factors.[14]

What are the impacts of the anti-homosexual bias, and the LGBT lifestyle on the educational experiences of the LGBT youth? One obvious negative educational impact is the negative peer pressure and verbal victimizations experienced by the LGBT young people in the school setting which negatively impact their school experience and their educational outcomes. This example from Cohn is a pertinent illustration of the point. Regardless of a boy's actual sexual orientation, if he shows extreme giftedness in an area of learning, acting or caring that is thought to belong predominantly to girls, the boy is likely to hear discouraging comments or rumors from his peers about him not being boy enough or being too girlish for them. In the same way, a girl who has extraordinary giftedness in academic skills or endeavors considered to belong mainly to boys, such as mathematical reasoning, engineering and athletics skills will, in all likelihood quickly learn from her schoolmates that she is on the queer side or that she is not girl enough for them.

11. Cohn, "Gay Gifted Learner"; Salend, *Creating Inclusive Classrooms*.

12. Grant and Sleeter, *Doing Multicultural Education*; Salend, *Creating Inclusive Classrooms*.

13. Gutierrez, "Counseling Queer Youth"; Grant and Sleeter, *Doing Multicultural Education*.

14. Wolff et al., "Evangelical Christian College Students," 218.

As a result of the incessant negative peer pressure, physical harassment or assault reported by 60 percent of LGBT students, and verbal victimizations experienced by over 80 percent of them, LGBT students face higher rates of school truancy and academic failure. They not only show lower GPAs, they also evidence lower rates of enrollment in postsecondary education.[15] About 32 percent of LGBT students miss school because of the harassments, as well as because of fear for safety. This is a high rate of missing school when compared to a national sample rate of 4.5 percent.[16] The literature on LGBT subject presents interesting information. The chapter will, therefore, proceed to discuss information from pertinent literature on homosexuality and seek to draw attention to the genesis of the subject and to promote dialogue from a Christian worldview point.

Perspectives on Homosexuality from a Christian Worldview

Our discussion of perspectives on homosexuality from a Christian worldview point will focus on a review of some relevant literature on the origins of homosexuality. This review reveals that the notion of a solely biological origin of homosexuality as a foregone conclusion is not tenable. Because of the heightened attention to this issue in society, in education in general, in multicultural education, as well as in the education of diverse learners, and because of its relevance to Christians in the academy, it is necessary to give the topic some attention from a Christian worldview approach.

The Origins of Homosexuality

Most people are heterosexual. It is estimated that close to 97 percent of people are sexually attracted to those of the opposite sex.[17] Among the minority (3 percent or more) who are attracted to people of their own sex, there are various intermediate forms of sexual attraction or orientation. For example, terms such as *asexual* (not the same as celibacy, people who generally do not feel sexual attraction or desire to any group of people), *intersex* (people whose sexual anatomy or chromosomes do not fit with the traditional markers of "female" and "male," such as people born with both

15. Morgan et al., "Creating Safe Environments," 5.
16. Ibid.
17. Balthazart, "Minireview."

"female" and "male" anatomy like penis, testicles, vagina, uterus; people born with XXY chromosomes), *kink/BDSM* (kink is an umbrella term for the practices of BDSM; bondage and discipline, dominance and submission, and sadism/masochism), *pansexual* (people who experience sexual, romantic, physical, and/or spiritual attraction for members of all gender identities/expressions), *polyamorous* (having more than one loving or erotic relationship), and others, belong to this (3 percent or more) category.[18]

There have been studies, discussions, speculations and debates about the origins of sexual orientation for this minority group.[19] While a lot of people believe that education and environmental factors are at the background of the sexual orientation of this group, some others hold strongly that biological causes, precisely prenatal factors, significantly determine human sexuality, including that of this minority group.[20]

Typically, there is no one explanation for what influences most human behavior and choices, especially this critical feature of human sexual behavior. Available relevant literature suggests that psychological, behavioral, environmental and biological factors contribute toward the determination of human sexual behavior, which includes behavior associated with sexual orientations.

Balthazart is very correct in describing sexual orientation as "a behavioral trait that displays one of the largest degrees of sexual differentiation."[21] While strongly arguing that biological factors determine sexual orientation, Balthazart correctly declares that "learning, education and expectations of society clearly play an important role in the genesis of behavioral and even sometimes physiological differences."[22] In a similar vein, James who is also a proponent of the biological explanation for the origins of sexual orientation strongly agrees that the LGBT sexual orientation can be triggered by

> situational factors such as exposure to an unusually gay-positive environment . . . play, exploration, lack of opposite-sex partners, hazing, initiation rituals, intoxication, sexual frustration, prostitution, boredom, opportunism, curiosity and mistakes. According

18. University of Michigan, "Student Life"; Balthazart, "Minireview"; Kattari, "Identity and Sexual Communication."

19. Dobson, *Bringing Up Boys*; James, "Biological and Psychosocial Determinants"; Balthazart, "Minireview"; Frisch and Hviid, "Childhood Family Correlates"; Kinsey et al., *Sexual Behavior in the Human Male*.

20. Balthazart, "Minireview"; James, "Biological and Psychosocial Determinants."

21. Balthazart, "Minireview," 2937.

22. Ibid., 2940.

to this view, the experience of some self-identified lesbians (the "situational" ones) is preceded by learning of some sort.[23]

Behavioral theory holds that what motivates humans to behave in certain ways depends on the reinforcement (stimulus) they get from such a behavior, and how powerful the reinforcement is. Behavioral theorists have, therefore, narrowed down the functions of all human behavior to just two—namely, positive reinforcement and negative reinforcement.[24]

Balthazart, though an advocate for the biological origins of homosexual behavior, strongly supports this behavioral theory of the influence of environmental events on human behavior. He states: "Sexual interactions between same sex partners (male mounting another male or female mounting another female) are observed quite frequently in a broad variety of animal species." Then he adds:

> Often, these behaviors are expressed only when a suitable partner of the opposite sex is not available due to captivity (zoo or other captive populations), or when a skewed sex ratio in the population, or the presence of dominant males is preventing access to females. These behaviors . . . serve as an outlet for sexual motivation in the absence of suitable partners of the opposite sex.[25]

The implication of the argument is that these behaviorally and environmentally motivated sexual behaviors frequently observed in a wide variety of animal species are equally applicable to some humans given the same environmental motivational stimuli.

Environmental factors do definitely impact sexual orientation. Throckmorton citing the monumental work of Danish epidemiologist Morten Frisch and statistician Anders Hviid, which analyzed data from over two million homosexuals for environmental factors in their decisions to marry homosexually, highlights the role of environmental factors in sexual orientation. Frissch and Hviid convincingly demonstrate, as other researchers have done, that environmental factors do influence sexual orientation. Their study established a strong link between environmental factors such as geographic birthplace and family relationships and the probability of marrying a partner of the same sex or opposite sex. The

23. James, "Biological and Psychosocial Determinants."

24. Umbreit et al., *Functional Behavioral Assessment*; Alberto and Troutman, *Applied Behavior Analysis for Teachers*; Corsini, *Dictionary of Psychology*; Kazdin, *Encyclopedia of Psychology*; Lane et al., *Managing Challenging Behaviors*.

25. Balthazart, "Minireview," 2939.

extensive study also found that among intact parents, bearing multiple children and living in rural areas increase the probability of their children marrying heterosexually.

While there are various reports which trace the origin of homosexuality to psycho-social, behavioral and environmental causes, others trace it to the human biological systems.[26] Some of the studies cited to support this viewpoint have been studies that did not provide conclusive evidence.[27] That is why Dobson categorically states that "there are no respected geneticists in the world today who claim to have found a so-called 'gay gene' or other indicators of genetic transmission."[28] For example, Balthazart states that although "50–60% of the variance in sexual orientation in humans has a genetic origin . . . the responsible gene(s) remain(s) unknown."[29] Similarly, James, in presenting his summary of a comprehensive theory of sexual orientation, states as follows: "Some homosexual men have genes that predispose to their sexual orientation. The same may apply to some lesbians, but such genes have not, as far as I know, been identified."[30]

Dobson, however, concedes that some kind of biological predisposition in the form of an inherited temperament is possible, and can make one vulnerable to environmental influences. The illustration of the out workings of temperament using an example that is unrelated to sexual orientation may be pertinent here. In special education, for instance, if a child has a naturally impulsive temperament, then usually that might predispose the child to resist guidance or supervision from others.[31]

Though there has been a lot of information put out and a lot of effort made to educate the public about the biological origins of, and therefore, the irreversibility of homosexuality, Dobson's contention is that people are not born homosexual. He adds the following points as further evidence to illustrate his point that homosexuality is not genetic:

> There is further convincing evidence that it is not. For example, since identical twins share the same chromosomal pattern, or DNA, the genetic contributions are exactly the same within each

26. James, "Biological and Psychosocial Determinants"; Gutierrrez, "Counseling Queer Youth."

27. Balthazart, "Minireview"; James, "Biological and Psychosocial Determinants."

28. Dobson, *Bringing Up Boys*, 116.

29. Balthazart, "Minireview," 2945.

30. James, "Biological and Psychosocial Determinants," 555.

31. Turnbull et al., *Exceptional Lives.*

of the pairs. Therefore, if one twin is "born" homosexual, then the other should inevitably have that characteristic too. That is not the case. When one twin is homosexual, the probability is only 50 percent that the other will have the same condition. Something else must be operating.

Furthermore, if homosexuality were specifically inherited, it would tend to be eliminated from the human gene pool because those who have it tend not to reproduce. Any characteristic that is not passed along to the next generation eventually dies with the individual who carries it.

Not only does homosexuality continue to exist in nations around the world, it flourishes in some cultures. If the condition resulted from inherited characteristics, it would be a "constant" across time. Instead, there have been societies through the ages, such as Sodom and Gomorrah and the ancient Greek and Roman empires, where homosexuality reached epidemic proportions. The historical record tells us that those cultures and many others gradually descended into depravity, as the apostle Paul described in Romans 1, resulting in sexual perversion in all its varieties. That ebbing and flowing with the life cycle of cultures is not the way inherited characteristics are expressed in the human family.

Finally, if homosexuality were genetically transmitted, it would be inevitable, immutable, irresistible, and untreatable. Fortunately, it is not. Prevention is effective. Change is possible. Hope is available. And Christ is in the business of healing. Here again, gay and lesbian organizations and the media have convinced the public that being homosexual is as predetermined as one's race and that nothing can be done about it. That is simply not true. There are eight hundred known former gay and lesbian individuals today who have escaped from the homosexual lifestyle and found wholeness in their newfound heterosexuality.

. . . I would be less than honest if I didn't admit that homosexuality is not easily overcome and that those who try often struggle mightily. But it would be equally dishonest to say that there is no hope for those who want to change. Credible research indicates otherwise.[32]

To further illustrate his points regarding the origin of homosexuality from a Christian worldview perspective, Dobson quotes from clinical psychologist Dr. Nicolosi's book entitled *Preventing Homosexuality: A Parent's Guide*:

32. Dobson, *Bringing Up Boys*, 117.

The fact is, there is a high correlation between feminine behavior in boyhood and adult homosexuality. . . . The most important message I can offer to you is that there is no such thing as a "gay child" or a "gay teen." [But] left untreated, studies show these boys have a 75 percent chance of becoming homosexual or bisexual. . . . Many clients have told me, "If only—back then when I was a child—someone had understood the doubts, the feeling of not belonging—and tried to help me." . . .

In my opinion, the father plays an essential role in a boy's normal development as a man. . . . Mothers make boys. Fathers make men. . . . The late Irving Bieber, a prominent researcher, observed that pre-homosexual boys are sometimes the victims of their parents' unhappy marital relationship. In a scenario where Mom and Dad are battling, one way Dad can "get even" with Mom is by emotionally abandoning their son. . . .

For a variety of reasons, some mothers also have a tendency to prolong their sons' infancy. A mother's intimacy with her son is primal, complete, exclusive; theirs is a powerful bond which can deepen into what psychiatrist Robert Stoller calls a "blissful symbiosis." But the mother may be inclined to hold onto her son in what becomes an unhealthy mutual dependency, especially if she does not have a satisfying, intimate relationship with the boy's father. She can put too much energy into the boy, using him to fulfill her own needs in a way that is not good for him. . . . Effeminate boys yearn for what is called "the three A's." They are: their father's affection, attention and approval.

. . . Growing up straight isn't something that happens. It requires good parenting. It requires societal support. And it takes time. The crucial years are from one and a half to three years old, but the optimal time is before age twelve. Once mothers and fathers recognize the problems their children face, agree to work together to help resolve them, and seek the guidance and expertise of a psychotherapist who believes change is possible, there is great hope.[33]

For his conclusion, Dobson adds:

The bottom line is that homo sexuality is not primarily about sex. It is about everything else, including loneliness, rejection, affirmation, intimacy, identity, relationships, parenting, self-hatred, gender confusion, and a search for belonging, This explains why the homosexual experience is so intense—and why there is such anger

33. Quoted in Dobson, *Bringing Up Boys.*

expressed against those who are perceived as disrespecting gays and lesbians or making their experience more painful. I suppose if we who are straight had walked in the shoes of those in that "other world," we would be angry too . . . Another major cause . . . results from early sexual abuse. One study indicated that fully 30 percent of homosexuals say they were exploited sexually as a child, many of them repeatedly. That experience can be devastating, and depending on when it occurs, it can be life changing.[34]

The differing views about homosexuality notwithstanding, school professionals must work together with all stakeholders as a team for the school success of every student.

Creation of School Success Environments

Regardless of a student's background, beliefs, sexual orientation or other categorizations, school professionals must work with students, families, and other stakeholders to ensure positive school experience and school success environments for all students. The creation of school success environments for LGBT students requires intentionally taking steps to address some important issues and concerns. It requires engaging in specific strategies. Here is a proposal by this author of such strategies which may be regarded as the ABCDE of the creation of school success environments for LGBT students. In summary, the strategies involve the building or enhancing of the following: (a) awareness, (b) bullying prevention, (c) curriculum, (d) diversity, and (e) education.

Awareness

Awareness is the crucial starting point. It has often been said that awareness is everything. Both at the school administration level, as well as at the classroom level, awareness should be created of the extent of social, relational, emotional, psychological and educational difficulties which the LGBT students go through. Many LGBT youth go through serious social, relational, emotional difficulties at home and in their communities. There is research evidence that more than 35 percent of LGBT adolescents face verbal abuse within their family as a result of their sexual orientation.[35] Studies also re-

34. Ibid., 119–24.
35. Fisher et al., "Promoting School Success."

veal that compared to their heterosexual peers, LGBT students experience more emotional and behavioral adjustment difficulties which include "higher rates of substance abuse, prostitution, truancy, encounters with law enforcement, and running away from home."[36] Other emotional and psychological difficulties that LGBT students experience more than their heterosexual counterparts in school, and which school professionals need to be clearly aware of, include: greater feelings of fear, anxiety, hopelessness, helplessness, worthlessness, alienation, extreme loneliness, clinical depression, drugs and alcohol abuse, suicidal ideation, and suicidal attempts.[37] The cumulative effect of the many emotional and psychological stressors on the LGBT students is that they become predisposed to extremely high risk for suicide, which is the leading cause of death among LGBT adolescents. There is research indication that as many as 40 percent of LGBT youth have made suicide attempts.[38]

Efforts should be made to bring awareness to school administrators, faculty, staff and students about these acute stressors, and various difficulties that LGBT students are constantly confronted with, and to create a school environment in which the pains that students are already carrying are not escalated. The creation of such awareness should instead help to provide all students a welcoming school climate in which all students, including the most vulnerable, such as the LGBT students, feel safe and valued members of the school community.[39] To create such a desirable school community environment, both the administration and the classroom teachers should use the school counselors, the school social events, as well as the school communication media to create and disseminate the necessary awareness. Make students aware of significant local, state, national or international news items or issues relevant to the LGBT community.

Awareness can further be created through the formation and encouragement, by school administration, of student-led interactional groups such as Gay Straight School Alliances (GSAs), an after-school club that welcomes all members of the school as well as community members who wish to learn more about issues of sexual orientation in a safe environment.

36. Ibid., 80.

37. Trammell, "Homosexuality Is Bad for Me"; Fisher et al., "Promoting School Success"; Morgan et al., "Creating Safe Environments"; Liboro et al., "Beyond the Dialectics and Polemics"; Salend, *Creating Inclusive Classrooms*; Russo, "Debate Is Growing."

38. Biegel and Kuehl, "Safe at School"; Grant and Sleeter, *Doing Multicultural*; Fisher et al., "Promoting School Success"; Salend, *Creating Inclusive Classrooms*.

39. Southern Poverty Law Center, "Best Practices."

GSAs are credited with promoting safe, nondiscriminatory, and supportive environment in which all students are valued.[40] Research has found that GSAs which exist in nearly 20 percent of high schools provide positive "environments in which students of all sexual orientations can meet and talk about issues that affect all students."[41] The success of GSAs in creating awareness, promoting an overall positive school climate of support and inclusivity, is attributable to the support of faculty, administrators, school staff, and non-sexual minority students for GSAs.[42]

Bullying

An environment of acceptance and safety for all students, including sexual minority students is an environment that fosters healthy interactions between students; it is a conducive environment for learning.[43] The unwanted, aggressive, angry or painful behavior by a child or group of children against a more vulnerable child or group of children, is a description of bullying. The high incidence and devastating effects of bullying in schools is comparable to the combination of the high incidence and destructive effects of cancer and coronary heart disease in the wider society today.

Bullying in schools directed against LGBT diverse learners is widespread, despite legal protections and provisions.[44] The sexual minority students daily face a unique set of safety concerns. More than 85 percent LGBT students face harassment because of their sexual or gender identity. Another 20 percent or more of these sexual minority students are physically attacked. In part because of the excessive harassment and safety concerns they face daily, the suicide rate for LGBT students is believed to be about four times higher than that of their peers in the straight population.[45] Yet, very often teachers and administrators seem to show little or no response. Many educational institutions have significantly failed to adequately address the serious bullying related issues and concerns of LGBT youth.[46]

40. Salend, *Creating Inclusive Classrooms*; Morgan et al., "Creating Safe Environments"; Fisher et al., "Promoting School Success."

41. Fisher et al., "Promoting School Success," 84.

42. Ibid.

43. Ibid.

44. Ibid.

45. Biegel and Kuehl, "Safe at School."

46. Ibid.

The first step in creating a bully-proof school community is for the administration to put in place a code of conduct which includes a clearly spelt out zero tolerance anti-bullying policy. The policy may need to include explicit guidance designed to safeguard LGBT students. It will be necessary to get the input of students, parents, guardians, educators and the community into the policy. The administration should use the code of conduct as well as the anti-bullying policy to do the following: (a) specify and clarify to students, faculty and staff what bullying is; (b) give bullying a face by using relevant examples of harassment based on actual incidents to illustrate harassment. Include specific examples of harassment based on sexual orientation.

The administration should also create an anti-bullying task force and designate a leader or coordinator. The name and contact information of the anti-bullying task force leader should be made visible by being posted in the cafeteria, the school nurse's office or clinic, the school office, the student handbook, and the school website. Counselors and staff trained in bullying prevention and intervention should work together as a team with the task force coordinator to develop and maintain the school's anti-bullying program. The anti-bullying task force and the administration should engage in frequent and effective communication with students, families and the community about ways to create more positive school climate, and ways to prevent or solve bullying problems.

Bullying usually takes place where or when adults are not present. As part of the effort to curb bullying, and further the school climate improvement process, it is necessary to identify places where bullying occurs and to take action to make such places safer. The anti-bullying task force, the administration and teachers in addition to working together to identify those places where bullying frequently happens, should find creative ways to help immediately remove them. For example, students or staff can be trained and assigned to monitor these locations, and cameras can be added to help with the monitoring.

The anti-bullying task force and teachers should respond appropriately to, and follow up on, all cases of bullying. The following guideline provided by Shore is helpful:

- Take all bullying incidents seriously, even those that seem minor.
- Take immediate action to ensure the student's safety.

- Tell the aggressor that bullying is unacceptable and reiterate the specific consequences for bullying (rules/consequences should have been clearly stated at the beginning of the year and clearly posted).

- If the bullying is verbal, intervene to stop ridicule immediately.

- Report the incident to the principal or designated person (per school policy).

- Follow school policy for disciplinary action and other required steps.[47]

Arm students with helpful anti-bullying strategies and skills, such as what Coloroso calls the four most powerful antidotes to bullying which are: "a strong sense of self, being a friend, having at least one good friend who is there for you through thick and thin, and being able to successfully get into a group."[48] Additionally, provide emotional support to a student who is bullied as soon after the bullying incident as possible. These guidelines provided by Shore should be helpful:[49]

- Listen sympathetically to the student's explanation of what happened. Make sure to convey in a calm voice that you take his concern seriously and understand his distress.

- Reassure him that the bully's behavior was wrong. If he has come to you to report the bullying, assure him that talking with you was the right thing to do. If you found out about the bullying but determined he kept it to himself, encourage him to alert you or another staff member immediately if he is bullied again.

- Tell him he is not to blame for the bullying.

- Let him know that you want to make sure the bullying does not happen again. Remind him that the school does not tolerate bullying and is committed to ensuring his safety.

- Explain that you will need to inform his parents and members of his IEP team about the bullying and that you will all work together to find ways to prevent future bullying.

- Explain that there are strategies he can use to avoid repeated bullying, which the school will help him learn.[49]

47. Shore, *Bullying Prevention for Students with Disabilities*, 3.

48. Coloroso, *The Bully, the Bullied, and the Bystander*, 137.

49. Shore, *Bullying Prevention for Students with Disabilities*, 3.

Curriculum

In their very popular teacher preparation book titled *The First Days of School: How to Be an Effective Teacher,* Wong and Wong very eloquently espouse that the goal of the school and of the teacher is to help students learn effectively. For Wong and Wong, effective learning is learning that impacts and touches lives. Many LGBT students are unable to focus on academic tasks and learn effectively because they frequently experience depression, fear, worry, anxiety, rejection, and isolation at school. As a result of safety concerns, they skip school about five times more than students in the general population; and they are twice more likely to report no plans for postsecondary education than their peers in the regular population.[50]

Packaging and presenting the curriculum in an inclusive manner, has the potential, not only of helping create a more positive school climate for LGBT students, it also has the potential of helping them engage in effective learning. Teachers, working in collaboration with school administration can play a big role in making this happen. A recent study in Canada found that teachers and administrators played a significant role in the effective implementation of strategies and programs that were found to be successful for supporting LGBT students in Canadian Catholic schools, just as the strategies and programs have been in the public, secular schools in the United States. According to the Canadian study, curricular changes were an essential component of the strategies and programs that yielded successful results for the support of LGBT students both in the United States and in Canada. With the support from the administration, the Canadian teachers became creative with their specific subject material. Consequently, they introduced "small but positive changes in the curriculum and the inclusion of LGBT-specific initiatives."[51] Here is an example of the incorporation of LGBT material into the curriculum by one of the Canadian teachers in the study:

> The head of one of the departments because he wants to put a number of frameworks and lenses to go through English literature . . . put the gay-lesbian lens as one of the lenses to choose from. So if they want to, students can choose to discuss a tale through the lens of queer studies.[52]

50. Fisher et al., "Promoting School Success."
51. Liboro et al., "Beyond the Dialectics and Polemics," 170.
52. Ibid., 171.

Other ways that teachers can incorporate LGBT material into the curriculum include: discussion of an article or editorial commentary in a newspaper or news magazine about the LGBT community, use of safe language (instead of words like "joto," "faggot," etc.), encourage students to read and discus works by sexual minority authors, give students the opportunities to write papers on popular artist, athlete or influential individual who is a member of the LGBT community, create projects or develop curriculum that portrays how people with divergent views or beliefs work collaboratively, harmoniously and productively together. Examples for such project or curriculum work might include: military people from different countries and divergent backgrounds fighting together against a common enemy, Russian Communist cosmonauts working together with American Christian astronauts on space projects, etc.

Wong and Wong , who are experts on curriculum implementation, theorize that in the process of effective learning, the teacher does more than make a difference. Their dictum is that the teacher is the difference. They, therefore, insist "it is essential that the teacher exhibit positive expectations toward all students."[53] It is common knowledge that for personal or religious reasons many teachers still feel uncomfortable addressing the topic of homosexuality. And we know that teachers' beliefs and attitudes toward students have important effects on teaching practices, and they have negative effects on students' achievements.[54] The negative effects may also include poor self-esteem for students. Regardless of the personal or religious feelings and persuasions of teachers, it is still their responsibility to create a safe learning environment for every student in their classroom.[55]

For LGBT youth, self-esteem is a huge factor in their school success efforts both academically and socially. With poor self-esteem, students are not likely to achieve their potential academically.[56] As Salend very correctly points out, "Promoting self-esteem in students and their own sense of self-efficacy can improve their learning and ability to advocate for themselves. . . . Students with low self-esteem often make negative statements about themselves that hinder their performance."[57] Consequently, if a student's self-esteem is low, it is helpful to give attention to raising self-esteem

53. Wong and Wong, *First Days of School*, 11.

54. Klehm, "Effects of Teacher Beliefs."

55. Morgan et al., "Creating Safe Environments."

56. Salend, *Creating Inclusive Classrooms*.

57. Ibid., 206.

before tackling any academic difficulty. Salend lists several ways to help promote self-esteem such as:

- helping structure academic activities and social situations in such a way that students succeed and reflect on the factors that help them be successful;
- recognizing students' achievements and talents;
- giving students moderately challenging tasks;
- focusing on student's recent successes;
- teaching students to use self-management techniques and learning strategies;
- asking students to perform meaningful classroom and school-based jobs and leadership positions;
- posting students work in the classroom and throughout the school.[58]

Since their sexual minority status does often affect the academic performance and social adjustment of LGBT youth, the individualized education plan (IEP) of LGBT students who receive special education services can be profitably utilized in their curriculum. The IEP is a federally mandated legal document required for each special education student. The document specifies the individualized plan of goals and objectives, instruction, services and supports for students with disabilities based on their individual needs, strengths and challenges. Developed by a team of school professional and other people who know the student, the IEP is intended to address the student's academic, behavioral, and social concerns. If a student with a disability is found to have self-esteem issues, such issues can be addressed in the IEP since self-esteem concerns do negatively affect a student's academic performance and social adjustment. Parents of students who receive special education services have the right to request an IEP meeting at any time and the school district is obligated to comply with the request. The IEP meeting, which may include the student, provides an opportunity for the IEP team to identify resources and strategies for promoting the student's self-esteem. If behaviors or skills deficits related to the student's disability are contributing to the child's self-esteem issues, the information will likely be contained in the formal evaluations that are part of the student's file, and such deficits should also be addressed in the IEP.

58. Ibid.

Let us consider how the IEP can be used as a tool for self-esteem building for LGBT students in special education. The self-esteem goals should be based on the student's past and present levels of performance, they should be relevant to the student's needs, and they should be stated positively. The student's progress should be monitored and targeted and specific praise and reward given to student as student shows progress. Such honest and appropriate feedback occurring on a regular basis will help to build student's self-esteem. As much as possible, the student should be involved in the IEP development as such involvement empowers the student and makes for more positive outcomes. In the development of an IEP to enhance self-esteem, academic expectations might be reduced or modified to ensure success. It will be necessary to specify exactly such curricular segments that will be modified, as well as where or how to compensate for them. The activities for an IEP targeting self-esteem might include:

- Identify words or actions from others that cause you to become angry (such as others calling you names, making unkind remarks and discussing you)
- Name ways people show approval or disapproval
- Express anger appropriately by using words to state feelings (when X happens, I feel Y, or Z)
- Identify way(s) to ease frustration in imaginary situations
- Describe situation(s) in which student experiences a given emotion
- Ask teacher or other appropriate adult for help or move away to a quiet, voluntary time out
- Make any criticism constructive and sandwich it between positives
- Being a peer mentor to another student
- Engage in small group esteem building activities
- Utilize opportunities to demonstrate strengths, for example, by doing oral presentation, sharing achievement, leading a class project, helping another peer in class
- Become involved in extracurricular activities that support your interests and strengths.

An IEP with self-esteem target for an LGBT student might look like the following:

By (date), given actions or words (e.g., teasing or name calling from peers) that evoke feelings of self-doubt, (student name) will use three (3) self-esteem activities (specify which ones; e.g., some of the activities mentioned above) to maintain positive self-esteem as shown by measurable progress on a progress monitoring checklist (e.g., a self-reflection checklist or questionnaire provided by teacher) for (4 out of 4) incidents which evoke self-doubt.

Diversity

It is desirable to have diversity in schools. It makes for richness and strength. No wonder it has been said that "diversity is the spice of life." In her blog in the Opinion section of the July 7, 2014, *US News & World Report*, Nina Rees affirms that "exposing students to different backgrounds and cultures makes everyone better off"; and that "students learn the most when they can learn from their peers." She concludes her blog with these profound words:

> As the demographics of our country shift and we welcome more people from other countries, today's students and tomorrow's workers will be enriched by the perspectives and experiences of people who don't have the same background they do. By broadening their perspectives, students can stretch their minds, seeing the world in new ways. Working together, students from every background can help each other take advantage of all the opportunities America offers.[59]

As student demographics in schools become progressively more diverse, it is important for school professionals to understand how gender identity, sexual orientation and culture intricately intersect for students. Sexual minority students in addition to dealing with stressors related to their gender identity and sexual orientation, also have to deal with stressors of how to adjust and adapt to the dominant culture.[60]

Various cultures tend to view the LGBT identity differently. Some cultures subscribe to a group identity. Such cultures usually emphasize the priority and values of the family; they emphasize respect for elders, and more traditional gender roles. In such cultures, the desires and choices of the individual are of secondary importance to the collectivistic identity of

59. Rees, "Diverse Schools."
60. Fisher et al., "Promoting School Success."

the larger family and ethnic community. Examples are Asian and Latino cultures, in which LGBT identity often represent a direct threat to the family system. In consequence, individuals are likely to put family preferences above personal desires.[61] In other cultures, such as some Native American cultures, and certainly the African American culture, heterosexual identity tends to be valued, and those who show LGBT identity openly are likely to be rejected and risk losing what is considered a vital support system.[62] White middle-class American culture, which predominantly accounts for the majority of the LGBT community in the United States, tends to subscribe to more fluid views of sexuality and gender, allowing for the possibility of greater acceptance of individuals who identify as LGBT.[63] In working with LGBT students, culture and ethnicity are, therefore, important aspects to consider. Though LGBT youth who are students of color may struggle with meeting the demands and expectations represented by various cultures and communities, these minority students may be in a position to provide to or derive from these communities some valuable contributions.[64]

The study by Liboro, Travers, and St. John, of strategies and programs that were found to be successful for supporting LGBT students in Canadian Catholic schools, found that fostering of school climates that value and promote tolerance and respect for LGBT individuals was a diversity enhancing strategy which raised awareness on LGBT issues among members of the different school communities. Such diversity strengthening strategies can be implemented by disseminating informational materials and resources in the school community that discourage adverse reactions and hostile attitudes toward diversity and inclusion, and by creating educational programs about LGBT rights, including the first amendment rights of LGBT youths, by discouraging the use of non-inclusive and derogatory language.[65]

Suggestions by Morgan et al. of terms to use within conversations about relationships that allow all students to feel connected to the classroom environment include "significant other, date, and partner." To further bring out the importance of appropriate language, Morgan et al. add:

> It is important to remember that words have power within a classroom environment and that students with disabilities place large

61. Ibid.
62. Ibid.
63. Ibid.
64. Ibid.
65. Liboro et al., "Beyond the Dialectics and Polemics."

emphases on the opinions and attitudes of the teachers. Therefore, use of language that supports students is greatly important.[66]

Faculty and other school professionals, who promote an inclusive school environment by use of language that is supportive of students, and by actively promoting the diversity program of the school in other ways, can be publicly recognized and praised. Such public recognition and praise not only affirms their positive action, it also creates a culture in which other professionals and members of the school community are encouraged to also show public support of the school's diversity effort as well as support of the school's positive school climate initiative. Those educators and school professionals who are praised and recognized for their positive, outstanding contributions to diversity throughout the year, could be presented with special awards, such as "Diversity Leader" certificates during the end-of-the-year award ceremonies.[67]

Education

The importance of education in creating inclusive, positive school communities for all students, including LGBT students, cannot be overemphasized.[68] Education and current knowledge about different facets of LGBT issues is limited. That probably explains (at least in part) the reason for the recent great outpouring of government research funds and media attention to LGBT matters.[69] For example, as Russo et al. correctly report, in August 2015 the National Institutes of Health awarded $5.7 million for research related to LGBT youth. Abundant research evidence indicate that there is lack of adequate knowledge at various levels necessary for creating inclusive, positive school environments for LGBT students.[70] Research also shows that education is beneficial in helping straight students develop more positive attitudes which help in creating inclusive classrooms. The study by Wolff, Himes, Kwon, and Bollinger indicates that efforts to educate students

66. Morgan et al., "Creating Safe Environments," 9.

67. Southern Poverty Law Center, "Best Practices."

68. Morgan et al., "Creating Safe Environments for Students."

69. Russo, "Debate Is Growing."

70. Ibid.; Wolff et al., "Evangelical Christian College Students"; Lim et al., "National Survey of Faculty"; Morgan et al., "Creating Safe Environments"; Liboro et al., "Beyond the Dialectics and Polemics"; Dessel, "Effects of Intergroup Dialogue"; Trammell, "Homosexuality Is Bad for Me."

about sexual minority issues by posting fliers, or speaking on a "peer panel" which allows LGBT students to share their experiences might be successful in significantly decreasing negative attitudes, and helping students become more tolerant.[71]

A good place to begin, therefore, is to invest time, money, manpower and all the resources necessary for educational development of the entire school community, starting with students. The bulk of sexuality education programs students receive in schools give little attention to homosexuality. Objective, factual educational information about homosexuality as some people's preferred expression of sexuality should be made available to both straight and LGBT students. The objective sexuality education should, for example, teach students the facts and dangers of unsafe-sex practices. It should also teach them about the factual implications of some homosexual practices, and what Russo et al., describe as "difficult trade-offs" that inevitably come into play sometimes. For example, it can help youth learn, and think through the fact that one of the implications of transgender treatment is that (though there are costly, non-guaranteed medical procedures to try to circumvent infertility) the young person "can never have biological children . . . they or their parents are consenting to lifelong infertility.[72]

Students, parents, teachers and other members of the school community also need education on issues pertaining to the LGBT community, such as issues about gender identity and sexual orientation, provision of community resources (for example, counseling centers for families), correcting misinformation related to the LGBT community. Creditable reports indicate that teachers lack the comfort or knowledge base to effectively address the issues related to the LGBT student population.[73] It is significant that "as of 2005, less than 40% of school districts offered any kind of education about sexual orientation, and only 30% of schools offered staff development activities."[74] Professional development opportunities can be provided by school administration for teachers that address their knowledge base on gender identity and sexual orientation issues, as well as other topics relevant to the LGBT population. In the classrooms, teachers can utilize their classroom rules and procedures to educate their students on the negative emotional feelings and consequences resulting from a student

71. Wolff et al., "Evangelical Christian College Students," 217.
72. Russo, "Debate Is Growing," 35.
73. Morgan et al., "Creating Safe Environments."
74. Fisher et al., "Promoting School Success," 82.

using another student's sexual identity to tease that other student or put them down.[75]

There is research evidence that addressing LGBT-related issues by key educational support personnel, such as counselors or teachers who are aware of community resources, and are sensitive to the needs of LGBT students, can have a positive impact on student feeling of acceptance, as well as provide educators' renewed confidence in addressing LGBT issues. These educational support personnel could also provide professional development training to families, and provide educational workshops for students on the school campus.[76] Though there are not many laws and policies that specifically protect the rights of LGBT youth, there are federal and state legal mandates that require for all students to have equal access to a safe, harassment-free school environment.[77]

Studies show that faculty, and other professionals do benefit from education that broadens their horizons on LGBT issues, and helps in the essential task of creating safer and more inclusive school environments. For example, in an experimental mixed methods field design by Dessel that tested outcomes of an intergroup dialogue intervention on public school teacher attitudes, feelings, and behaviors toward LGB students and parents, the quantitative findings of the research indicated that dialogue participation resulted in statistically significant positive changes in attitudes, feelings, and behaviors. The qualitative data analysis of the study confirmed positive changes as a result of dialogue participation. Another example, which is a recent research by Lim, Johnson and Eliason, found limited knowledge, experience, and readiness for teaching LGBT health among baccalaureate faculty who are heterosexual. It also found that the estimated median time devoted to teaching LGBT health was 2.12 hours. In addition, the study highlighted the need for improvement in the design of faculty development programs and provision of better guide in aligning the curricula with current LGBT health priorities.

Education for LGBT youth can also be provided in the form of books, movies, periodicals and other library resources that are LGBT-friendly which can allow LGBT students to have their questions answered. These library resources can as well enable other none-LGBT students on campus

75. Morgan et al., "Creating Safe Environments."
76. Ibid.
77. Fisher et al., "Promoting School Success."

because nearly 90 percent know someone (a friend, teacher, parent, future coworker, or significant associate) who is part of the LGBT community.[78]

Conclusion

The concluding question of our focus on the school success of LGBT diverse learners from a Christian worldview point is "What is the obligation of the Christian educator and the Christian community in the face of the fact of homosexuality, and in the face of the fact of the adverse circumstances, and poor school outcomes of students who identify as LGBT?" What should the Christian response be?

The School Success of LGBT Diverse Learners and the Obligation of Christian Educators, and the Christian Community

This chapter has demonstrated that the plight of LGBT diverse learners in schools is currently poor socially, emotionally, physically, psychologically, and educationally. The chapter has also shown that scientifically the "gay gene" has so far not been found, and that temperament, behavior, environment, etc., seem to be some of the multiple pathways to the LGBT sexual orientation. The chapter ended by proposing five ways to create environments, pathways and trajectories for the school success of LGBT diverse learners., called the ABCDE of the creation of school success environments for LGBT students.

The obligation of the Christian community vis-à-vis homosexuality is obviously indicated in the Scriptures. The Bible in several places is clearly not supportive of homosexuality (Lev 18:22; 20:13; 1 Cor 6:9–10; Rom 1:26–28). Gay rights advocates have offered "other interpretations" of such passages.[79] We have, however, chosen not to engage in theological debates about the hermeneutics (proper theological interpretation and meaning) of these scriptures. First, engaging in an exegesis of the Bible passages referenced above, or elaborating on what Trammell referred to as "seemingly understood belief that homosexuality is inherently incongruent with evangelicalism"[80] is outside the space constrains of this chapter. Second,

78. Morgan et al., "Creating Safe Environments."
79. Wolff et al., "Evangelical Christian College Students," 215.
80. Trammell, "Homosexuality Is Bad for Me," 5.

and more importantly, we agree with the views of Wolff et al. that such debates only tend to ignite "heated theological debates" which are not as important and beneficial as "building personal relationships that challenge core beliefs and negative emotional responses."[81]

While the Bible categorizes homosexuality as sinful, the Bible also lists a number of other things that are equally sinful such as killing, stealing, lying, committing adultery, impure thoughts, hatred, fighting, jealousy, anger, constant effort to get the best for yourself, complaints, criticisms, and others (Exod 20:13–16; Gal 5:19–21 Living Bible). Christians are not called to throw stones at people who do these wrong things, but as salt and light are to draw them in love to God for repentance and restoration. Christians are all called to be a community of love.

The command is to truly "love God, and to love our neighbors as we love ourselves" (Mark 12:30–31 NKJV). However, love does not mean glamorizing sin, or compromising the Christian witness; it means to be understanding, to be tolerant, and to be accepting of the person, not for what they do, but for who they are; someone created in the image of God, for whom Jesus died so that believing in him, they might be saved.

Jesus did not condemn the Samaritan woman with less than perfect sexual history (John 4). He does not condemn those who wrestle with the lifestyle issues that he has not endorsed. Instead, he genuinely reaches out to them and makes a difference in their lives. To the woman caught in adultery (John 8: 1–11), Jesus said: "Go and sin no more" (v.11). Christians who are called upon to defend the weak and oppressed (Ps 82: 3–4; Isa 1:17), to be patient with everyone (1 Thess 5:14), to be salt and light (Matt 5:13, 16), and to be good neighbors (Luke 10:25–37), should join the effort to ensure the creation of inclusive, school success environments for LGBT diverse learners.

Bibliography

Alberto, P. A., and A. C. Troutman. *Applied Behavior Analysis for Teachers*. 7th ed. Englewood, NJ: Prentice-Hall, 2006.

Balthazart, J. "Minireview: Hormones and Human Sexual Orientation." *Endocrinology* 152 (2011) 2937–47.

Biegel, S., and S. J. Kuehl. "Safe at School: Addressing the School Environment and LGBT Safety through Policy and Legislation." National Education Policy Center, September 30, 2010. http://nepc.colorado.edu/publication/safe-at-school.

81. Wolff et al., "Evangelical Christian College Students," 215.

Cohn, S. "The Gay Gifted Learner: Facing the Challenge of Homophobia and Antihomosexual Bias in Schools." In *Youth at Risk: A Prevention Resource for Counselors, Teachers, and Parents*, edited by D. Capuzzi and D. Gross, 123–34. 4th ed. Upper Saddle River, NJ: Prentice Hall, 2006.

Coloroso, Barbara. *The Bully, the Bullied, and the Bystander: From Preschool to High School; How Parents and Teachers Can Help Break the Cycle of Violence*. New York: HarperResouce, 2004

Corsini, R. J. *The Dictionary of Psychology*. New York: Brunner-Routledge, 2002.

Dessel, A. B. "Effects of Intergroup Dialogue: Public School Teachers and Sexual Orientation Prejudice." *Small Group Research* 41 (2010) 556–92.

Dobson, J. *Bringing Up Boys: Practical Advice and Encouragement for Those Shaping the Next Generation of Men*. Wheaton, IL: Tyndale, 2001.

Fisher, E. S., et al. "Promoting School Success for Lesbian, Gay, Bisexual, Transgendered, and Questioning Students: Primary, Secondary, and Tertiary Prevention and Intervention Strategies." *California School Psychologist* 13 (2008) 79–91.

Friend, M. *Special Education: Contemporary Perspectives for Schools and Professionals*. 4th ed. Boston: Pearson, 2014.

Frisch, M., and Hviid, A. "Childhood Family Correlates of Heterosexual and Homosexual Marriages: A National Cohort Study of Two Million Danes." *Archives of Sexual Behavior* 35 (2006) 533–47.

Grant, C. A., and C. E. Sleeter. *Doing Multicultural Education for Achievement and Equity*. New York: Routledge, 2007.

Gutierrez, F. J. "Counseling Queer Youth: Preventing Another Matthew Shepard Story." In *Youth at Risk: A Prevention Resource for Counselors, Teachers, and Parents*, edited by D. Capuzzi and D. Gross, 331–71. 4th ed. New Jersey: Prentice Hall, 2006.

James, W. "Biological and Psychosocial Determinants of Male and Female Human Sexual Orientation." *Journal of Biosocial Science* 37 (2005) 555–67.

Kattari, S. "Identity and Sexual Communication for Sexual and Gender Minorities with Physical Disabilities." *Sexuality & Culture* 19 (2015) 882–99.

Kazdin, A. E. *Encyclopedia of Psychology*. Oxford: Oxford University Press, 2000.

Kinsey, A.C., et al. *Sexual Behavior in the Human Male*. Philadelphia: Saunders, 1948.

Klehm, M. "The Effects of Teacher Beliefs on Teaching Practices and Achievement of Students with Disabilities." *Teacher Education and Special Education* 37 (2014) 216–40.

Lane, K., et al. *Managing Challenging Behaviors in Schools: Research-Based Strategies That Work*. New York: Guilford, 2011.

Liboro, R. et al. "Beyond the Dialectics and Polemics: Canadian Catholic Schools Addressing LGBT Youth Issues." *High School Journal* 98 (2015) 158–80.

Lim, Fidelindo, et al. "A National Survey of Faculty Knowledge, Experience, and Readiness for Teaching Lesbian, Gay, Bisexual, and Transgender Health in Baccalaureate Nursing Programs." *Nursing Education Perspectives* 36 (2015) 144–52.

Morgan, J. J., et al. "Creating Safe Environments for Students with Disabilities Who Identify as Lesbian, Gay, Bisexual, or Transgender." *Intervention in School and Clinic* 47 (2011) 3–13.

Rees, N. "Diverse Schools Bring Many Benefits." *US News & World Report*, July 7, 2014. http://www.usnews.com/opinion/blogs/nina-rees/2014/07/07/school-choice-allows-students-to-take-advantage-of-diversity.

Russo, F. "Debate Is Growing about How to Meet the Urgent Needs of Transgendered Kids." *Scientific American Mind* 27 (2016) 27–35.

Salend, S. J. *Creating Inclusive Classrooms: Effective and Reflective Practices.* 5th ed. Upper Saddle River, NJ: Merrill / Prentice Hall, 2005.

———. *Creating Inclusive Classrooms: Effective and Reflective Practices.* 8th ed. Boston: Pearson, 2016.

Sexton, T. L., et al. "Levels of Evidence for the Models and Mechanisms of Therapeutic Change in Family and Couple Therapy." In *Bergin and Garfield's Handbook of Psychotherapy and Behavior Change,* edited by M. J. Lambert, 590–646. 5th ed. New York: Wiley, 2004.

Shore, K. *Bullying Prevention for Students with Disabilities.* Port Chester, NY: DUDE, 2014.

Smith, T. E. C., et al. *Teaching Students with special Needs in Inclusive Settings.* 7th ed. Boston: Pearson, 2016.

Southern Poverty Law Center. "Best Practices: Creating an LGBT-Inclusive School Climate." Teaching Tolerance, a project of the Southern Poverty Law Center. 2013. http://www.tolerance.org/lgbt-best-practices.

Trammell, J. Y. "'Homosexuality Is Bad for Me': An Analysis of Homosexual Christian Testimonies in *Christianity Today* Magazine." *Journal of Media and Religion* 14 (2015) 1–15.

Turnbull, A., et al. *Exceptional Lives: Special Education in Today's Schools.* 8th ed. Boston: Pearson, 2016.

Umbreit, J., et al. *Functional Behavioral Assessment and Function-Based Intervention: An Effective, Practical Approach.* Upper Saddle River, NJ: Merrill / Prentice Hall, 2007.

Wolff, J. R., et al. "Evangelical Christian College Students and Attitudes Toward Gay Rights: A California University Sample." *Journal of LGBT Youth* 9 (2012) 200–224.

Wong, H. K., and R. T. Wong. *The First Days of School: How to Be an Effective Teacher.* Mountain View, CA: Wong, 2009.

7

Depression and Anxiety in the Classroom for Children with Mild to Moderate Disabilities

How Can the Educational Community and the Family Help?

Ben C. Nworie PhD, MDiv, LPC
Professor of Special Education
School of Education, Biola University

Abstract

THE CHAPTER HIGHLIGHTS THE symptoms of the internalizing problems of depression and anxiety in the classroom for children with mild to moderate disabilities. A discussion of possible causes of depression and anxiety for these children follows. The chapter then reflects on how these rampant problems impact children's education. The paper ends with recommendation of strategies and ways for the school community and the family to help.

Keywords: depression, anxiety, disabilities, school, family

Introduction

Mental health problems, especially depression and anxiety, are real and rampant inside and outside of the classroom. It is estimated that 25 percent of the United States population will experience some degree of mental illness during their lifetime, and that half of this number will develop disabling mental health problems requiring medication or long-term disability or both.[1] Depression in young people is a significant problem that affects well over 30 percent of the school age population; especially when it is considered that over 33 percent of school children diagnosed with attention deficit hyperactivity disorder (ADHD) are actually students with bipolar disorder.[2] A similarly significant number of students experience anxiety disorders which include generalized anxiety disorder, panic disorders, social phobia, separation anxiety disorder, or a combination of these disorders.[3]

Anxiety disorders have been identified as the most common mental health disorders among children and adolescents, and the median onset age among this population is eleven years.[4] Prevalence rates of anxiety disorders in children and adolescents with intellectual disability were identified to be up to 22 percent[5] while students with separation anxiety disorder alone are believed to make up about 80 percent of younger school children.[6]

Depression and anxiety are called internalizing problems or behaviors. Behavioral and psychological problems are often dichotomized into two patterns referred to as internalizing and externalizing problems. Internalizing symptoms are more inward focused, and tend to distress mainly the individual. Externalizing problems such as disruptive behavior and aggression, on the other hand, are more outward-directed and usually generate discomfort and conflict to others in the surrounding environment.[7] According to the *Diagnostic and Statistical Manual of Mental Disorders, 5th edition (DSM-5)*, internalizing disorders include such things as depression, anxiety, trauma and stressor-related disorders. Other internalizing

1. Selix and Goyal, "Postpartum Depression."
2. Capuzzi and Gross, "Defining Youth at Risk"; Hammen, "Adolescent Depression."
3. Salend, *Creating Inclusive Classrooms.*
4. Mammarella et al., "Anxiety and Depression in Children."
5. Reardon et al. "Anxiety Disorders in Children and Adolescents."
6. Dryden-Edwards, R. "Separation Anxiety Disorder."
7. Forns et al., "Internalizing and Externalizing Problems."

symptoms include poor self-esteem, suicidal behaviors, self-injury, short attention span, decreased academic progress, bulimia, anorexia, and some also include schizophrenia.[8] Internalizing and externalizing problems are not mutually exclusive. Just as students can experience both anxiety and depression together,[9] they can also exhibit both Internalizing and externalizing problems concurrently.[10]

Symptoms of Depression and Anxiety in the Classroom for Children with Disabilities

Depression and anxiety are common internalizing problems among school-aged children, especially students with disabilities. Reliable research on teenage depression indicates that rates of youth depression are the highest of all psychological disorders of children.[11] And the co-morbidity of depression and anxiety, that is, the fact that they occur together is well-known in the field of mental health.[12]

These children with depression and anxiety can be found in any of the thirteen special education disability categories.[13] Available studies clearly indicate the prevalence of elevated rates of depression and anxiety symptoms among students of various ages and IQs who are in the disability category of autism spectrum disorders (ASDs), as well as among those who are categorized as students with learning disabilities.[14]

Let us consider the preponderance of anxiety and depression among students in the disability category of learning disabilities (LD). They make up over 35 percent of students between ages three and twenty-one in the United States who under the federal mandate guiding special education,

8. Hallahan et al., *Exceptional Learners*; Turnbull et al., *Exceptional Lives*.

9. Orinstein et al., "Psychiatric Symptoms in Youth."

10. Hallahan et al., *Exceptional Learners*.

11. Hammen, "Adolescent Depression."

12. Bella and Omigbodun, "Social Phobia in Nigerian University Students"; Mannion et al., "Investigation of Comorbid Psychological"; Newby et al., "Internet Cognitive Behavioural Therapy"; Siddique et al., "Prevalence of Anxiety and Depression"; Ashraf, and Najam, "Comorbidity of Anxiety Disorder and Major Depression."

13. Vohra et al., "Access to Services"; Reardon et al., "Anxiety Disorders in Children and Adolescents.

14. Strang et al., "Depression and Anxiety Symptoms in Children and Adolescents"; Gallegos et al., "Anxiety, Depression, and Coping Skills"; Ashraf and Najam, "Comorbidity of Anxiety Disorder and Major Depression."

the Individuals with Disabilities Education Act (IDEA), receive special education and related services.[15] Students with LD make up about 50 percent of referrals to special education in Mexico.[16] Several studies confirm that students with LD, in comparison with their typically developing peers, show more elevated levels of anxiety and depression.[17]

In the classroom, students with LD, as well as those with other disabilities, frequently exhibit symptoms of depression and anxiety such as crying, worrying, avoidant behavior, and acting without thinking due to nervousness. Friend and Bursuck have correctly pointed out that some of these students "may choose not to act on their previous knowledge because their attempts at socially appropriate behavior may have gone unrecognized, and they would rather have negative recognition than no recognition at all.[18] They give the example of a student, James, who was rebuffed by one group of students so often that he began to say unkind things to them just to provoke them. The student James also began going out together with other students who chronically misbehaved because James felt at least appreciated by the misbehaving students.

Other symptoms of depression and anxiety frequently exhibited in the classroom by students with disabilities include showing little confidence in their own abilities due to poor self-concept. The poor self-image in turn leads to learned helplessness. As Friend and Bursuck have aptly remarked,

> Students with learned helplessness see little relationship between their efforts and school or social success. When these students succeed, they attribute their success to luck; when they fail, they blame their failure on a lack of ability.[19]

In the classroom, students with disabilities who are depressed or anxious also often show somatic symptoms such as headaches, cramps, tics and selective mutism.[20] Students with selective mutism, despite possessing the

15. Turnbull et al., *Exceptional Lives*; Yell, *Law and Special Education*.

16. Gallegos et al., "Anxiety, Depression and Coping Skills."

17. Ibid.; Friend and Bursuck, *Including Students with Special Needs*; Salend, *Creating Inclusive Bathrooms*.

18. Friend and Bursuck, *Including Students with Special Needs*, 227.

19. Ibid.

20. Kauffman, "Characteristics of Emotional and Behavioral Disorders"; Cohen and Wysocky, *Front of Class*; Gallegos et al., "Anxiety, Depression, and Coping Skills"; Friend and Bursuck, *Including Students with Special Needs*; Salend, *Creating Inclusive Classrooms*.

ability to speak, have been known not to communicate in selective social situations or environments. Consequently, although they may use verbal communication at home, they may refrain from verbally interacting with others in school in order to avoid social interactions.[21] These students with depression or anxiety along with refusing to speak in class sometimes may show other symptoms in the classroom such as being visibly nervous when given an assignment, becoming ill when it is time to go to school, or showing a lack of self-confidence when performing common school and social tasks.[22]

Possible Causal Factors of Depression and Anxiety for Children with Disabilities

There are various biological, sociological and psychological causal factors and conceptual models of depression and anxiety in children with disabilities. The biological models of mood and anxiety disorders fall into two main categories: those focusing on the role of genetic factors, and those emphasizing biochemical processes. In the genesis of depression and anxiety, though the specific details of the nature of the genetic transmission of these disorders have not been determined, studies in this field suggest that there is a strong genetic aspect in the causation of these mental health problems in the general population, as well as in children with disabilities. For example, genetic factors account for about 50 percent of mood disorders in twin studies; children of parents who are depressed are three times more likely to experience major depression in their lives and for parents who experience bipolar disorder, there is a much stronger genetic link for bipolar among their offspring.[23] Some pediatric anxiety cases such as generalized anxiety disorder (GAD) and obsessive compulsive disorder (OCD) are biologically inherited and may persist into adulthood.

The biological model of the causation of mood and anxiety disorders also focuses on biochemical routes such hormones, hypothalamus-pituitary-adrenal axis, neurotransmitters, and others. Research findings have established a close link between abnormalities in the ebb and flow of neurotransmitters, especially serotonin, in the brain of people who experience depression and anxiety; the studies have also shown the effect of

21. Salend, *Creating Inclusive Classrooms.*

22. Friend and Bursuck, *Including Students with Special Needs.*

23. Capuzzi and Gross, "Defining Youth at Risk."

antidepressant medications in the effective control of the symptoms of the mood and anxiety disorders.[24]

There are other biological causal factors such as physical and emotional stress. A recent study by Dyches, Christensen, Harper, Mandleco, and Roper[25] of 122 single mothers of children with autism spectrum disorders found that hassles and caregiver burden were positively correlated with clinical depression. Some medical problems associated with abnormalities or complications in the normal biological functioning of the systems of the human body are also seen as biological causal factors of internalizing problems. For example, studies have shown that children with neurological disorders such as migraine headaches, and seizures, or other various medical conditions may also have symptoms associated with depression or anxiety.[26] The study by Tietjen and Khubchandani, which involved a total of 34,525 individuals, suggests that headache, depression, and pain have a mutual pathogenesis.[27]

Psychologically, there are behavioral and cognitive conceptual models of the causal factors of depression and anxiety. For behaviorists, mood and anxiety problems stem from significant loss, as well as the absence of adequate or sufficient reinforcement. Indeed in behaviorism, every behavior, positive or negative, hinges on the availability of appropriate positive and negative reinforcement schedules or lack thereof.[28] According to this model, lack of sufficient reinforcement in children and adolescents can often give rise to other behaviors, such as: "anxiety, aggressiveness, delinquency, somatic complaints, substance use, poor peer relationships, negative body image, poor school performance, school phobia."[29]

The cognitive conceptual models of depression and anxiety focus on the role of cognition. According to this model, especially as espoused by Aaron Beck, it is believed that our moods and behaviors are determined by our thinking, based on the belief that "cognition and affect are interactive and that the prior occurrence of cognition will determine a person's

24. Ibid.

25. Dyches et al., "Respite Care for Single Mothers."

26. Reilly and Balantine, "Epilepsy in School-Aged Children."

27. Tietjen and Khubchandani, "Depression Has Additive Effect."

28. Umbreit, *Functional Behavioral Assessment*; Alberto and Troutman, *Applied Behavior Analysis*.

29. Capuzzi and Gross, "Defining Youth at Risk," 118.

affective response to an event."[30] Subsequently, others in the cognitive school of thought, such as Albert Ellis, expanded the model by suggesting that mood and anxiety disorders are caused by cognitive errors that consist mainly of three negative thinking patterns which include "a negative view of self, of the world, and of the future."[31]

Sociologically, depression and anxiety in children are often associated with causal factors such as poverty, language and literacy difficulties, socialization difficulties, school difficulties, and other internalizing problems. Separation anxiety disorder (SAD), which is triggered by separation of students from their primary caregivers, accounts for a significant number of younger school children. Some studies report an overrepresentation of girls with separation anxiety disorder.[32] Gender, therefore, also seems to be a causal factor as significantly more girls than boys experience mood and anxiety disorders.[33]

Sociologically, bullying has been identified as a causal factor for depression and anxiety. A study by Campbell, Missiuna, and Vaillancourt on peer victimization and depression in children with and without motor coordination difficulties found that children with and without disabilities who experience bullying are at increased risk of experiencing depression.

Similarly, all types of abuse, especially family abuse and maltreatment are strongly connected with the internalizing problems of depression and anxiety. The analyses of a study of over 1348 participants with a diagnosis of migraine and co-morbid depression and anxiety found that "all types of childhood abuse and neglect are strongly associated with depression and anxiety, and that the relationship strengthens with increasing number of maltreatment types."[34] These internalized disorders of depression and anxiety if ignored for long enough could precipitate explosive externalizing problems.

30. Ibid., 124.

31. Ibid.

32. Austin and Sciarra, *Children and Adolescents.*

33. Capuzzi and Gross, "Defining Youth at Risk."

34. Tietjen et al., "Childhood Maltreatment and Migraine," 33.

Impact of Depression and Anxiety on the Education of Children with Disabilities

The internalizing problems of depression and anxiety considerably impact children's education as the children show symptoms such as irritability, fatigue, fear, worry, dysphoria, psychomotor retardation, social withdrawal, poor concentration and poor academic engagement.[35] For these students with disabilities, the combination of low self-esteem and learned helplessness stemming from their anxiety and depression usually results in lack of motivation, school avoidance behavior and poor school performance.[36] Friend and Bursuck amply illustrate this point with the example of Denny, a fifteen-year-old sophomore in high school who despite being in special education since the second grade mainly received grades of D and F, but never a grade better than a C. Denny, who eventually started to skip classes feeling that his going to class did not help him do well, plans to drop out of school on his sixteenth birthday.[37]

Denny's behavior is typical for children with anxiety problem. Anxiety has to do with a person's response to stress. While some students with anxiety may obsess about specific things, most of these students often feel overwhelmed, exhausted, and under a lot of stress. Some of them, even when they look calm outwardly, are unable to concentrate because their brain, being overstimulated, never stops. They are not able to stop thinking, and the constant brain stimulation can get so intense that it interrupts their sleep and negatively affects their quality of life, including the quality of their school work. Rarely living in the present, such students typically worry constantly about the future or live in the past. In consequence their school performance is negatively impacted.

Often children with neurological disorders such as migraine headaches, and seizures, as well as various other medical conditions also experience symptoms associated with depression or anxiety. This co-morbid symptomatology usually has significant impact on a child's schooling. In most of these cases the children do qualify to receive special education services under one of the thirteen special education categories. Even with special education support for them, schooling can still be quite a struggle

---

35. Austin and Sciarra, Children and Adolescents.

36. Friend and Bursuck, *Including Students with Special Needs*; Salend, *Creating Inclusive Classrooms*.

37. Friend and Bursuck, *Including Students with Special Needs*.

for most of these students.[38] In such situations, students in inclusive placements seem to show more positive gains in social and emotional functioning. In addition students in inclusive settings tend to be more accepted by peers, have more satisfying relationships with their best school friends, have higher self-perceptions of academic competence, and fewer problem behaviors than their peers in receiving resource room special education support, or their counterparts in self-contained special education classes.[39]

Strategies and Ways for the School Community and the Family to Help Students with Disabilities Who Also Have Depression and Anxiety

On December 10, 2015, the US Congress reauthorized the Elementary and Secondary Education Act and the No Child left Behind (ESEA/NCLB) by passing the Every Student Succeeds Act (ESSA). This new law addressed a number of issues that should contribute to the success of every student. However, the mental health provisions of this new law is an indication of the national significance of the main subject of this chapter, which is giving attention to the mental health needs of many students. As part of the mental health provision of the new law, it approves "significant investments for states and districts to implement: comprehensive school mental health services, efforts to improve school climate and school safety, strategies to reduce bullying and harassment, and activities to improve collaboration between school, family and the community."[40]

The school community and the family are in a position to utilize various strategies and ways to help in the prevention and treatment of depression and anxiety in students with disabilities. The schools, to begin with, have available to them simple instruments and checklists which school psychologists and counselors could utilize to ascertain the presence of mood and or anxiety disorders in students. For effectiveness and to rule out other concerns, the assessment needs to take into consideration the student's life circumstances such as their home and social environment, their life stressors, interpersonal relationships, as well as their cognitive and affective characteristics.

38. Reilly and Ballantine, "Epilepsy in School-Aged Children."

39. Wiener and Tardif, "Social and Emotional Functioning"; Friend and Bursuck, *Including Students with Special Needs*; Salend, *Creating Inclusive Classrooms*.

40. See www.ed.gov/ESSA; all4ed.org/essa; cecblog.typepad.com/files/cecs-summary-of-selected-issues-in-every-student-succeeds-act-essa-1.pdf.

Once the determination of the presence of anxiety and depression has been made through authentic assessment and evaluation, the school can use a combination of affective, cognitive, and behavioral strategies to help the affected students in the areas that they struggle the most, such as building their self-esteem and enhancing their self-acceptance, enhancing their problem-solving, decision-making and task completion skills, improving their interpersonal relationships and social skills, and others.

Since students with disabilities who receive special education services are also entitled to related services such as counseling and psychological services, the students can be helped through the utilization of these various services. The utilization of these related services can be built into the individualized education plan (IEP) of the students. The effective execution of IEPs usually calls for the collaborative efforts of teachers, related services providers, other school professionals, school administrators and the family. Under such arrangements, the students can receive individual help, as well as group interventions. Group interventions have the advantage of reaching students in larger numbers, can be cost-effective, can be adaptable to classroom formats, and can facilitate the teaching and learning of skills in a more congenial, communal, peer context.

Schools can also help by providing early prevention which, according to Capuzzi and Gross, "can take the form of educational programs focused on forming friendships (social skills), nonviolent conflict resolution, assertiveness training, and skills for relating to adults, dealing with peer pressure, and improving critical school competencies such as basic academic skills and academic survival skills."[41] Effective early prevention programs usually focus on social skills or life skills training which, as Capuzzi and Gross, correctly pointed out, involve "behaviors and attitudes necessary for coping with academic challenges, communicating with others, forming healthy and stable relationships, and making good decisions."[42] It is helpful to recall that theoretically, life skills training is founded on perspectives of earlier scholars like Bandura and others in whose views children and adolescents are not held responsible for causing their problems but are considered capable of learning new behavioral patterns that decrease the likelihood of future problems.

Schools can provide families with the clues and resources to assess and build the self-determination skills of their children with disabilities who

41. Capuzzi and Gross, "Defining Youth at Risk," 132.
42. Ibid.

have mood and anxiety issues. As Zheng, Maude, Brotherson, Summers, Palmer, and Erwin correctly noted, building initial skills in the early years for the later growth in the area of self-determination in the postsecondary years is essential for individuals with disabilities who also experience depression and anxiety. Families should observe and seek to promote in their children some of the foundational skills for self-determination, such as choice making, self-regulation, and engagement.[43]

Some of these students come from ethnically and culturally diverse backgrounds, and do present with self-esteem and life skills deficit issues. It is vital for special education teachers, therefore, to have in their repertoire of practice some understanding of how to integrate self-esteem building and life skills training.[44] School psychologists, counselors, other teachers and family members can all help in teaching life skills which essentially involves breaking down tasks into smaller stages or component parts and demonstrating how to move methodically and incrementally from simple to more complex skills. The five-step model of effective life skills training sessions moves from instruction (teaching) through modeling (showing), to role-play (practicing), feedback (reinforcement), and homework (application).[45] Along with teaching life-skills, schools can utilize stress reduction techniques such as relaxation training, meditation, and guided visual imagery which may be helpful in the prevention or reduction of mood and anxiety disorders among students with disabilities. Additionally, schools can help by providing leadership training programs which also enhance life skills training. Leadership training opportunities help students exercise decision-making skills, learn the importance of self-control, increase problem-solving and decision-making skills.[46]

The school working collaboratively with the family can utilize advances in neuroscience to help students with anxiety by devising ways to help reduce the increased rates of metabolic impulses occurring in specific segments of the brain of a student who has anxiety disorder. For example, for people with generalized anxiety disorder (GAD), the hyperactive brain circuits are located in the occipital, temporal and frontal lobes as well as the cerebellum and thalamus sections of the brain.[47]

43. Zheng et al., "Foundations for Self-Determination."

44. Austin and Sciarra, *Children and Adolescents.*

45. Capuzzi and Gross, "Defining Youth at Risk."

46. Ibid.

47. See www.cnsforum.com/educationalresources/imagebank/brain_struc_anxiety

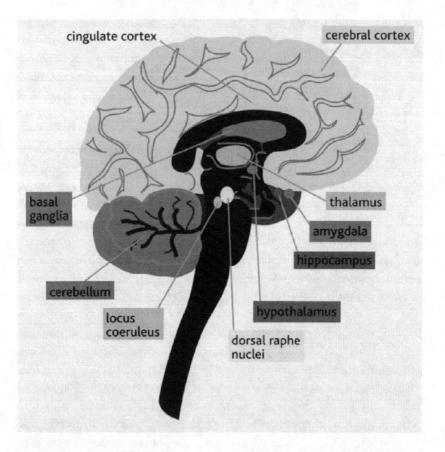

Consequently teachers can use brain training techniques and strategies within the classroom such as drawing, simulation which is the use of a model of behavior to gain a better understanding of such a behavior, and other forms of techniques utilized in the Neuro-Education model to help effect significant positive learning and behavior outcomes for students with anxiety. For students with anxiety, this effective Neuro-Education model of teaching and learning helps to engage students in "deep learning" that empowers understanding as opposed to "surface learning" that requires memorization alone. In consequence it shifts the educational paradigm from teacher to learner.[48]

Also the family and school communities can work collaboratively to provide prevention and treatment benefits to students with disabilities

/neuro_biol_gad.

48. Arwood et al., *Pro-social Language*.

who experience mood and anxiety problems through utilization of exercise, nutrition, and improved self-care habits which can be very helpful to these students. Studies have shown that several weeks of aerobic exercise program can help male and female students experience lowered incidence of depression, anxiety, and enhance positive symptoms such as improved vigor and self-efficacy. For example, Balkin, Tietjen-Smith, Caldwell, and Yu-Pei[49] found aerobic exercise to be an effective intervention for depression among young college age female students. Their study found that the college women students who participated in aerobic exercise experienced a significant and meaningful decrease in depressive symptoms. Findings from the study also suggested an apparent link between depression and overall physical fitness. An obvious advantage of the use of exercise and nutrition as helpful strategies is that the formation of these healthy habits early in life is easier and more cost effective than changing poor habits later in life.

The family and the school should collaborate to ensure that students with mood and anxiety issues engage in healthy nutritional habits. Healthy nutrition can make significant impacts in the mood, anxiety level, and productivity of students. For example, during my high school soccer coaching career, in the 1999–2000 school year, I inherited the worst performing soccer team in a school district in the Midwest of the United States. As I began to work with the students, my earliest observation was that while the students greatly loved soccer, some of them who had promising skills frequently appeared weak or withdrawn. My initial investigations and assessments revealed that for many of these students their free school lunch was the only meal they ate or were sure of during the day. They came from homes where they did not eat breakfast, were usually not assured of after school dinner, and when they ate other meals, such meals almost invariably consisted of unhealthy fast foods. To add to their poor nutritional habits, some of these students also smoked and abused alcohol. Upon making these discoveries, I took steps to provide help in this area for the students. Through collaboration with the school administration, the parents teacher association and some businesses in the community, we were able to raise funds for the team. Through such funds, healthy breakfast and other meals were provided for the soccer players. Counseling services were also provided for those who needed such support. Consequently, this team eventually became a winning (undefeated) team. They turned around from being

49. Balkin et al., "Utilization of Exercise."

the worst performing team in the school district to becoming the district champions.

The family can play a pivotal role in the treatment and prevention of internalizing disorders of children particularly when parents work together in the family as a team. A recent study that investigated the parenting behaviors of mothers and fathers of clinically anxious young children, with or without depressive comorbidity, highlights the importance of including both mothers and fathers in the prevention and treatment of internalizing disorders of children, especially at the preschool age.[50]

Effective instructional coaching of these students with internalizing problems by special education teachers and other school professionals will yield equally significant results. Teachers and school professionals should, therefore, make use of best practices such as creating a positive, safe learning environment, understanding behavioral assessment and intervention, finding each student's strengths and utilizing the student's strengths in creating an educational plan that works best for the student, tracking each student's progress by monitoring successes and setbacks, so as to quickly provide effective intervention plans for sustained success, by mastering differentiated instruction and Universal Design for Learning (UDL) through providing students with various teaching styles. For example see the figure below.

Table 1.1. Using Best Practices to Provide Effective Instruction for Students with Depression and Anxiety

Identify Student's Anxiety/Depression Symptoms in Jr. High Classroom	Identify Student's Strengths/Needs/Deficit.	Create a Positive and Safe Learning Environment. Monitor Student's Progress	Create Best Education Plan for Student: Use Accommodations or Differentiated Instruction
Forgetful of class rules, does not keep track of due dates and class assignments.	Strengths: Good peer to peer relationship skills Needs: Very disorganized	Use peer verbal & visual cues & reminders. By 6 months, use notebook, calendar, helpful materials independently. No peer or staff reminders.	Provide specific instructions and helpful materials like notebook, calendar and/or checklists. Model expected behavior, check, praise.

50. Otto et al., "Parenting Behaviors of Mothers and Fathers."

Needs more time to complete class work, and all written assignments.	Strengths: Good handwriting Needs: Poor time management.	Adjust amount of required work. By 3 months complete all written assignments & class work satisfactorily with a "B."	Teach time management skills. Pair with a focused peer with poor handwriting skills. Extend time for work completion.
Not attending class on time and frequently does not attend at all; acts worried, sad or sleepy in class.	Strength: Likes to draw. Has good drawing skills Needs: Lacks focus, or concentration on task. Gives up easily.	Assess why student is late or absent for class. Teach life skills for attendance and punctuality. In 6 months, attend class regularly and punctually 90% of the time without use of reinforcement.	Provide student reinforcement for attendance and punctuality, based on assessment result as to why student is late or absent for class. Help student use artistic talent in solving class problem. Give bonus points for attendance.
Student finding it difficult to work together with peers, especially those who tease or bully student.	Strength: Good listening and oral communication skills. Needs: Help with anger management issues.	Change seating so student does not sit close to peers who tease or annoy him/her. By 6 months, respond assertively to 90% of teasing or bullying.	Provide assertiveness training one hour weekly for 3 months for learning to deal with teasing and/or bullying with assertiveness.
Finds textbook difficult to read. Makes reading errors which interfere with proper comprehension; and makes student discouraged and unhappy in class.	Strengths: Good retentive memory. Loves hearing stories Needs: Poor motivation to read. Gives up easily.	Provide remedial reading that emphasizes accuracy in proper comprehension. Good candidate for class dramatizations.	Provide digital textbook. Highlight student text. Use student's interest in hearing and telling stories to motivate him or her to read with a coach or a peer.

Has problem with math test involving multiplication and division. Has some somatic symptoms of headaches and cramps during math tests.	Strengths: Loves playing computer games. Able to use calculator. Needs: Has test anxiety. Has difficulty being able to concentrate.	Give computerized division and multiplication practice and drill 20 mins. each school day. In the IEP, allow use of calculator. By end of school year, student will be able to correctly complete 90% of multiplication and division problems on the district math test.	Provide extra instruction on multiplication and division skills. During math class, pair student with peer who is able to easily solve multiplication and division problems. Give student 15 mins. of small group remedial math instruction 4 times weekly. Give extra time as test accommodation.

Effective instruction of these students with internalizing problems by special education teachers and other school professionals also calls for effective collaboration with the families of the children in the area of communication. Collaboration with the family in this area is especially significant because the school has for long had the reputation of communicating with the family only when problem situations with students emerge; consequently, the school has not always come across as being a fully communicative partner with the family or solidly on the side of parents in that sense.[51] One way to improve this collaborative communication is by improving school to-home communication. The TRIBE checklist below provides helpful strategies for improving home-to-school communication.

School-to-Home Written Communication Improvement Strategies Using the TRIBE Checklist

T = Type: It is neater, more professional looking, and more efficient to type documents instead of hand writing them. This improves legibility and minimizes grammatical and spelling errors. If the intent is to personalize the note or document, consider adding a brief handwritten footnote at the end.

R = Readability: The more readable the document, the clearer and better the communication. Whether or not the family is highly educated, instead of writing at the college or graduate level, it is better to write at the level at

51. Thomas, *Public School Law*.

which the newspapers are written which is usually between the 4th and 6th grade level. An example of a long, complex sentence contrasted with the same sentence broken down into few shorter sentences is a good illustration of readability. It saves the reader time, communicates the message of the note clearer, and is therefore more effective.

I = Images: Since a picture is worth more than a thousand words, make effective use of simple pictures, images, diagrams graphs and charts. Incorporate images and media that the reader can more easily relate to or track with. If possible, use links that most clearly convey your message, links that are easy to follow.

B = Brief: Make the communication brief. Ideally limit it to one page. If it must be more than one page, insert page numbers. Consider breaking contents down into sections, use bullet points or numbering.

E = Example: Examples more than anything else help to drive home the point of the communication. As much as possible, make use of real life examples which the reader can relate to.

Table 1.2. TRIBE checklist for improving school-to-home written communication[52]

T	Type Type documents instead of hand writing them. Use consistent font size. Use highlighting, or bold print only for emphasis.
R	Readability Write at the 4th to 6th grade level. Use short, clear, readabile sentences.
I	Images Use pictures, images, diagrams graphs and charts. Use images and media that the reader can more easily relate to. Use easy to follow links that clearly convey your message.
B	Brief Limit document to one page. If more than one page, insert page numbers. Break contents down into sections. Use bullet points or numbering.
E	Example Use examples to drive home the point of the communication. Use real life examples which the reader can relate to.

52. See Nagro, "PROSE Checklist," for additional home-to-school communication improvement strategies.

Furthermore, the effective instruction of these students requires the utilization of assistive devices and supplemental services.[53] Above all, successful instruction of these students recognizes that effective, learner-centered environments identify, nurture, and utilize students' strengths to promote positive academic achievements.[54]

Finally, it may be necessary for the school to help educate some families who may have some wrong ideas about mental health problems. For example, some families may come from cultures or backgrounds that still hold on to the erroneous notion that depression is a sin or the result of sin, and that anxiety disorder or depression (or both) do result from demonic possession which has occurred in consequence of moral or spiritual lapses.[55] Families who adopt these cultural or traditional folk ideas about mental health issues typically resort to secular folk psychiatric treatment which in some parts of Africa and South America involves utilizing the services of the witch doctor or the curandero, which is not best practice, and certainly not Christian practice.

Bibliography

American Psychiatric Association. *Diagnostic and Statistical Manual of Mental Disorders.* 5th ed. [*DSM-5*]. Washington, DC: American Psychiatric Association, 2013.

Arwood, E., et al. *Pro-social Language: A Way to Think about Behavior.* Portland, OR: APRICOT, 2015.

Ashraf, F., and N. Najam. "Comorbidity of Anxiety Disorder and Major Depression among Girls with Learning Disabilities." *Pakistan Journal of Medical Research* 54 (2015) 109–12.

Austin, V. L., and D.T. Sciarra. *Children and Adolescents with Emotional and Behavioral Disorders.* New York: Pearson, 2010.

Balkin, R. S., et al. "The Utilization of Exercise to Decrease Depressive Symptoms in Young Adult Women." *Adultspan Journal* 6 (2007) 30–35.

Bella, T. T., and O. O. Omigbodun. "Social Phobia in Nigerian University Students: Prevalence, Correlates and Co-morbidity." *Social Psychiatry & Psychiatric Epidemiology* 44 (2009) 458–63.

Campbell, W. N., et al. "Peer Victimization and Depression in Children With and Without Motor Coordination Difficulties." *Psychology in the Schools* 49 (2012) 328–41.

Capuzzi, D., and D. R. Gross, eds. "Defining Youth at Risk." In *Youth at Risk: A Prevention Resource for Counselors, Teachers, and Parents,* 3–19. Upper Saddle River, NJ: Pearson Education, 2006.

53. Nworie, "Future Trends for Special Education."
54. Weed, "Culturally Responsive Schooling."
55. Scrutton, "Is Depression a Sin or a Disease?"

Cohen, B., and L. Wysocky. *Front of the Class: How Tourette Syndrome Made Me the Teacher I Never Had*. New York: St. Martin's Griffin, 2008.

Dryden-Edwards, R. "Separation Anxiety Disorder." MedicineNet.com. http://www.medicinenet.com/separation_anxiety/article.htm.

Dyches, T., et al. "Respite Care for Single Mothers of Children with Autism Spectrum Disorders." *Journal of Autism & Developmental Disorders* 46 (2016) 812–24.

Forns, M., et al. "Internalizing and Externalizing Problems." In *Encyclopedia of Adolescence*, edited by R. J. R. Levesque, 1464–69. New York: Springer, 2014. Retrieved from http://link.springer.com/referenceworkentry/10.1007%2F978-1-4419-1695-2_261.

Friend, M., and W. Bursuck. *Including Students with Special Needs: A Practical Guide for Classroom Teachers*. Boston: Pearson, 2015.

Gallegos, J., et al. "Anxiety, Depression, and Coping Skills among Mexican School Children: A Comparison of Students With and Without Learning Disabilities." *Learning Disability Quarterly* 35 (2012) 54–61.

Hallahan, D. P., et al. *Exceptional Learners: An Introduction to Special Education*. 13th ed. Upper Saddle River, NJ: Pearson Education, 2015.

Hammen, C. "Adolescent Depression: Stressful Interpersonal Contexts and Risk for Recurrence." *Current Directions in Psychological Science* 18 (2012) 200–204. Retrieved from https://www.cnsforum.com/educationalresources/imagebank/brain_struc_anxiety/neuro_biol_gad.

Kauffman, J. M. *Characteristics of Emotional and Behavioral Disorders of Children and Youth*. 8th ed. Upper Saddle River, NJ: Merrill / Prentice Hall, 2006.

Mammarella, I. C., et al. "Anxiety and Depression in Children with Nonverbal Learning Disabilities, Reading Disabilities, or Typical Development." *Journal of Learning Disabilities* 49 (2016) 130–39.

Mannion, A., et al. "An Investigation of Comorbid Psychological Disorders, Sleep Problems, Gastrointestinal Symptoms and Epilepsy in Children and Adolescents with Autism Spectrum Disorder." *Research in Autism Spectrum Disorders* 7 (2013) 35–42.

Nagro, S. A. "PROSE Checklist: Strategies for Improving School-to-Home Written Communication." *Teaching Exceptional Children* 47 (2015) 256–63.

Newby, J. M., et al. "Internet Cognitive Behavioural Therapy for Mixed Anxiety and Depression: A Randomized Controlled Trial and Evidence of Effectiveness in Primary care." *Psychological Medicine* 43 (2013) 2635–48.

Nworie, B. C., ed. "Future Trends for Special Education: A Brief Overview." In *Central Issues in Special Education: Engaging Current Trends and Critical Issues in Contemporary Practice*, 275–76. Boston: Pearson, 2013.

Orinstein, A., et al. "Psychiatric Symptoms in Youth with a History of Autism and Optimal Outcome." *Journal of Autism and Developmental Disorders* 45 (2015) 3703–14.

Otto, Y., et al. "Parenting Behaviors of Mothers and Fathers of Preschool Age Children with Internalizing Disorders." *Journal of Child & Family Studies* 25 (2016) 381–95.

Reardon, T. C., et al. "Anxiety Disorders in Children and Adolescents with Intellectual Disability: Prevalence and Assessment." *Research in Developmental Disabilities* 36 (2015) 175–90.

Reilly, C., and R. Ballantine. "Epilepsy in School-Aged Children: More than Just Seizures?" *Support for Learning* 26 (2011) 144–51.

Salend, S. J. *Creating Inclusive Classrooms: Effective and Reflective Practices*. 8th ed. Boston: Pearson, 2016.

Scrutton, A. P. "Is Depression a Sin or a Disease? A Critique of Moralizing and Medicalizing Models of Mental Illness." *Journal of Religion, Disability & Health* 19 (2015) 285–311.

Selix, N. W., and D. Goyal. "Postpartum Depression among Working Women: A Call for Practice and Policy Change." *Journal for Nurse Practitioners* 11 (2015) 897–902

Siddique, I., et al. "Prevalence of Anxiety and Depression in Patients with Dissociative Disorders." *Journal of Pakistan Psychiatric Society* 12 (2015) 21–23.

Strang, J. F., et al. "Depression and Anxiety Symptoms in Children and Adolescents with Autism Spectrum Disorders without Intellectual Disability." *Research in Autism Spectrum Disorders* 6 (2012) 406–12.

Thomas, S. B., et al. *Public School Law: Teachers' and Students' Rights.* New York: Pearson, 2008.

Tietjen, G. E., et al. "Childhood Maltreatment and Migraine (Part II). Emotional Abuse as a Risk Factor for Headache Chronification." *Headache: Journal of Head & Face Pain* 50 (2010) 32–41.

Tietjen, G., and J. Khubchandani. "Depression Has Additive Effect on Headache Associated Pain Comorbidities." Paper presented at the 56th Annual Scientific Meeting, American Headache Society, Los Angeles, June 26–29, 2014.

Turnbull, A., et al. *Exceptional Lives: Special Education in Today's Schools.* 8th ed. Boston: Pearson, 2016.

Umbreit, J., et al. *Functional Behavioral Assessment and Function-Based Intervention: An Effective, Practical Approach.* Upper Saddle River, NJ: Merrill / Prentice Hall, 2007.

Vohra, R., et al. "Access to Services, Quality of Care, and Family Impact for Children with Autism, Other Developmental Disabilities, and Other Mental Health Conditions." *Autism: International Journal of Research and Practice* 18 (2014) 815–26.

Weed, K. Z. "Culturally Responsive Schooling." In *Azusa Pacific University English Language Learner and Diversity Manual,* edited by N. J. Thorsos and I. Yee-Sakamoto, 46–73. Boston: Pearson, 2007.

Wiener, J., and C. Y. Tardif. "Social and Emotional Functioning of Children with Learning Disabilities: Does Special Education Placement Make a Difference." *Learning Disabilities Research and Practice* 19 (2004) 20–32.

Yell, M. L. *The Law and Special Education.* 4th ed. Upper Saddle River, NJ: Pearson, 2016.

Zheng, Y., et al. "Foundations for Self-determination Perceived and Promoted by Families of Young Children with Disabilities in China." *Education and Training in Autism and Developmental Disabilities* 50 (2015) 109–22.

8

Three Models of Constructivist Learning Utilized by Jesus Christ

HeeKap Lee, PhD
Professor
Department of Education, Azusa Pacific University

and

Ie May Freeman, EdD
Assistant Professor
Department of Teacher Education, Azusa Pacific University

Abstract

CONSTRUCTIVISM IS A LEARNING theory that explains how learners construct knowledge and meaning from their experiences. In spite of confusion with the term constructivism, it is divided into three known categories: (1) inquiry-based learning (IBL); (2) discovery learning (DL); and (3) problem-solving based learning (PBL). This article deals with Jesus Christ's teaching utilizing the three modes of constructivist learning. This article also seeks to provide knowledge of each constructivist category in suitable learning environments.

Introduction

Every person who encountered Jesus Christ was amazed by his teachings. So what are the characteristics of his teaching? This article identifies the critical aspects of his teaching through the lens of constructivism. Three modes of constructivist teaching procedures and tactics are addressed. In addition, applicable ideas for the other educational settings will also be provided.

Characteristics of Jesus' Teaching

Teaching is the most universal and appreciated role of the Christian teaching ministry throughout the ages.[1] Jesus' major ministry while he was on the earth was to teach (Matt 26:55). Jesus asked his disciples to teach everything he had commanded them when ascended to heaven. His teaching was truly amazing as it showcased what effective teaching should look like. Pazmino pointed out the following five principles of Jesus' teaching practices: (1) Jesus' teaching was authoritative; (2) Jesus' teaching was not authoritarian; (3) Jesus' teaching encouraged people to think; (4) Jesus lived by what he taught; and (5) Jesus loved those whom he taught.[2]

Jesus' teaching purpose, method, target and outcome was very different from those of Jewish rabbis. His approach was to train his disciples to become fully like him (Luke 6:40) by changing their mindsets. It even prepared them to transform the world. This was different to that of the Jewish religious leaders who emphasized the dissemination of the law through recitation. Table 1 shows the basic differences between Jesus and the Jewish leaders' teaching styles.[3]

---

1. Nouwen, *Creative Ministry.*
2. Pazmino, *God Our Teacher,* 72–73.
3. Lee, "Jesus Teaching through Discovery."

Table 1. Comparison of the Teaching between Jewish Leaders and Jesus

	Jewish Leaders	Jesus
Purpose of teaching	Dissemination of information Remembering the Law	Teaching disciples to become fully like Jesus (Luke 6:40)
Teaching methods	Recitation, memorization Mouth-to-mouth	Reasoning (listening & questioning) Luke 2:46–47 Relations-oriented (heart-to-heart)
Teaching target	Behavioral change by observing customs and Laws	Integrating heart and behaviors, visible and invisible areas
Outcomes	Mastery of content	Transform their lives by applying the learning

Jesus stimulated his learners' internal motivation to learn through a variety of instructional strategies. The process of inquiry, questions, discovery, and parables was his main teaching method through which Jesus challenged his followers to apply what they learned. Upon reviewing the teaching methods that Jesus utilized, Lee concludes that Jesus provided constructivist pedagogical strategies. Constructivism is a new mode of education, which emphasizes that learners construct knowledge based upon their own backgrounds and prior experiences. What is learned cannot be separated from the context of where the learning took place. Duffy and Jonassen summarized it as a set of assumptions such as:

- The world is real, but structure is not a part of this reality;
- Meaning is imposed on the world by our experience;
- There are many ways to structure the world; many meanings or perspectives may be generated from the same data;
- None of the meanings are inherently correct; and
- Meaning is rooted in experience.[4]

Even constructivism has been readily accepted in the field of education over the last few decades, however, confusion has emerged with the term constructivism. Critics view it as an educational philosophy while

---

4. Duffy and Jonassen, "Continuing the Dialogue."

others adopt it as a learning theory. To clarify the term constructivism, the authors suggest the adoption of three constructivist modes based on the role of teacher/learners and the complexity of a task. These three modes are: inquiry-based learning (IBL), discovery learning (DL), and problem-based learning (PBL). Table 2 below depicts the summary of these three modes of constructivist learning.

Table 2. Three Modes of Constructivist Pedagogy

Modes	Role of Teacher/Learner	Task
Inquiry-based learning (IBL)	A teacher-centered individual inquiry process, learners are dependent on a teacher, but gain new understanding at the end of the inquiry.	The learning task is academic and instructional. It should be understood via an inquiry led by a teacher.
Discovery learning (DL)	A teacher-led individual inquiry, where learners are actively involved in the learning process. Through the inquiry process, the learners investigate the issues and propose viable solutions.	The learning task is either an instructional or real task brought by a learner.
Problem-solving based learning (PBL)	Learners-oriented problem-solving inquiry. A teacher introduces a real problem that is to be solved by the learners.	The learning task is a real, authentic task to be solved by students via collaboration.

The three modes of constructivism have their own purposes, implication processes, and evaluation strategies. The table 3 below depicts the general features of these three modes and explains it in detail. Table 3. Three Modes of Inquiry-Based Pedagogies

	Purpose	Process	Evaluation Method
IBL	Expanding the learner's knowledge through well-prepared questions by a teacher. Individualistic inquiry process. Learners understand new concepts, rules, and principles.	Connecting new concepts, information, and theories to previous knowledge sets. Leading questions from a slightly higher intellectual level than the learner's capacity (zone of proximal development).	Checking for understanding, learning evaluation.
DL	Transforming students' lives by challenging their worldview, value, and perspective through an inquiry process.	One to one, or group debate, educational tasks with reflective thinking procedures emphasized.	Students' self-realization/reflection, personal change by applying their learning.
PBL	Solving the real/authentic problems and issues.	Team/collaboration with the authentic tasks.	Problem-solving, peer-evaluation, self-reflection.

Three Modes of Constructivism Teaching and Learning

This section will explain the three modes of constructivist pedagogies, their general characteristics, and how Jesus used each effectively when he taught.

Inquiry-Based Learning (IBL)

A unique feature of Jesus' teaching lies in the major question he continually asks his students. They were as follows. "Have you understood?" (Matt 13:51) or "Are you still lacking in understanding?" (Matt 15:16), "Do you not yet understand?" (Matt 16:8), "Don't you understand?" (Mark 7:18; Mark 4:13).

Inquiry is a process to gain understanding by engaging students in open-ended and hands-on activities. A typical example of inquiry-based learning is the 5 E's that was adapted by Bybee in a science class.[5] The five stages of learning are identified as: Engaging, Exploring, Explaining, Elaborating, and Evaluating. During the engaging stage, students become mentally engaged by making connections between past and present learning experiences. In the exploring stage students identify concepts, processes,

---

5. Bybee, *Achieving Scientific Literacy*.

and skills through hands-on activities with the teacher's guidance. Following this is where students explain their understanding of concepts and processes. In the elaborating stage, students expound on their understanding of concepts and skills. They usually conduct additional activities that require an application of what was learned. In the last stage of evaluating, the teacher assesses students' understanding and abilities through formal and informal assessments. Formal assessments are identified as pre-diagnostic, formative and summative assessments. Informal assessments can be checking for students' understanding verbally or in written form.

Therefore, inquiry-based learning (IBL) is a teacher-led pedagogy where a teacher facilitates a set of questions in order to inspire students to think and learn critically. The purpose of IBL is to expand students' knowledge and skill through a well-designed inquiry process. The role of a teacher is to conduct organized questioning and challenge students to find the answer. Hence, the teacher may possess expert knowledge and facilitation skills to involve students in the learning process actively. Colburn identifies the characteristic behaviors of a teacher to initiate an effective IBL process as:

- asking open-ended, or divergent, questions;

- waiting a few seconds after asking the questions, giving students time to think;

- responding to students by repeating and paraphrasing what they have said without praise or criticism;

- avoiding telling students what to do, praising evaluation, or rejecting/ discouraging student ideas and behaviors; and maintaining a disciplined classroom.[6]

IBL is a practical teaching method in the Bible. As Paul clarifies in 1 Corinthians 2:14, students are able to understand when a spiritually discerning teacher instructs them in a carefully designed inquiry process. Jesus successfully led many inquiry-based learning sessions when he taught. A few examples included his teaching to the disciples on the road to Emmaus (Luke 24). Another examples were his instruction to Nicodemus in John 3; James and John (Mark 10:25–45); a Samaritan woman at the well (John 4); a paralyzed man at Bethesda (John 5); Peter (John 21 and Matt

---

6. Colburn, "Inquiry Primer," 44.

14:22–36); and Pilate (John 18). These purposeful interactions were identified as inquiry-based learning.

Jesus utilized a three-step inquiry process in his approach to teaching: (1) begin with an intriguing question; (2) lead contextualized inquiry; and (3) allow learners to explore new learning. Jesus would open up the conversation with a critical and engaging question. He asked a Samaritan woman, "Will you give me a drink?" (John 4:7). He asked an invalid at Bethesda, "Do you want to get well?" (John 5:6). He inquired of the disciples on the road to Emmaus, "What are you discussing together as you walk along?" (Luke 24:17). He began a conversation with Peter with the question, "Simon son of John, do you truly love me more than these?" (John 21:15). Like the Master, his disciples employed IBL as a main form of teaching. Phillip, one of seven deacons of the Jerusalem Church, taught an Ethiopian eunuch through a set of inquiry processes. He began by asking the eunuch, "Do you understand what you are reading?" (Acts 8:30).

During his ministry Jesus led the conversation while considering his students' backgrounds and contexts. Nicodemus was a member of the Sanhedrin. When Nicodemus came to him, Jesus initiated the conversation with the question, "You are Israel's teacher but do not understand these things?" (John 3:12).

IBL can be found with Jesus's approach with the Samaritan woman. He considered her agony in marrying five husbands. By utilizing inquiry-based teaching, he effectively shifted the direction of the conversation from her personal problems to that of worship. This topic was undoubtedly of genuine interest to her. Another example of IBL happened when Jesus met two discouraged disciples on the road to Emmaus. They thought Jesus had failed to redeem Israel. Jesus led the conversation by explaining what was said in all the scriptures concerning himself (Luke 24:27). The last example of contextualized questioning occurred with Peter one of Jesus' disciples. The Bible noted that Peter in deep distress for denouncing his master (Jesus) three times. Jesus restored him by asking him thrice, "Simon son of John, do you truly love me?" (John 21:15, 16, 17). His contextualized teaching resulted in learners being eager to acquire information that helped them answer questions, meet their needs, or help them cope with their situations.[7]

Inquiry-based learning had a powerful and effective impact on Jesus' audience. He allowed them to understand a deep meaning with their

7. Lee, "Jesus Teaching Through Discovery."

hearts. The disciples on the road to Emmaus said, "Were not our hearts burning within us while [Jesus] talked with us on the road and opened the Scriptures to us?" (Luke 24:32). The Samaritan woman learned about the concept of real worship in spirit and truth. Peter now realized the true meaning of being his disciple after Jesus commanded, "Follow me" (John 21:19). The ultimate goal of IBL is to inspire students to recognize new concepts and experiences.

In a structured inquiry, the teacher provides students with a question or instructional task to investigate as well as the procedures and materials. The teacher doesn't inform them of the expected outcomes.[8] Rather than simply making declarative statements about truth, Jesus posed questions that held within them startling answers. It is critical for teachers to contextualize the inquiry process and possess effective facilitation skills. Teachers need to initiate conversations in a well-organized format along with carefully asking their students to consider new ways of seeing the truth.[9] Throughout the inquiry process, the purpose of learning is to understand things that are hard to comprehend and easy to misconstrue.

Discovery Learning (DL)

In inquiry-based learning (IBL), a teacher leads the inquiry process by motivating students to answer questions. It is a teacher-centered format where the instructor's facilitation skills are highly emphasized. In the inquiry process, students understand new concepts, principles and regulations. However, it is different to that of discovery learning which is a type of inductive reasoning in which students move from studying specific examples to formulating general rules, concepts and principles.[10] It is an internal shift in the students' frame of reference. Piaget said that understanding comes from discovery and that without understanding production and creativity are lost.[11]

In discovery learning, students are asked to review their perspectives, values, and worldviews. Bruner believes that students must be active by identifying key principles for themselves rather than simply accepting

---

8. Colburn, "Inquiry Primer."

9. Schultz and Schultz, *Why Nobody Learns*.

10. Schunk, *Learning Theories*.

11. Piaget, *To Understand Is to Invent*.

teacher explanations.[12] Students realize a new way of learning that will replace a consciousness dominated by the hegemony of conventional wisdom.[13] Bicknell-Holmes and Hoffman identify three main attributes such as:

- Through exploration and problem-solving students create, integrate, and generalize knowledge;
- Student driven, interest-based activities which the student determines the sequence and frequency;
- Activities to encourage integration of new knowledge into the learners' existing knowledge base.[14]

Discovery learning usually takes several steps including hypothesis generation, experiment design, data analysis and prediction.[15] Throughout discovery process, students gain a new way of understanding that replaced a consciousness dominated by conventional wisdom.[16] That is why Jesus employed discovery learning when he taught. He utilized discovery learning for instilling a transformation of perception in his listeners by exploring and reorganizing their worldviews, mindsets or values.

Several cases that Jesus implemented discovery learning are found in the Bible. For example, Jesus mentioned the story of the prodigal son (Luke 15:11–32) as a typical example of discovery. Through a set of discovery processes, Jesus challenged the learners' narrow and legalistic worldview. He helped them to gain a new grace-based perspective. This worldview included loving all pagans and sinners. It was about a humble sinner who was favored by God over the one who self-righteously adhered to the dictates of custom and law. Jesus tried to teach that the father does not judge his son's errant behavior by conventional standards. The father compassionately and unconditionally welcomed him home.

Another example where Jesus employed the discovery learning was the story of the Good Samaritan. This story was told in response to the question, "Who is my neighbor?" The traditional definition of a neighbor to the Jews only included their fellow Israelites because they were known

---

12. Bruner, "Act of Discovery."

13. Wanak, "Jesus' Questions," 168.

14. Bicknell-Holmes and Hoffman, "Elicit, Engage, Experience, Explore."

15. Njoo and De Jong, "Exploratory Learning with a Computer Simulation."

16. Wanak, "Jesus' Questions."

as descendants of Abraham. Rather than offering the answer, Jesus challenged the conventional definition of a neighbor by sharing the story of a Samaritan who has become a long-time enemy of Israelites. Jesus invited his listeners to distance themselves from the rules and roles of traditional wisdom. Even a Samaritan can be considered a neighbor.

The discovery learning that Jesus employed usually took three stages: unlearning (forgetting the old wisdom), learning (adopting the new way of thinking), and relearning (stabilizing new learning to their future lives) based on an organizational development theory suggested by Lewin.[17] First, Jesus challenged his audience by framing a question that brings a degree of disequilibrium or cognitive dissonance (unlearning stage). In order to confront traditional teachings, Jesus communicated a story, parable, or allegory. This made the audience reflect on their principles and beliefs learned from their forefathers or traditional wisdoms. When Jesus told the prodigal's son story, it made the audience rethink the old Jewish convention which was to confront their conventional thoughts that that only Jews are chosen as God's people. His hidden intention of sharing the story of the Good Samaritan was to convict the audience who were mainly Jews to part with traditional thoughts. They adhered to the notion that only the healthy and wealthy have allowed to participate in the kingdom of God. Through this kind of discovery learning, Jesus challenged people to realign their thinking and cultural patterns with the kingdom of God. The paradigm shifted from worldly thinking to divine wisdom.[18] The point of Jesus' discovery learning methods was to transform viewpoints and perspectives from a life based on conventional wisdom to a life centered on God.

Throughout the discovery learning process, audiences achieved a deeper level of understanding from Jesus' teachings. After sharing the story of the Good Samaritan, the teacher of the law now learned who was the neighbor to the man who fell into the hands of robbers (Luke 10:36). A neighbor can be anyone who helps the Jews regardless of custom, tradition, and/or nationality. The teacher of the law sparked a paradigm shift about the treatment of neighbors. This type of inquiry process is indirect. At no time did Jesus force the audience to accept his ideas, values and perspective. Throughout this process, the audience discovered insights and spiritual discernment. This allowed them to change their thinking by gaining a new perspective. Finally, Jesus asked his audience to apply what they have

17. Lewin, "Group Decisions and Social Change."
18. Wanak, "Jesus' Questions."

learned. After explaining the parable of the Good Samaritan, Jesus encouraged the expert of the law to apply what he had learned, saying to him, "Go and do likewise" (Luke 10:37).

Is there any limitation to discovery learning? A possible concern is that not all students may understand all the new concepts. In order for discovery of learning to be successful, learners need to understand the domain at a higher level than when the necessary information is just presented by a teacher or an expository learning environment.[19] That's why all of Jesus' followers might not understand the meaning of his teaching through discovery unless he was asked. He didn't pursue followers and make sure they understood what he meant. In tying this in to the inquiry process, students "may be ever seeing but never perceiving, and ever hearing but never understanding" (Mark 4:12). To grasp the structure of information, a shift should be made in the teacher's conception of planning for exploration rather than to achieve a set of predetermined, observable outcomes.[20] The teacher presents examples and the students work with them until they discover the interrelationships. Learning takes place through inductive reasoning.

Problem-solving Based Learning (PBL)

Problem-based learning (PBL) is the highest level of inquiry-based learning in which teachers instruct students using authentic tasks and real problems. Therefore, this form of learning requires teachers to be equipped with high levels of knowledge and communication skills to handle real problems. The key characteristics of PBL involve teamwork, communication skills, problem-solving capacities, and analytical/creative competencies. It also centers around individual research.[21]

Parnes identifies six stages of creative problem-solving learning such as: (1) objective-finding; (2) fact-finding; (3) problem-finding; (4) idea-finding; (5) solution-finding; and (6) acceptance-finding.[22]

What makes problem-based learning different? Students tackle authentic, ambiguous, open-ended problems that may have many potential solutions. Students plan, organize, and evaluate during the problem solving

19. Van Joolingen, "Cognitive Tools for Discovery Learning."
20. Hammer, "Discovery Learning and Discovery Teaching."
21. Wood, "ABC of Learning and Teaching in Medicine."
22. Parnes, *Source Book for Creative Problem-Solving.*

process.[23] In addition, students become engaged in the problem-solving process in teams. Learning objectives are formulated through consensus. Students divide into teams. Each team is responsible for handling a part of the problem. They identify what is known, what information is needed, and what strategies or steps to take. The teachers' role in PBL is to model high-order process skills while probing for student understanding. Checking for students' understanding and assessing group achievement is the final approach.

There are many cases where Jesus implemented PBL in the Bible. This is found when Jesus asked his disciples to preach the gospel by sending them two by two (Matt 10:1; Mark 6:7). He gave a clear mission (problem) to his disciples saying, "Preach the message . . . heal the sick, raise the dead, cleanse those who have leprosy, drive out demons" (Matt 10:7–8). The twelve disciples were trained for public ministry before being sent out by Jesus. They were taught the doctrines and witnessed his miracles. Now, Jesus provided the real, authentic tasks to solve in teams. Again, Jesus sent seventy-two disciples to a mission field (Luke 10:1). The disciples successfully implemented the mission work and returned. They reported to Jesus, saying, "Lord, even the demons submit to us in your name" (Luke 10:17).

Another example of PBL occurred when Jesus asked the disciples to feed five thousand people on a mountainside (John 6). Feeding this vast amount of people seemed daunting, as there was little food to provide. However, before performed his miracle of feeding them, Jesus intentionally posed the problem of feeding the hungry crowd to the disciples. Phillip claimed the task as impossible. All twelve disciples didn't give up on this idea and began to discuss strategies. Only Andrew attempted to deal with the problem by presenting a boy's small lunch. Even though the disciples did not solve the situation successfully, they learned that Jesus is a prophet who is to come into the world (John 6:14). Finally, before Jesus ascended to heaven he asked all his disciples to go and make disciples of all nations (Matt 28:19). All of the disciples obeyed their master's command preaching the gospel in all locations.

PBL is the highest level of learning. It prepares students to be equipped with advanced skills and competencies. This can help them handle difficult situations. Jesus affirms the place of PBL learning when difficult problems are faced or perplexing questions are raised. In such cases, learners are encouraged to seek solutions for themselves by communicating with each

23. Wood, "ABC of Learning and Teaching in Medicine."

other. Teamwork and collaboration are essential in PBL. Students come together to exchange ideas, articulate their problems, and construct meanings that make sense to them.

When and How to Use Each Mode of Constructivism Pedagogies?

Each mode of constructivism has unique strengths that might be applied to other educational contexts. Inquiry-based learning may fit into a task where a teacher wants students to understand a new concept, principle, or theory by providing a well-processed question and answer session. While leading an inquiry, teachers ask questions to check for students' understanding. Inquiry-based learning is beneficial to students who are not ready for a self-directed learning process yet. A teacher or mentor may scaffold them by facilitating a well-designed question-and-answer session.

Discovery learning is valuable when a teacher desires students to gain new insights and in-depth meaning of a theory or principle. This is accomplished by exploring their worldview, perspective and values. Internal reflections and intuitive insights are gained through the discovery process. Even though teachers lead the discovery process, students become active participants in learning by exploring concepts. They can answer their own questions through testing and experience. Discovery learning is most successful when students have prerequisite knowledge. Students are involved with meaningful experiences.

PBL is a powerful option if a teacher wants students to solve a problem collaboratively. The focus is on the learner. Students collect data, discuss intervention strategies, and solve a real problem. Students are equipped with a high level of knowledge and competencies in order to solve the problem. The role of a teacher is to serve as facilitator or a resource provider. Teachers can provide tips every now and then if need be.

How do we use these three modes of constructivism? When students are dealing with a simple learning task, inquiry-based learning should be implemented under a teacher's leadership. For students to solve a moderately complex problem, a teacher can provide discovery learning. Problem-solving learning is probably the best option if the task is very complicated. Of course, the students should be relatively advanced in critical thinking skills. How do we evaluate the successful implementation of these three modes of teaching? The table below is the summary of evaluation strategies for each mode of constructivist teaching.

Table 4. Three Modes of Constructivism: The Characteristics

	Role of Assessor	Assessment Method	Areas to Be Assessed
IBL	Checking for understanding	Questions, survey, essay	Cognitive domains
DL	Exploring the deep meaning of the hidden wisdom Meaning-making	Interview, observation, self-reflection	Invisible area: mindset, values and worldview
PBL	Help students monitor themselves, provide hints, facilitate students	Self-assessment Peer-evaluation Evaluated by real-world assessment	Applied competence, critical thinking, PB, communicative competency, collaborative/ leadership competency

Concluding Remarks

Jesus was the epitome of an outstanding teacher. He effectively connected with his audiences by utilizing all three modes of constructivism: inquiry-based learning (IBL); discovery learning (DL); and problem-based learning (PBL). These three modes have their own strengths in the classroom. For maximum learning to take place, teachers need to discern when it is feasible to execute these models.

Bibliography

Bicknell-Holmes, T., and P. S. Hoffman. "Elicit, Engage, Experience, Explore: Discovery Learning in Library Instruction." *Reference Services Review* 28 (2000) 313–22.

Bruner, J. S. "The Act of Discovery." *Harvard Educational Review* 31 (1961) 21–32.

Bybee, R. W. *Achieving Scientific Literacy: From Purposes to Practical Action.* Portsmouth, NH: Heinemann, 1997.

Colburn, A. "An Inquiry Primer." *Science Scope* 22 (2000) 42–44.

Duffy, T. M., and D. H. Jonassen. "Continuing the Dialogue: An Introduction to This Special Issue." *Educational Technology* 32 (1991) 9–11.

Hammer, D. "Discovery Learning and Discovery Teaching." *Cognition and Instruction* 15 (1997) 485–529.

Lee, H. "Jesus' Teaching Model and Its Embedded Constructivist Principles." In *Faith-Based Education That Constructs*, edited by H. Lee, 71–83. Eugene, OR: Wipf & Stock, 2010.

———. "Jesus Teaching through Discovery." *International Christian Community for Teacher Education Journal* 1 (2006). http://www.icctejournal.org/ICCTEJournal/past-issues/volume-1-issue-2/jesus-teaching-through discovery.

Lewin, Kurt. "Group Decisions and Social Change." In *Readings in Social Psychology*, edited by E. E. Maccobby et al., 330–44. New York: Holt, Rinehart & Winston, 1958.

Njoo, M., and T. de Jong. "Exploratory Learning with a Computer Simulation for Control Theory: Learning Processes and Instructional Support." *Journal of Research in Science Teaching* 30 (1993) 821–44.

Nouwen, H. M. *Creative Ministry*. Los Angeles: Image, 1971.

Parnes, S. J. *Source Book for Creative Problem-Solving: A Fifty Year Digest of Proven Innovation Processes*. Buffalo, NY: Creative Education Foundation, 1992.

Pazmino, R. W. *God Our Teacher: Theological Basics in Christian Education*. Ada, MI: Baker Academic, 2001.

Piaget, J. *To Understand Is to Invent*. New York: Grossman, 1973.

Schultz, T., and J. Schultz. *Why Nobody Learns Much of Anything at Church: And How to Fix It*. Loveland, CO: Group, 1993.

Schunk, D. H. *Learning Theories: An Educational Perspective*. 4th ed. Cranbury, NJ: Pearson Education, 2004.

Van Joolingen, W. "Cognitive Tools for Discovery Learning." *International Journal of Artificial Intelligence in Education* 10 (1999) 385–97.

Wanak, L. "Jesus' Questions." *Evangelical Review of Theology* 33 (2009) 167–78.

Warden, M. D. *Extraordinary Results from Ordinary Teachers: Learning to Teach as Jesus Taught*. Loveland, CO: Group, 1998.

Wood, D. F. "ABC of Learning and Teaching in Medicine: Problem Based Learning." *British Medical Journal* 3 (2003) 213–16.

Authors' Notes

HeeKap Lee, PhD, is a professor in the Department of Teacher Education at Azusa Pacific University. He may be contacted via hlee@apu.edu.

Ie May Freeman, EdD, is an assistant professor in the Department of Teacher Education at Azusa Pacific University. You may contact her at ifreeman@apu.edu.

9

Integrating Faith in Teacher Education Pedagogy and Scholarship

A Personal Story and Reflective Discourse

Chinaka S. DomNwachukwu, PhD

Professor of Multicultural Education and Associate Dean of Diversity and Values
School of Education, Azusa Pacific University

Introduction

EFFECTIVE FAITH INTEGRATION DEMANDS a competent professional practice that is balanced by an effective infusion of faith and sound theological and doctrinal foundations. Faith integration is not just how we share our faith in our disciplines, but how we communicate the important topics, issues, and principles of our disciplines to our students using solid theological foundations through application of the Christian worldview and values. My faith integration experience and activities have expanded and increased as my roles in the academic setting have changed over the years.

In this essay I share the process by which I have integrated faith in two areas of practice within the university setting: teaching and scholarship. I provide both the scholarly and theological basis for faith integration in each area with the goal of clearly distinguishing the independent process of faith integration within each area. I will reflect on how my faith informs my practice as well as how my practice informs my faith.

Faith Integration in Teaching

One of the courses I teach—Teaching and Cultural Diversity—has been a perfect course, as a professor of teacher education, to tap into the integral relationships which exist between Christian faith and human knowledge, particularly as expressed in my academic discipline of teacher education.[1] This course focuses on preparing beginning level teachers with the skills and competencies needed to effectively meet the needs of students from diverse ethnic, socio-cultural, and linguistic backgrounds. As I teach, my faith integration focus has been to help my students develop a perspective of teaching in a diverse setting, with underlying assumptions that are based on sound biblical perspectives and evangelical Christian values. To accomplish these goals, the class is required to read two important materials, among many others. The first is Lederhouse's "Dual Citizenship" article and the second is a combination of two documents that include President George W. Bush's and President Bill Clinton's statements on prayer in schools. These two documents are archived on the US Department of Education website.

Starting with these government papers, my class engages in a discussion of the challenge of religion in the context of the public school classroom, which is usually the "elephant in the room." Many of my students come to class believing that it is illegal to mix their faith with their practice as teachers. A critical study of these government documents highlights to these new teachers the freedoms we have as teachers and the freedoms our students have to practice their faith even within the four walls of public schools. Like all of the freedoms Americans enjoy, there are limitations. We address the limitations that exist as part of the demands of our democratic system, and discuss how those limitations deserve our respect as Christian professionals and practitioners who operate within a democratic society. After we have clearly identified both the freedoms and limitations, the context is set for these beginning teachers to go beyond the "dos and don'ts" of religion in schools to engage with their own roles and practices as educators from a Christian perspective. Lederhouse's article is a qualitative

1. Cf. Haskar, "Faith-Learning Integration."

study of three teachers who are professing evangelicals. The study builds upon an article titled "Worldview, Modernity, and the Task of Christian College Education."[2] Lederhouse examined how a Christian worldview influences a teacher's "educational philosophy, sense of identity, and the nature of classroom ethos the teacher seeks to establish."[3] Students read the article at home and on the second day of class we analyze it and identify the critical issues raised by the article that relate to our profession and the Christian worldview. For the rest of the course, these documents form the theoretical basis for engaging a variety of questions about the intersection of the teaching profession and the Christian worldview. Some of the questions we address through the subsequent weeks include the following:

1. *How can evangelical Christian teachers reconcile and balance their sometimes theologically conservative beliefs with their work in the increasingly liberal and pluralistic atmosphere of the American public school?* This question allows these beginning teachers to confront the fact that some of them are often too conservative for an increasing liberal educational setting. They are brought to a place where they are able to understand the need to be respectful of differences, while at the same time not compromising their faith and values.

2. *How do your core beliefs, or worldviews, make claims on other dimensions of your life and influence your choices and professional practice?* Again this question leads us to engage the fact that regardless of how much people claim that they are religiously unbiased, most people come to the educational setting with some type of religious bias. Identifying and dealing with these biases allows them to better serve all students in their classrooms.

3. *Considering the pedagogical issues of classroom management, instructional planning, and delivery, how does your faith speak to or lead you to deal with these facets of your professional practices and behaviors?* The focus here is helping these teachers to articulate positive philosophies of teaching that can be anchored on their faith traditions and the Christian worldview.

While these questions and many others guide our conversations about the extent to which our faith speaks to our practices and vice versa, I have

2. Walsh, "Worldview, Modernity, and the Task of Christian College Education."
3. Lederhouse, "Dual Citizenship," 12–13.

another activity that runs parallel to the conversations. As mentioned earlier, a primary focus of this course is on preparing beginning-level teachers to meet the needs of all students in their classrooms—especially students with disabilities, non-native English language speakers, and students from diverse cultural, religious, and socio-economic backgrounds. I have found my student teachers to more easily connect with the demands to meet the students in the K–12 classrooms at their points of need when viewed from the perspective of what I have termed the "shepherding pedagogy." This exercise is a blend of spiritual devotionals and reflections on teaching practices anchored on Psalm 23. Each reading introduces a piece from the psalm combined with pedagogical issues that overlap with our Christian values. It identifies pedagogical practices that are anchored on Christian values that each teacher candidate reflects on and writes responses to how these practices could inform their educational activities.

In another course, Senior Seminar: Education and Professional Ethics, which targets undergraduate students who are preparing to enter the teaching profession, the focus is on teaching and professional ethics. The primary texts for this course are:

- Sproul, R. C. *Lifeviews*. Grand Rapids: Revell, 1995.
- Colson, C., and R. George. *Doing the Right Thing*. Grand Rapids: Zondervan, 2011.
- Dean, K. C. *Almost Christian*. Oxford: Oxford University Press, 2010.

Sproul's book contrasts secular worldviews with the Christian worldview. It addresses such topics as existentialism, pragmatism, pluralism, and relativism. It engages a variety of contemporary issues that stretch and challenge the Christian worldview. Dean's book focuses on an analysis of the faith of an average American Christian teen and what Dean calls their "watered down faith." The text contrasts contemporary Christian culture with true Christian faith. Colson and George's book is actually a six-part book on Christian ethics. These materials combine to provide my students strong literary and practical bases to engage the Christian worldview and articulate how it should shape their professional practices as they go into the world upon graduation. This class, which is conducted using the Socratic dialogue approach, stretches the worldviews of graduating seniors and often pushes them to better articulate their positions on essential issues that challenge the Christian worldview such as homosexuality, abortion, and other controversial topics. The goal of this class is to prepare "students to understand and express a Christian perspective on issues critical to the education profession" and to help them define who they are as Christians and professionals with the goal that they will be enabled through intense dialogue and a variety of writing assignments to purposefully establish a link between their faith and their intended professions.

Challenges

The challenges I have faced with the course on education and cultural diversity relate to the fact that it is a graduate-level class and the population is more diverse than in the undergraduate program. A good number of students in the class are often non-Christians or are Roman Catholics. The evangelical Christian worldview does not readily appeal to some of these individuals and there is often a struggle to justify to them the relevance of these exercises and the rationale for placing a demand on them to engage in faith integration exercises. I have had to find ways to explain to these graduate students that it is important to our Christian institution that they are familiar with our faith positions and values so that as they graduate and enter the professional setting, their fidelity to the institution as their alma mater can be demonstrated as they uphold the values and ethical principles that make our institution unique. I take time to explain to them that we are not interested in producing degrees but rather we want to produce difference makers who can positively impact their communities. In the undergraduate class, the challenge has been to ensure that the conversations are not overwhelmingly religious and theological and at the same time ensure that the core educational issues and principles that form the main focus of the course remain at the center of the conversations for students to view the course as an academic (rather than a theology) course that focuses on teacher education.

Faith Integration in Scholarship

In 2009 I published a chapter in the book *Doing Good and Departing from Evil*, edited by Carol Lambert. My chapter was titled "Through the Eyes of Faith: The Mandate of Teacher Goodness." The goal of the chapter was to provide a theological basis for teachers to conceptualize their practices as a divine mandate. The goal was to compel teachers to begin to see teaching as more than just a profession, but as a vocation.

In the chapter I engaged the concept of goodness: the idea of education as the highest good along with the concept of teacher goodness. I shared data from a study I conducted among teachers, using a focus group. The study asked these teachers from an urban Southern California school to describe a good teacher and identify the characteristics that set good teachers apart. Findings from that focus group study revealed certain attributes that they saw as essential in good teachers. Using these findings as the basis, I engaged the idea of teacher goodness from three theological streams: Jewish, Islamic, and Christian. The study revealed that within these three religious traditions, the idea of teacher goodness finds very strong theological footing, but more so in the Christian faith as exemplified in the person of Christ, who took delight in being called a teacher (rabbi). This makes faith integration in the teaching field a seamless endeavor.

Recently I coauthored a book with a colleague titled *Multiculturalism: A Shalom Motif for the Christian Community*. In that book we engaged around the ways the Christian community has not only resisted the idea of multiculturalism, but has often argued against it. We presented ways in which the Bible lends credence to the discipline of multicultural education and also presented ways in which we see our discipline speaking to our faith in a language that can not only enhance its effect and credibility in the world, but also makes it more kingdom minded. This is possibly one of my best efforts at faith integration in scholarship. As I move forward in my teaching and research, I am continuing to explore biblical principles that make service and social justice more appealing to my discipline. Books like Henri Nouwen's *In the Name of Jesus: Reflections on Christian Leadership* introduce another dimension which speaks to Christian leaders in either educational or other settings. The field is wide open and we have yet to scratch the surface.

Personal Reflections on Faith Integration in Teaching and Scholarship

A major challenge of faith integration in my teaching comes in the nature of diversity within our graduate student population. As mentioned earlier, a good number of my graduate students are not Christians and those who are Christians are not all from the evangelical tradition, which makes it challenging to connect with them on the intersection of the teacher education discipline and Christian faith. Those of the non-Christian tradition sometimes feel that faith issues are out place, and in some cases they make comments in their course evaluations that they do not see the benefit of faith integration activities since they do not share the Christian worldview. The reality is that these are legitimate concerns from the individuals who come to our Christian institution not because of our faith values but because of the quality of education we have to offer or the appropriateness of our programs to meet their academic needs. As a professor, I am therefore compelled to explore ways to present the Christian worldview in non-threatening and academically appealing ways. This has led to a continuous study and experimentation on ways I can directly connect the academic content and skill sets in my courses to expose my teacher candidates to the Christian values and worldview issues that we consider important for all our graduates to leave with. In my cultural diversity class this has been quite effective, as I have realized how effectively Christian worldviews on love of neighbor, caring for aliens and the destitute, and the issues of immigration, equity, poverty and social justice have sound biblical bases that anyone who is committed to those issues can easily identify with. I have learned to present these diversity issues in ways that speak directly to the disconnect that exists in the church today, and using biblical references I have made a strong case on how the discipline of multicultural education appeals directly to biblical principles that Christians should already be familiar with and which non-Christians should have no problem endorsing if they are going to be effective multicultural educators. I have discovered that when the ways in which diversity speaks to the Christian faith are presented as critical inquiry, non-Christian students are attracted to engage in this discourse with a healthier spirit.

Conclusion

Faith integration activities in any field, including education, psychology, mathematics, and sciences, must be seen as a journey. It is a journey characterized by twists and turns as one must balance academic integrity, respect for individual freedom and human dignity, and the faith foundations of your institution. All of these must, however, become opportunities for personal and professional growth for the Christian professor. People who come to teach in faith-based institutions must appreciate the fact that there is a fundamental difference between Christian institutions and secular institutions. While our professional academic classes must not be transformed into Sunday school classes, we have a mandate to permeate what we do with our Christian values and worldview issues in ways that are more visible and more measurable than are possible in any secular settings. Faith integration is a journey, not a destination. The more we engage it, the more we discover who we are intellectually, spiritually, and socially. We will never arrive, but we can continue to grow.

Bibliography

Colson, C., and R. George. *Doing the Right Thing*. Grand Rapids: Zondervan, 2011.

Dean, K. C. *Almost Christian*. Oxford: Oxford University Press, 2010.

De Pree, M. *Leading Without Power*. Holland, MI: Shepherd, 1997.

DomNwachukwu, C. S. "Through the Eyes of Faith: The Mandate of Teacher Goodness." In *Doing Good, Departing from Evil: Research Findings in the Twenty-First Century*, edited by Carol J. Lambert, 89–112. New York: Lang, 2009.

Hagberg, J. O. *Real Power: Stages of Personal Power in Organizations*. Salem, WI: Sheffield, 1994.

Hasker, W. "Faith-Learning Integration: An Overview." *Christian Scholar's Review* 21 (1992) 234–38.

Lederhouse, J. N. "Dual Citizenship: Can Christians Still Teach in Today's Public Schools?" In *Nurturing Reflective Teachers: A Christian Approach for the 21st Century*. Proceedings of the Third Biennial Symposium for Christian Professional Education Faculty, April 1998, Wheaton College, Illinois, 1999.

Palmer, P. J. *The Courage to Teach*. San Francisco: Wiley, 1998.

Sproul, R. C. *Lifeviews*. Grand Rapids: Revell, 1995.

Walsh, B. "Worldview, Modernity, and the Task of Christian College Education." *Faculty Dialogue* 18 (1992) 1–29.

Wilkes, C. G. *Jesus on Leadership*. Wheaton, IL: Tyndale, 1998.

10

Jesus, Justice, and Special Education Inclusion

A Case for the Shalom Model of Inclusion

Ben Nworie, PhD, MDiv
Professor of Special Education
School of Education, Biola University

and

June Hetzel, PhD
Professor and Dean
School of Education, Biola University

Abstract

This chapter is a theoretical discourse that proposes a justice-infused, biblically based special education inclusion model, the Shalom Model of Inclusion. After discussing justice, inclusion, incarnationality, the Hebrew concept of shalom, and agape love which form the foundational thinking for the proposed Shalom Model of Inclusion, the authors introduce the central concept of imago Dei and the four domains of the Shalom Model of Inclusion which are: shared curriculum experience, shared strengths and needs, effective and differentiated pedagogy, as well as community and collaborative praxis. The model is illustrated with the love, compassion and collaboration shared in the L'Arche communities where disabilities, instead of being viewed negatively as problems to be solved, are viewed as gifts, and opportunities to learn new ways to love, to be faithful, to live together in recognition of the naturalness and goodness of difference, as well as discover the importance of weakness and vulnerability. L'Arche tangibly demonstrates the practicality and effectiveness of shalom inclusion.

Keywords: justice, inclusion, special education, love, shalom

Introduction

If the practice of special education inclusion continues based on best practices as we know it, that is, our best human ideology, knowledge, and skills, etc., it will bring about *some* beneficial outcomes. However, even though we will see *minor* benefits, we will continue to get exactly what we have been getting—that is, lower educational outcomes in comparison with general education,[1] litigations,[2] teacher attrition,[3] lack of love and justice from the Christian perspective (1 Cor 13:2–3, 8–9; 2 Cor 5:19), and lack of human flourishing. On the other hand, if we conduct special education inclusion based on best practices of the finest human ideology, knowledge, and skills, in combination with Jesus' model of love and justice as seen through the healing miracles and demonstrated existentially and pedagogically by him, then we will realize a system of special education inclusion that is wholesome, biblically based, and characteristic of shalom. The proposed Shalom Model of Inclusion will be characterized by positive and measurable educational outcomes; less litigation; more thriving practitioners, who teach not only out of a sense of obligation, but out of a sense of vocational calling to shalom; and flourishing students who experience love, justice, and shalom demonstrated by their teachers, and service providers.

This chapter is a proposal for a paradigm shift in the practice of special education inclusion. The basic idea of inclusive special education, as it is

1. Bremer et al., "Public Reporting."

2. Yell, *Law and Special Education* (3rd ed); Pudelski, "Rethinking the Special Education Due Process System"; Minnesota Department of Education, "Special Education Litigation Costs Report."

3. Mamlin, *Preparing Effective Special Education Teachers.*

currently understood in schools, is the practice of educating children with and without disabilities in the same setting, which is usually understood to be the general education setting.[4] Some essential components of the proposed Shalom Model of Inclusion, which are often missing in the traditional setting include acceptance (which encompasses the biblical concept of justice), innovative curriculum design, belonging (which incorporates the biblical idea of love), and community.[5]

This chapter is a theoretical discourse that proposes a move from current conventional special education models of inclusion, to a more dynamic, incarnational and biblically based special education inclusion model, the Shalom Model of Inclusion. After discussing justice and inclusion, the concept of incarnationality, the Hebrew concept of shalom, and the concept of agape love, which form the foundational thinking for the proposed model, the Shalom Model of Inclusion, will be introduced. Following this foundational discussion, the four domains of the Shalom Model of Inclusion—shared curriculum experience, shared strengths and needs, effective and differentiated pedagogy, and community and collaborative praxis—will be examined, along with the central concept of imago Dei. The Shalom Model of Inclusion, is illustrated with the love, compassion and collaboration shared in the L'Arche communities where disabilities, instead of being viewed negatively as problems to be solved, are viewed as gifts, and opportunities to learn new ways to love, to be faithful, to live together in recognition of the naturalness and goodness of difference, as well as discover the importance of weakness and vulnerability. Our conclusion will be that L'Arche tangibly demonstrates the practicality and effectiveness of Shalom inclusion.

Foundational Concepts

The Shalom Model of Inclusion foundationally encompasses the concepts of justice, inclusion, incarnationality, shalom, and agape love.

---

4. Hallahan et al., *Exceptional Learners*; Salend, Creating Inclusive Classrooms.

5. Salend, *Creating Inclusive Classrooms*; Gargiulo, *Special Education in Contemporary Society.*

Justice

According to the *Oxford Dictionary*, justice is to do, treat, or represent with due fairness or appreciation. As a noun, it is the quality of being fair and reasonable. Justice means giving each person what he or she deserves. It is something everyone seems to desire for themselves. Here is a good illustration of the meaning of justice. Heather and Mark were living comfortable, safe lives, yet they became concerned about the most vulnerable, poor, and marginalized members of society, and they made long term personal sacrifices in order to serve the interests, needs and cause of those other people. That according to the Bible is what it means to "do justice."[6]

Justice *(mishpat)* in the Old Testament combines the abilities both to judge and to acquit which emanate from God.[7] In other words, justice in the Old Testament illustrates the idea of the juxtaposition of God's law against God's love. By abiding in love, we allow the justice *(mishpat)* of God to prevail in our lives.[8] As the Bible clearly teaches, *"The one who abides in love, abides in God and God abides in him"* (1 John 4:16b).

Inclusion

Most dictionaries define inclusion as being really and truly an insider. In the educational context, it is being actively and essentially a part of the regular education curriculum. It refers to educating students with disabilities in general education settings.[9] Inclusive education is to create a fair, collaborative, supportive, and nurturing learning environment for all students.

The federal law that regulates special education practice in the United States, the Individuals with Disabilities Education Act (IDEA), mandates the education of every child with a disability in the least restrictive environment (LRE), which means educating them in settings as close to the regular class as possible where an appropriate program can be provided, and where the child can make satisfactory educational progress.[10]

6. Keller, *Generous Justice.*

7. Doty, *Eden's Bridge.*

8. Ibid.

9. Heward, *Exceptional Children*; Salend, *Creating Inclusive Classrooms* (7th ed.); Gargiulo, *Special Education in Contemporary Society.*

10. Heward, *Exceptional Children.*

Though the concept of inclusion grew out of mainstreaming and shares many of its philosophical goals and implementation strategies, inclusion is different from mainstreaming. In mainstreaming, a special needs student is temporarily placed in a general education classroom for content instruction at a time that the student's individualized education plan (IEP) team thinks that the student will be successful. Students in mainstream placements are "pulled out" for services or for direct instruction in a more restrictive special education classroom. In full inclusion, on the other hand, a special needs child is placed in a general education classroom 100 percent of his/her day. The student's services and service providers all go to that classroom to assist the student in being successful. Inclusion in this full sense is not right for every student. The decision for a full or partial inclusion placement rests with the student's individualized education plan (IEP) team. For maximum benefit, inclusion must, therefore, be decided on an individualized basis.[11]

Including special education students in the general education population has obvious benefits to it. That is why "most educators favor some degree of integration of students with disabilities with nondisabled students."[12] There seem to be no detrimental effects or significant loss of instructional time due to the presence of a student with severe disability.[13] On the contrary, inclusive programs tend to yield increased accomplishment of IEP objectives, in the same way that increased academic improvement tends to result from heterogeneous grouping of students rather than from grouping by ability level.[14] In addition, in full inclusion, students' instruction time is better utilized as they stay in one classroom for services.[15]

The special education student often wants to emulate what the general education student is doing. When the general education student helps the special education student in a learning process it often increases the general education student's learning skills and knowledge base. Students learn to work with students who are different from what they see around them normally. Many students are willing to help accomplish social integration

11. Salend, *Creating Inclusive Classrooms* (8th ed.).

12. Hallahan et al., *Exceptional Learners*.

13. Aldridge and Goldman, *Current Issues and Trends in Education*; Gargiulo, *Special Education in Contemporary Society*.

14. Nworie, "Central Issues in Special Education"; Gargiulo, *Special Education in Contemporary Society*.

15. Aldridge and Goldman, *Current Issues and Trends in Education*.

goals. When a general education student becomes a friend with a special education student they often become the special education student's biggest champions.[16]

Special education students who are educated in inclusive regular education classrooms, have more opportunities for "normal" relationships with their peers and to learn the normal cultural patterns.[17] Special education students learn to work together, develop friendships, collaborative skills, communicative and interactive skills as they collaborate with their regular education peers in inclusion settings. Conversely the regular education students develop tolerance and appreciation of differences when they work with their special education peers through inclusion practices.[18]

Special education students taught in a self-contained special education classroom tend to have lower self-esteem and tend to be employed less than their counterparts in the regular education classroom.[19] Since the special education teacher's job is to prepare students for the work world, this sounds like a sad commentary on self-contained, non-inclusive special education classrooms.

Shalom (as will be defined in the next section) happens when special education inclusion is done right. For example, Klingner and Vaughn, from their study which investigated the perceptions of 4,659 students, found that students with disabilities want the same activities, books, homework, grading criteria, and grouping practices as their classmates without disabilities. The study also found that students with and without disabilities in inclusion setting value teachers who "slow down instructions when needed, explain concepts and assignments clearly, teach learning strategies, and teach the same material in different ways so that everyone can learn."[20]

Incarnationality

The noun *incarnation* comes from two Latin roots, namely *in*, meaning "into," and *carn*, meaning "flesh." The Latin and the Greek equivalent (*en sarki*) of the word incarnation literally means "in-flesh." Though the word

16. Salend, *Creating Inclusive Classrooms* (8th ed.)

17. Aldridge and Goldman, *Current Issues and Trends in Education*.

18. Ibid.; Salend, *Creating Inclusive Classrooms* (7th ed.)

19. Aldridge and Goldman, *Current Issues and Trends in Education*; Salend, *Creating Inclusive Classrooms* (8th ed.); Gargiulo, *Special Education in Contemporary Society*.

20. Klinger and Vaughn, "Students' Perceptions of Instruction."

incarnation is not used in the Bible, it is used in certain references in the New Testament about the person and work of Jesus Christ "in the flesh" (Eph 2:15; Col 1: 22).[21] Incarnation is the theological term for the coming of Jesus, the idea that "God was in Christ, reconciling the world to himself" (2 Cor 5: 19). *Incarnation* is used figuratively to convey the idea of putting an abstract concept or idea into concrete form.[22] The Shalom Model of Inclusion proposed is *incarnational* because it illustrates the idea of inclusion as concrete, ongoing tangible acts of love through the teacher and the community members toward the special needs student.[23]

Shalom

The Hebrew word *shalom* (שָׁלוֹם), generally translated in English as peace, has a much broader and deeper meaning and application than peace. Shalom (שָׁלוֹם) in Hebrew means completeness, soundness, wholeness, welfare, and peace. It is from *shalam*, which encompasses the meaning of safety, wellness, happiness, restored, good health, and prosperity (*Strong's Concordance*). Shalom is used in the Bible for salvation, justice, and peace.[24] The Old Testament usage of shalom has these three shades of meaning: "A material and physical state of being, relationships, and a moral sense of duty."[25] As a material and physical state, shalom seeks harmony for peoples' physical and material well-being. A biblical example of this is seen in Genesis 37:14 when Jacob asked his son Joseph to go to his brothers and check on their shalom (or well-being). So a *state of shalom* ensures good physical health as well as the absence of deprivations. A state of shalom is what we desire for our special needs students.

In the Old Testament, another idea of this multifaceted concept, shalom, is illustrated in relationships that embody personal harmony with others, and harmony with God, as illustrated in the life and relationships of Abraham, especially in his relationship with Lot (Gen 13:8). Shalom, in this sense of harmonious relationships, is also seen in Leviticus 19:18: "You shall not take vengeance, nor bear any grudge against the children of your people, but you shall love your neighbor as yourself: I *am* the Lord." Here

21. Packer, "Incarnation."
22. Neal, "Incarnational Theology."
23. Billings, "Problem with 'Incarnational Ministry.'"
24. Yoder, *Shalom*.
25. DomNwachukwu and Lee, "Multiculturalism," 98.

the justice that is in view is that of a holistic and communal state of well-being, peace, love, good health, and prosperity.[26] Shalom, as harmonious community state, is characterized by unity and obvious equality. Shalom, therefore, is accomplished when we go beyond mere tolerance, and delight to "live in right relationship with God, each other, and nature."[27] This state of shalom is greatly needed in special education.

In the Old Testament, shalom is also "the presence of moral and ethical relationships characterized by honesty, integrity, and straightforward character; it is the absence of deceit, lies, and hypocrisy."[28] These qualities of shalom such as completeness, wholeness, welfare, peace, physical and material well-being, communal harmony, honesty, integrity, and straightforward character, are embodied by God, and their potentialities are built into humans who are made in his image. In Genesis 1: 26 the triune God said, "Let us [*Elohim*, plural] make man in our image." Since man and woman are made in the image of God who embodies these qualities of shalom, it should be within the repertoire of man to exhibit, share, practice and experience shalom. The idea of the image of God (imago Dei) within humankind supports and sustains the possibility of a lived experience of the Shalom Model of Inclusion in special education. Wherever shalom is experienced, there is always present a God kind of love called agape.

Agape Love

The Bible describes the love that motivated Jesus ministry as the first and greatest commandment: "'Love the Lord your God with all your heart and with all your soul and with all your mind.' This is the first and greatest commandment. And the second is like it: 'Love your neighbor as yourself.' All the Law and the Prophets hang on these two commandments." (Matt 22:34–40). It is the exceptional God kind of love called agape. "It is the love that is used of God for man . . . based on the fact of a solid, unwavering love commitment. . . . This *agape* love is the kind of love that chooses to understand the needs of another and then responds to those needs by expending available resources to meet those needs."[29] Agape and justice are integral

26. Crisp, "Jesus and Affluence"; Fowler and Pacino, *Faith Integration and Schools of Education.*

27. DomNwachukwu and Lee, "Multiculturalism," 112.

28. Ibid., 98.

29. Stowell, *Shepherding the Church*, 182.

and essential components of shalom. Where the two are lacking it will be difficult to find shalom. Conversely, where the two converge, as is the case in the life and ministry of Jesus, shalom is present. Agape love in the proposed Shalom Model of Inclusion for special education, is based both on God's Word and on the words and ways of Jesus (his love and justice).

The Shalom Model of Inclusion

The L'Arche experience outside the classroom (described below) is proof positive that the Shalom Model of Inclusion can be actualized in the school setting. The Shalom Model of Inclusion has in its center the concept of imago Dei. That is, that humankind is created in the image of God, with all the potentialities of shalom living. Yes, we actually have this capacity to live incarnationally, to love with agape love, and to create communities characterized by shalom and inclusiveness. Built around this concept of imago Dei are four domains: shared curriculum experience, shared strengths and needs, reflective and differentiated pedagogy, and community and collaborative praxis.

Figure 1.1. The Shalom Model of Inclusion

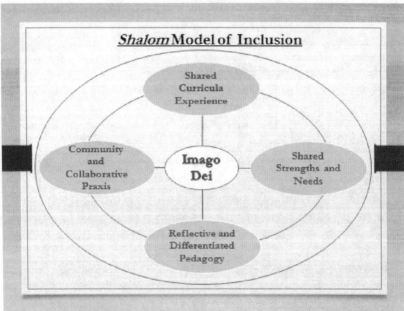

Imago Dei

The Shalom Model of Inclusion for special education is founded primarily on the realization that human beings are created in God's image (imago dei). What does it mean to be created or made in the "image of God"? Genesis 1:26–28 states:

> Then God said, "Let Us make man in Our image, according to Our likeness; let them have dominion over the fish of the sea, over the birds of the air, and over the cattle, over all the earth and over every creeping thing that creeps on the earth." So God created man in His own image; in the image of God He created him; male and female He created them. Then God blessed them, and God said to them, "Be fruitful and multiply; fill the earth and subdue it; have dominion over the fish of the sea, over the birds of the air, and over every living thing that moves on the earth."

"Made in the image of God" (v. 27), means that humans are a snapshot or facsimile of God. That is, we are godlike and have godlike aptitudes.[30] Humans have great value, and occupy a higher place in the created order than animals and plants because we alone are imprinted with godlike characteristics. We, humans, though finite and imperfect share the same attributes with God the Creator who is infinite and perfect. We bear the image of God and are godlike because we share attributes of God.[31] We reflect God's creative, spiritual, intelligent, communicative, relational, moral, and purposeful capacities.

The image of God we bear impacts our relationship with God as well as our relationship with fellow men. It is God's desire that humans enjoy fellowship with him as well as with each other. Just as the image of God is reflected in and through all people regardless of their needs, status, culture, or gender, the image of God we bear makes people of all races and ethnic groups of the same status and unique value before God. This *imago Dei* concept negates the idea of social or racial superiority or inferiority, segregation, divisions, or separations. The fact that the entire human race shares common origins as well as this common bond of divine identity should produce a concern and empathy for all people.[32]

---

30. Staub, *About You.*

31. Ibid.

32. Lee, "Building a Community of Shalom."

The image of God is, therefore, the core, uniting piece of the Shalom Model of Inclusion for special education. Imago dei, the central piece, ties together, supports and strengthens the four essential components of the Shalom Model of Inclusion. The four components are: (1) shared curricular experience, (2) shared strengths and needs, (3) reflective and differentiated pedagogy, and (4) community and collaborative praxis. Below is a brief explanation of each component.

Shared Curricular Experience

An inclusive special education environment is where all students are learners, and are provided with fairness instead of identicalness, through being educated together in high-quality, age-appropriate, general education classrooms in their neighborhood schools.[33] Such inclusivity is essential for a shalom-based educational environment. Before the enactment of the federal legislation, the Americans with Disabilities Act (ADA) in 1990, people with disabilities in the United States faced all kinds of barriers,[34] including access to school, access to basic services, inclusion in regular classrooms, and so forth.

In his ministry, Jesus exemplified this aspect of shalom in various ways. He gave his hearers the shared curricular experience by teaching the different ability groups together, by teaching his disciples and answering their questions together, by teaching the people publicly in the synagogue, by openly teaching while answering the questions of his Jewish opponents, and while associating with several classes of people (e.g., Sermon on the Mount in Matt 5–7; Luke 4:14–30; Mark 6:2; Matt 13:54, etc.). Jesus also exemplified the shared curricular experience component of shalom when he took his disciples with him and taught them while he ate with and spent time talking with those who were despised. Keller put it most eloquently this way: "He ate with and spoke to tax collectors, the wealthiest people in society, yet the most hated, since they acquired their gains through collaborating with the Roman forces of occupation."[35] Jesus welcomed all into his presence, without being a respecter of persons, and provided simultaneous

33. Salend, *Creating Inclusive Classrooms*; Gargiulo, *Special Education in Contemporary Society.*

34. Yell, *Law and Special Education* (4th ed.); Nworie, *Central Issues in Special Education.*

35. Keller, *Generous Justice,* 45.

lessons for people of all different walks of life (Matt 26:6–13; Mark 14:3–9; Luke 5:27–32; Luke 7:44–46; Luke 19:1–10).

Shared Strengths and Needs

A shalom-based, inclusive special education calls for a community where *all students* are valued as worthwhile individuals who have strengths and needs, are capable of learning and contributing to society. It is a situation where *all students* are taught to appreciate diversity and to value and learn from each other's similarities and differences.

This shalom-based, inclusive special education model, where all students are taught to love, value and learn from the similarities and differences of their peers, can best be illustrated by the worldviews and way of life of the L'Arche communities. L'Arche was founded in 1964 by Jean Vanier and Father Thomas Philippe based on Jesus' teaching that the person who is poor in what the world commonly values is, actually, blessed and endowed with deep gifts to offer. The L'Arche communities are "an international network of inclusive communities within which people with developmental disabilities live together with people who do not have such disabilities."[36]

There is a radically new system of valuing in L'Arche. It is a place where disabilities exist, but they do not really matter. In other words, within L'Arche, disability has a totally different meaning from the cultural norm. The worldview and theology of L'Arche is such that "disabilities are not viewed as problems to be solved, but rather as particular ways of being human which need to be understood, valued, and supported."[37] According to Swinton, the emphasis is on "discovering ways of loving and living together that recognize the naturalness and beauty of difference and the theological significance of weakness and vulnerability."[38]

The act of loving, welcoming and accepting has such a central place at L'Arche that "within the L'Arche communities people with developmental disabilities are accepted and welcomed not for what they can or cannot do, but simply for what they are."[39] At L'Arche all people are welcomed with thankfulness and love as "*gifts* which have divine dignity, meaning

---

36. Swinton, "Body of Christ Has Down's Syndrome."

37. Ibid., 68.

38. Ibid.

39. Ibid.

and purpose . . . not for what (the *gift*) might become or for what it is not."[40] Swinton further adds "offering care and support to people with profound developmental disabilities is thus not an act of charity, but rather it is an act of faithfulness within which people respond in love to those whom God has given to them."[41] This practice of offering care and support to people with special needs as an act of faithful, loving response which is experienced at L'Arche foreshadows what the Shalom Model of Inclusion portends inside of the classroom.

As we have just discussed, in the L'Arche community, all people are welcomed with thankfulness and love as divine gifts which have marvelous dignity, meaning and purpose. One person is not valued above another; all persons are valued for their personhood, their imago Dei. All persons have strengths to contribute to the community and all persons have needs that can be met by others in the community. This is the type of shalom-based inclusiveness that embraces each member with agape love and demonstrates the incarnational capacity of loving the different other.

This quality of love carries with it the kind of compassion that Jesus profusely demonstrated in the course of his earthly ministry (Luke 7:13; Matt 8:3, 16–17; 9:36; 14:14; 15:32). As Berkowicz and Myers have rightly stressed, for effective learning, compassion is indispensable. They have also very correctly pointed out that Schools with compassionate leaders increase their students' potential for academic success. It is not an overstatement that compassionate learning environments, by helping decrease stress levels, do lower students' cortisol levels thereby increasing their ability to learn.[42]

Reflective and Differentiated Pedagogy

In the shalom inclusive practices environment, there is instructional integrity and integration. According to Friend and Bursuck, instructional integration which has integrity is practiced by "adjusting how teaching and learning are designed, (delivered) and measured."[43] Instructional integration is also practiced by ensuring that all students are afforded the services

40. Ibid., 68–69.

41. Ibid., 69.

42. Nworie, *Central Issues in Special Education*; Berkowicz and Myers, "Leadership, Learning, and Compassion."

43. Friend and Bursuck, *Including Students with Special Needs*, 18.

and the accommodations they need to succeed. That is, individualized education and differentiated instruction for *all students* is extended in terms of assessment techniques, general education curriculum accessibility, teaching strategies, technology, universal and physical design, accommodations, modifications, classroom management techniques and a wide array of resources and related services based on their needs.[44]

In his ministry, Jesus exemplified this aspect of the Shalom Model of Inclusion as he utilized various pedagogical skills and techniques. For example, he utilized questioning, storytelling, miracles, and parables at different times in his teaching ministry, depending on the needs of the listeners.

Disabilities can present real handicapping conditions for special education students. Consequently, effective inclusive practices require that students with special needs be provided with appropriate aids, supports and services that can help level the playing field for them, and enable these students to transition to independence, to flourishing and shalom. Some of the necessary aids, supports and services include occupational therapy, physical therapy, speech-language therapy, audiology services, psychological services, assistive technology, medical and school health services, and others. Without the provision of these needed supports and services, the academic and occupational outcomes for most of these students will continue to lag behind those of their peers without disabilities.[45]

The good news is that with advances today in modern science and technology, it is very possible to live a full and satisfying life with a disability. The sad commentary, however, is that for a number of reasons, many students with special needs are not getting the aids, supports and services (including assistive technology and the kinds of instructional services) that they actually need. According to Scruggs and Mastropieri, "The reason for this is not known, but perhaps has to do with limited time, training, or support for general education teachers; or because of teacher reluctance to implement strategies perceived to be of particular utility for only a small number of students in the class."[46]

44. Salend, *Creating Inclusive Classrooms*; Friend and Bursuck, *Including Students with Special Needs*.

45. Scruggs and Mastropieri, "What Makes Special Education Special?"; Gargiulo, *Special Education in Contemporary Society*; Friend and Bursuck, *Including Students with Special Needs*.

46. Scruggs and Mastropieri, "What Makes Special Education Special?," 31.

Community and Collaborative Praxis

The shalom inclusive practices environment needs and invites parents, pupils, school personnel, other professionals and service providers to pull together as partners for best outcomes. Generally, parents prefer that their children be educated in the general education classrooms along with their peers in those settings.[47] This kind of preference by parents is based on the perception that their children perform better academically in inclusive settings. Overall, more positive academic outcomes have been found in inclusive schools. For example, as correctly reported by Friend and Bursuck, research findings from a statewide study showed that students with disabilities who spent more time in general education had a higher passing rate in the eight-grade state test than similar students with disabilities who were educated in special education settings. Friend and Bursuck, also report other research findings which demonstrate that inclusive practices make positive impacts on students' achievement in math, problem solving skills, and discipline referrals. When parents participate in collaborative decision making regarding the educational services of their children, those parents tend to be more positive.[48] Such positive partnerships and social integration between parents, teachers, other professionals, students with disabilities and their peers, contribute to shalom experience and flourishing for students. Shalom inclusion thrives in collaborative, supportive, and nurturing learning environments.[49]

Pupils who are involved and participate actively in their schooling enjoy the benefits of inclusion, and show more positive learning outcomes.[50] All students should be encouraged to attend their individualized education plan (IEP) meetings (if they are able to attend). Students in 9th grade or who are fourteen years old should always be invited to their IEP, and should be encouraged to show full school participation, and fully attend their other school meetings such as the parent-teacher meetings if they possibly can.

Inclusion is more effective when schools and school districts intentionally plan for it. For example, by providing professional development, program-enhancing or restructuring resources and materials, administrative,

47. Friend and Bursuck, *Including Students with Special Needs.*

48. Ibid.

49. Salend, *Creating Inclusive Classrooms* (8th ed.); Friend and Bursuck, *Including Students with Special Needs.*

50. Greenwood, "How Should Learning Environments Be Structurd"; Salend, *Creating Inclusive Classrooms* (8th ed.).

financial and other needed support, which enable school personnel, other professionals, service providers and other stake holders to work collaboratively and reflectively in addressing students' strengths and challenges.[51]

The ministry of Jesus portrayed real community and collaborative engagement. He reached out to and involved a cross section of his community. For example, Jesus ministry was inclusive of the Samaritans (a hated and despised group by the Jews). He collaborated with a Samaritan woman in witnessing (John 4). One of his most profound teachings was about a "Good Samaritan." As Keller noted, "The first witnesses to Jesus's birth were shepherds, a despised group considered unreliable, yet God revealed the birth of his Son first to them. The first witnesses of Jesus's resurrection were women, another class of people so marginalized that their testimony was not admissible evidence in court. Yet Jesus revealed himself to them first."[52] Hence, Jesus modeled and included members of the community from all classes and walks in life. These shalom inclusive practices by Jesus enhanced his teaching and evangelistic ministry and ensured shalom. Such inclusiveness, peace, harmony, love and justice define full shalom.[53]

Conclusion

The proposed Shalom Model of Inclusion for special education which combines best practices of finest human ideology, knowledge, and skills, with the biblically based principles of love and justice, is an ideal approach to ensure flourishing students, successful practitioners, and thriving communities with positive educational outcomes, and transformational benefits characteristic of shalom. At the core of the Shalom Model of Inclusion is the concept that humankind is created in the image of God, with the full capacity to live incarnationally, to love with agape love. Surrounding this concept of imago Dei are the four important domains of shared curriculum experience, shared strengths and needs, reflective and differentiated pedagogy, as well as community and collaborative praxis. The successful combination of these components, in concert with loving service and justice, results in communities characterized by wholesome inclusiveness (or shalom).

51. Salend, *Creating Inclusive Classrooms* (8th ed.).

52. Keller, *Generous Justice*, 45.

53. Fowler and Pacino, *Faith Integration and Schools of Education*; McColl and Ascough, "Jesus and People with Disabilities."

The experience of the L'Arche community where care and support are offered to people with special needs, not as an act of benevolence, but as an act of faithful, loving response was portrayed as concrete evidence that the Shalom Model of Inclusion can be actualized in the school setting. The importance of compassion which pervaded Jesus' earthly ministry is highlighted in connection with the experience of the L'Arche communities where love and compassion go together resulting in shalom. It was, pointed out in the paper that compassion is indispensable for lowering student stress, and improving school success outcomes.

There are negative consequences of the disregard of this biblically based incarnational model of inclusion which unites the best of Christian virtues and ethical norms with the best of educational principles and practices. The failure of special education professionals and other stakeholders to abide by the bedrock ethical principles of justice and inclusion, as well as incarnationality, and the foundational moral virtue of love (*agape*), has the potential to lead to a continued decline in the quality of educational performance, rise in litigations, rise in teacher attrition, lack of student flourishing, and lack of teacher thriving which is not in the best interest of the future of society.

Conversely, infusing best practices with the Shalom Model of Inclusion which includes the biblical and ethical principles of justice, inclusion, incarnationality, compassion, and love (*agape*) through the work of the Spirit, creates the shalom community that portends the flourishing of students with disabilities, and the thriving of practitioners, while affirming the value and contribution of every child and teacher, all who have been created with imago Dei capacities.

Bibliography

Aldridge, J., and R. Goldman. *Current Issues & Trends in Education*. New York: Pearson, 2007.

Barton, B. B., et al. *Luke*. Life Application Bible Commentary. Carol Stream: Tyndale, 1997.

Berkowicz, J., and A. Myers. "Leadership, Learning, and Compassion: The Indispensables of Education." *Education Week*, 2014. http://blogs.edweek.org/edweek/leadership_360/2014/07/leadership_learning_and_compassion_the_indispensables_of_education.html.

Billings, J. T. "The Problem with 'Incarnational Ministry': What If Our Mission Is Not to 'Be Jesus' to Other Cultures, but to Join with the Holy Spirit?" *Christianity Today* 56 (2012) 58–64.

Blanchett, W. J., et al. "Urban School Failure and Disproportionality in a Post-Brown Era." *Remedial & Special Education* 26 2 (2005) 70–81.

Bremer, C., et al. "Public Reporting of 2007–2008 Assessment Information on Students with Disabilities: Progress on the Gap Front." Technical Report 57. *National Center On Educational Outcomes, University Of Minnesota*, 2011.

Coutinho, M. J., and D. P. Oswald. "Disproportionate Representation in Special Education: A Synthesis and Recommendations." *Journal of Child & Family Studies* 9 (2000) 135–56.

Crisp, T. M. "Jesus and Affluence." Unpublished article. Biola University, 2014.

DomNwachukwu, and Lee. *Multiculturalism: A Shalom Motif for the Christian Community.* Eugene, OR: Wipf & Stock, 2014.

Doty, David. *Eden's Bridge: The Marketplace in Creation and Mission.* Eugene, OR: Wipf & Stock, 2011.

Fowler, M., and M. Pacino, eds. *Faith Integration and Schools of Education.* Indiana: Precedent, 2012.

Friend, M., and W. D. Bursuck. *Including Students with Special Needs: A Practical Guide for Classroom Teachers.* Boston: Pearson, 2015.

Gargiulo, R. M. *Special Education in Contemporary Society.* Los Angeles: Sage, 2015.

George, S. "God of Life, Justice and Peace: A Disability-Informed Reading of Christology." *Ecumenical Review* 64 (2012) 454–62.

Greenwood, C. R. "How Should Learning Environments (Schools and Classrooms) Be Structured for Best Learning Outcomes?" In *Enduring Issues in Special Education: Personal Perspectives*, edited by B. Bateman et al., 303–21. New York: Routledge, 2015.

Hallahan D., et al. *Exceptional Learners: An Introduction to Special Education.* New Jersey: Pearson Education, 2015.

Heward, W. L. *Exceptional Children: An Introduction to Special Education.* 10th ed. Boston: Pearson, 2013.

Keller, T. *Generous Justice: How God's Grace Makes Us Just.* New York: Riverhead, 2010.

Klingner, J. K., and S. Vaughn. "Students' Perceptions of Instruction in Inclusion Classrooms: Implications for Students with Learning Disabilities." *Exceptional Children* 66 (1999) 23–37.

Lee, H. "Building a Community of Shalom: What the Bible Says about Multicultural Education." *Journal of the International Christian Community for Teacher Education* 10 (2015). https://icctejournal.org/issues/v5i2/v5i2-lee.

Mamlin, Nancy. *Preparing Effective Special Education Teachers.* New York: Guilford, 2012.

McColl, M. A., and R. S. Ascough. "Jesus and People with Disabilities: Old Stories, New Approaches." *Journal of Pastoral Care and Counseling* 63 (2009) 1–11.

Minnesota Department of Education. "Special Education Litigation Costs: FY 2012 Report to the Legislature." 2013.

Neal, G. S. "Incarnational Theology." Grace Incarnate Ministries, 2006. Retrieved from http://www.revneal.org/Writings/incarntheol.htm.

Nworie, B. C., ed. *Central Issues in Special Education: Engaging Current Trends and Critical Issues in Contemporary Practice.* New York: Pearson, 2013.

Packer, J. I. "Incarnation." In *New Bible Dictionary*, edited by I. H. Marshall et al., 501–4. Downers Grove: IVP Academic, 1996.

Parrish, Thomas. "How Should We Pay for Special Education?" In *Enduring Issues in Special Education: Personal Perspectives*, edited by B. Bateman, 410–27. New York: Routledge, 2015.

Pudelski, S. "Rethinking the Special Education Due Process System: A Proposal for the Next Reauthorization of the Individuals with Disabilities Education Act." Part 1. American Association of School Administrators, 2013. http://www.aasa.org/uploadedFiles/Policy_and_Advocacy/Public_Policy_Resources/Special_Education/AASARethinkingSpecialEdDueProcess.pdf.

Sack-Min, J. "From Funding to Teaching to Litigation: A Look at What Prevents the Landmark Special Education Law from Meeting Its Core Principles." *American School Board Journal* 194 (2007) 20–25.

Salend, S. J. *Creating Inclusive Classrooms: Effective and Reflective Practices*. 7th ed. Upper Saddle River, NJ: Merrill / Prentice Hall, 2011.

———. *Creating Inclusive Classrooms: Effective and Reflective Practices*. 8th ed. Boston: Pearson, 2016.

Scruggs, T. E., and M. A. Mastropieri. "What Makes Special Education Special?" In *Enduring Issues in Special Education: Personal Perspectives*, edited by B. Bateman, 22–35. New York: Routledge, 2015.

Smith, D. D., and N. C. Tyler. *Introduction to Special Education: Making a Difference*. Upper Saddle River, NJ: Merrill, 2010.

Staub, D. *About You: Fully Human, Fully Alive*. Hoboken, NJ: Wiley, 2010.

Stowell, J. M. *Shepherding the Church: Effective Spiritual Leadership in a Changing Culture*. Chicago: Moody, 1997.

Sullivan, A. L. "Disproportionality in Special Education Identification and Placement of English Language Learners." *Council for Exceptional Children* 77 (2011) 317–34.

Swinton, J. "The Body of Christ Has Down's Syndrome: Theological Reflections on Vulnerability, Disability, and Graceful Communities." *Journal of Pastoral Theology* 13 (2003) 66–78.

Tate, W. R. *Biblical Interpretation: An Integrated Approach*. Grand Rapids: Baker Academic, 2011.

US Department of Education. *Children with Disabilities Receiving Special Education under Part B of the Individuals with Disabilities Education Act*. Office of Special Education Programs, Data Analysis System, 2010. Retrieved from http://www.ideadata.org.

Yell, M. L. *The Law and Special Education*. 3rd ed. Upper Saddle River, NJ: Pearson, 2012.

———. *The Law and Special Education*. 4th ed. Upper Saddle River, NJ: Pearson, 2016.

Yoder, P. B. *Shalom: The Bible's Word for Salvation, Justice, and Peace*. Nappanee, IN: Evangel, 1998.

Index

Index

Index